Brewing up entrepreneurial adventures and
pioneering tales with the Prince of Ales

David Bruce OBE

The Firkin Saga
ISBN 978-1-915483-96-6 (paperback)
ISBN 978-1-915483-97-3 (hardback)
eISBN 978-1-915483-98-0
Audio ISBN 978-1-915483-99-7

Published in 2025 by Right Book Press

Manufactured by
Sue Richardson Associates Ltd.
Studio 6,
9, Marsh Street
Bristol
BS1 4AA
info@therightbookcompany.com

EU Safety Representative
eucomply OÜ
Parnu mnt 139b-14
11317 Tallinn
Estonia
hello@eucompliancepartner.com
+33 756 90241

© David Bruce OBE

The right of David Bruce OBE to be identified as the author of this work has been asserted in accordance with the Copyright, Designs and Patents Act 1988.

A CIP record of this book is available from the British Library.

All rights reserved. No part of this book may be reproduced, stored in a retrieval system, or transmitted in any form or by any means, electronic, mechanical, photocopying, recording or otherwise, without the prior written permission of the copyright holder.

David Bruce is not only a legend in brewing, he is also one of the great serial entrepreneurs in modern history. His stories make great reading, with a pageant of colourful characters surmounting one improbable challenge after another. I devoured the whole thing in one sitting!
– John Hickenlooper, founder of the Wynkoop Brewery and United States senator for Colorado

David Bruce's career has taken him from working as a humble brewer at Theakston's Brewery to pioneering pub brewing in Britain with his Firkin pub chain to becoming a successful investor in craft breweries around the world. *The Firkin Saga* is a fast-paced and instructive account of how he earned his title and played a key role in the global craft beer revolution.
– Steve Hindy, co-founder of the Brooklyn Brewery and author of *Beer School* and *The Craft Beer Revolution*

David Bruce is a true Prince of Ales. He put personality back into pubs and made locals feel local. This is a memoir of how to make the impossible happen.
– Sir Simon Jenkins, former editor of *The Times* and former chair of the National Trust

David Bruce reached a generation and inspired a mood, and this book explains how he did it: imagination, determination and sheer hard work. This fascinating book isn't really about beer. It's about a man and his ludicrously patient wife who together wilfully ignored the experts and naysayers to achieve something new and exciting and have left their mark, not just on pubs, but also on the lives of the thousands of families they have helped to enjoy life.
– Rob Dean, CMG, president of the Kennet & Avon Canal Trust

If it weren't for David Bruce's alternative view on the brewing and pub sector – a mixture of the comedic and the anarchic – the industry would be a very bleak place indeed. The self-styled Prince of Ales has not only written an entertaining book on his first 50 years as a brewer, but also a useful guide for the budding entrepreneur, with ten key business lessons that blend the serious with the silly.

    – Dominic Walsh, former business editor for the leisure and drinks
       industry at *The Times*

This book tells the rich story of David Bruce's life as a brewer and an entrepreneur. But it is so much more than a memoir. It details the highs and the lows of a world that many people know little about, and draws from them the essence of what it means to live life to the full.

    – Laura Farris, former member of Parliament for Newbury

A moment with David Bruce is all you need to be swept away by his enthusiasm for life. He is also a person of courage, real inspiring leadership, and a true philanthropist. This book not only tells the story of how one man beat the system and succeeded, but also sets out where things didn't go right and what lessons can be learned from these mistakes. A really good read.

    – The Rt Hon the Lord Benyon GCVO, Lord Chamberlain

Dedication

I dedicate this book to my long-suffering wife, Louise, who has shared my entrepreneurial journey for over 52 years. None of it would have been possible without her love, loyalty, support and friendship. Additionally, her innate business acumen as my co-shareholder in our private investment company since 1978 has proven invaluable on all too many occasions.

Contents

Introduction	1
My ten key business lessons	3

Part 1

Foreword by Roger Protz	7
1. My first Firkin	9
2. How the Duke of York became a Goose	15
3. From early days to Old Peculier	33
4. Learning the hard way with punch-ups and pythons	45
5. The Goose spreads its wings	59
6. A Fox, a Frog and battles with bureaucracy	69
7. Fun runs, a busted nose and seeing red in Bristol	89
8. Booming pubs, a tax threat and brewing a Barbarian	105
9. Making tracks at Denmark Hill while the Balloon is going up	113
10. Battles with bureaucrats and other lowlifes	123
11. Skirmishes with squatters, losing directors and becoming a dad	133
12. Avoiding trains and finding a helpful bank	141
13. Fishy work in Highbury and finding out the Queen is my Hackney landlord	149
14. A Falcon, a Phantom, a Fuzzock and a Flamingo all join the Firkin menagerie	159
15. A Firkin farewell	171

Part 2

Foreword by Charlie Papazian	187
16. From Firkins to philanthropy	189
17. Back to brewing and pubs	205
18. Off to the Big Apple in the Land of the Free	213
19. Honeypot buzzes along to a sticky end	229
20. Brewing up some capital ideas	237
21. From pubs to farm shops and a vineyard	251
22. Success breeds success	255
Epilogue	263
Brewing Bruce's brilliant beers!	265
Pros and cons for the Firkin sale	267
Acknowledgements	269
Index	271

Introduction

Having spent my whole career in the international brewing and pub industries, I want to share in this business memoir my first 50 years as a brewer and my many roller-coaster, helter-skelter, entrepreneurial escapades in the hope that this will inspire current and aspiring entrepreneurs.

My first entrepreneurial venture started in 1979, when I created the first pub in London for more than a century to revive the ancient custom of pubs brewing their own beer. I opened my eponymous Bruce's Brewery in the cellar of a closed-down pub in south-east London, which became the Goose & Firkin, thereby defying the many prophets of doom who claimed it would fail immediately. Nine years later, having opened several more breweries and 11 more Firkin pubs in London and Bristol, I sold them all for millions in cash just before my 40th birthday.

Looking back, much of my journey seems stranger than fiction, as it highlights the many triumphs and failures I encountered while creating or investing in new businesses from Paris to Seattle via London and New York.

After somewhat lacklustre schooldays and a failed entry to university, I needed a job, so I joined a brewery as an 18-year-old management trainee. Real ale and subsequently craft brewing were soon to be in the ascendant, so I used my training to climb on the beery bandwagon, having experienced early on the wrong end of nepotism. By then, I'd proven myself to be completely unemployable. I hated having a boss and had no money of my own, but I nurtured a passionate, burning desire to start and run my own business, focused on the world I knew best: brewing and pubs.

The first part of this book recounts how I became a disrupter and brewing provocateur by taking on Britain's big brewers and beating them at their own game. The second part is about how I became not only an international, serial entrepreneur but also a philanthropist, by putting some of my hard-won business experience and equally hard-won cash back into the community.

I'm happy to share the innumerable business lessons I learned, all too often the hard way, in the hope that other entrepreneurs will be made aware of the many challenges and pitfalls that inevitably occur while carving out a niche as a pioneer rather than being content to be a mere follower. On the next page, you'll find my ten key business lessons and, at the end of each chapter, short points detailing how these lessons emerged from my own varied experiences.

It hasn't been an easy journey and I would not have succeeded without the unwavering support for more than half a century of my wife, Louise, and the many brilliant and loyal colleagues I've enjoyed working with in so many different businesses across the world.

My ten key business lessons

- Lesson 1: Follow your instincts and demonstrate your motivation to succeed.

- Lesson 2: Build a trusted support network.

- Lesson 3: Be brave, ambitious and determined to overcome all obstacles.

- Lesson 4: Seize opportunities as they arise.

- Lesson 5: Delegate as soon and as often as possible.

- Lesson 6: Control the cash.

- Lesson 7: Inspire and educate others and put something back into your community.

- Lesson 8: Encourage and nurture free PR, even if it entails fancy dress.

- Lesson 9: Look after yourself and your family.

- Lesson 10: Savour the special moments.

Part 1

Foreword

By Roger Protz

The first time I met David Bruce was in 1979 when he was digging out a brewing tank in the cellar of the Goose & Firkin in Southwark. We got on straight away as I liked his infectious grin and self-deprecating humour.

I wasn't certain that someone who said he was 'too thick' to go to university would succeed with a run-down old boozer in the back streets of South London but the Goose was packed from opening day and spawned a chain of Firkins in all parts of the capital.

I kept in close touch with David as his small empire grew. I went several times to the brilliant Phoenix & Firkin in Denmark Hill, once in the company of Terry Jones of the Monty Python clan, who was a great beer lover.

When I worked in Islington for a few years I would regularly drink in the Flounder & Firkin, enjoying the beer and watching the fish gyrating in their giant tank.

David's genius – and genius is not too strong a word – was to make pub-going fun. Back in the 1970s and 80s, pubs were utilitarian in the extreme. They were what the Scots call 'drinking shops': you went for a bevvy, not for a laugh. David understood that if the beer was drinkable and the food edible he could draw big crowds to the Firkins as he also offered a laugh. There were outrageous puns and T-shirts based on the odd word firkin that you didn't use in the presence of your maiden aunt.

The Firkins succeeded against the odds. He faced opposition from powerful brewers with their large estates of pubs. He had to clamber over high walls built by licensing authorities and health and safety departments. He had to remove squatters from one pub and was threatened by football hooligans in another.

David survived the traumas with his mission to transform the British pub. Before writing this, I visited several pubs, and on each occasion I was greeted with warmth and courtesy. That would never have happened pre-Firkins where in too many pubs the greeting would have been, 'Whaddyer want in here? You're not a regular – clear off.'

It's important to point out that David's run-in with CAMRA over his use of malt extract in the Goose was confined to narrow minds in one branch and was not a national reproach. Brian Glover, who edited the campaign's national newspaper, *What's Brewing*, was also the author of the *New Beer Guide* that featured David on the cover outside the Phoenix & Firkin.

Front cover image from Brian Glover's book, 1988

Minor distractions aside, this is a wonderful memoir about faith in the good old British pub and its unique style of beer. Order a pint and prepare for what David would undoubtedly call a firkin good read.

Roger Protz has written more than 20 books about beer and pubs, including the best-selling 300 Beers to Try Before You Die *and the award-winning* Family Brewers of Britain. *He edited 24 editions of the annual* CAMRA Good Beer Guide.

My first Firkin

1979

On the fateful day of 18 July 1979, I opened the doors of the Goose & Firkin in Elephant and Castle, south London, with two thoughts in mind. Would anyone come to the pub? And would the words of one financial advisor whom I'd approached for his professional opinion ring horribly true: 'This project has absolutely no chance of succeeding and I suggest you abandon it immediately'?

The first question was soon answered. I couldn't believe that people would pay good money to drink what I'd produced in my subterranean brewery but, as I stood in the bar in my white boiler suit and wellies, I watched in amazement as droves of people poured through the door. As if by magic, the word had got around the neighbourhood that London's first pub to brew its own beer on the premises for more than a century had finally opened.

My wife Louise had taken the day off work to help with the opening. Half an hour before I unlocked the doors, we were still sweeping out builders' rubble. We hadn't advertised that we were opening and merely put a poster in the window saying 'Opening today'. I realised I hadn't made a price list and decided to charge 5p more than the most expensive beer in London pubs, as Bruce's Borough Bitter, with a strength of 4.5 per cent, was stronger than the average for that time in London.

We couldn't believe the reaction. The first lunchtime was so crowded that we had to ask customers to help with collecting and washing glasses and even serve behind the bar while I spent most of the time clumping up and down stairs to the brewery and cold beer store to ensure supplies didn't run out during our first session. Each time I left the bar to go to the brewery, I went through a door marked 'Ladies' and received some funny looks from the customers who must have wondered why this man in overalls and wellies kept rushing in and out of the ladies' loo. In fact, once through the door, I turned right and went down to the brewhouse.

Where it all started

Disaster struck during that first lunchtime. At the busiest moment, Dick Putland, the manager from Lloyds Bank who'd loaned me £10,000 to help finance the project, arrived and announced he wanted to see exactly how I'd spent his loan. I took him down to the cellar and proudly showed him the brewery. Dick stepped back to admire what he'd financed and caught the turn-up of his trousers in the plastic outlet tap at the bottom of one of the two fermenting vessels. As he jumped back, the tap came out and beer shot across the floor.

I dived down and jammed my thumb in the gushing orifice in an attempt to stem the flow of my liquid gold as it started to trickle down the drain. As my staff were all busy serving upstairs, I asked Dick to go up and shout above the cacophony if anyone knew a plumber, as the bank manager had knocked the tap out of the fermenting vessel. He was greeted with loud hisses and boos from the good-natured crowd but a plumber from a local building firm emerged from the throng and came to my rescue.

As the crowds continued to come to sup my beer, Louise and I knew we had a winning formula and could tell that financial advisor that his doom-laden forecast was hopelessly wide of the mark. Early the next morning, I ordered a taxi and went to Dick Putland's bank branch. I was in my wellies, covered in brewing sugar and with hops sticking to my bobble hat. I had a large carrier bag stuffed with £2,500 of wet notes, stuck it on his desk and said: 'Well, that's our first week's projected turnover... in a day.'

I'd built my brewing equipment to produce a maximum of 3,000 pints a week. However, the pub kept running out of beer, so I had to order additional kit to reach a capacity of 6,000 pints, twice my original estimate. Strong beers were added to the range with such names as Earthstopper, Mindboggler, Kneetrembler and, eventually, my legendary Dogbolter.

The customers were predominantly young, affluent and mobile, most of them from outside the immediate area. They weren't put off by a hostile reception from the Campaign for Real Ale (CAMRA). In its magazine, CAMRA said the Goose was 'too crowded, too noisy and too expensive'. In spite of that criticism, by October the pub's weekly takings were running at £4,500. Big brewers said spirit sales were the most profitable part of a pub's income but 80 per cent of the Goose's takings came from beer.

I did all the brewing myself and Louise helped in the evenings and served behind the bar. By the end of the year, the Goose had a team of eight, including a manager and full-time brewer. They were all paid above the average for the time. The manager, for example, earned £2,000 a year more than the standard union rate and had the added incentive of a 10–20 per cent sliding scale commission on net trading profit. We added food alongside the beer. I thought most pub food was awful – all soya beans and gravy – so we sold large, well-filled baps with the slogan 'Fill that gap with a Firkin bap!' As the pub was so crowded, there was seldom room for plates, cutlery, etc, so people just used to hold a bap in one hand and a pint in the other.

By the end of 1979, the Goose, which had formerly grossed £50,000 a year as the Duke of York, was heading for a projected turnover of £270,000 in its first year. As the term 'firkin' – meaning a nine-gallon beer cask – became a talking point throughout London and created a large number of puns, not all of them decent, we planned further pubs that would enable us to reach a target of £1 million annual turnover.

Having successfully opened the Goose & Firkin and my first Bruce's Brewery, little did I know then that 11 more Firkin pubs would eventually follow, such was my determination to operate and develop my own business.

Lessons and learnings

🍺 **Lesson 1: Follow your instincts and demonstrate your motivation to succeed**
Thank goodness I ignored the gloomy advice of the City brewing and leisure analyst who scrawled across my business plan 'This project has absolutely no chance of succeeding and I suggest you abandon it immediately'. His negative views were shared by innumerable others, especially among the big brewers, but I was determined to prove them all wrong. My advice is to be the eternal optimist and have faith in your judgement.

🍺 **Lesson 3: Be brave, ambitious and determined to overcome all obstacles**
No one had started a brewery in a London pub for more than a century, so it was a brave and unprecedented move on my part to become a pioneer against all the odds and the prophets of doom! Do your research and make sure you know what you need to know to take the leap.

🍺 **Lesson 10: Savour the special moments**
After gaining years of relevant experience and following months of research and hard work, it was wonderful to witness the moment that my first customer smacked his lips and declared that Bruce's Borough Bitter was absolutely delicious before ordering his second pint. Even at the busiest times, or if you're not sure how business is going, make time to enjoy the good moments as they may boost you to move on to the next steps.

2

How the Duke of York became a Goose

1979

I'd worked in various parts of the leisure industry, including nightclubs and pubs, mainly in the north of England and the East End of London. As an employee during my many and varied early jobs, I generally thought that most of my bosses were completely useless and that I could do a much better job than they were. I was determined to go it alone. Louise and I decided to move to London, where she could get a good secretarial job while I looked for possible outlets to run my own business. Louise had experience of running a small business. In Yorkshire, she and a friend had started a catering company called Crumpets that provided for private dinner parties.

We moved to Clapham in south London, and Louise got a well-paid job with BUPA, the private health company. But at the start of 1979, I was unemployed. I enjoyed athletics and was keen to keep fit, so spent a part of every day running through the streets of London. It wasn't wasted time, as I was on the lookout for possible sites to open a café, pub, sandwich bar or wine bar. In order to eke out Louise's salary and my unemployment benefit, we took in students, up to four at a time, at £25 a week each. They took over the top two bedrooms of our five-bedroom Victorian terraced house in Clapham that had cost us £19,500 – cheap by today's standards!

I became interested in taking the tenancy of the Charrington

Brewery's Moss Hall Tavern in Finchley, north London, a large roadhouse with bags of potential. Louise and I spent many hours touring the pubs in the area and we became increasingly enthusiastic about taking on the pub. A detailed feasibility study was drawn up that Louise typed after work. We were duly summoned to Charrington's regional office at Park Royal. We felt we did well at the interview and Charrington's seemed suitably impressed with our feasibility study. However, the weeks went by and we heard nothing. We felt frustrated at the lack of response as we felt the pub really was for us and we could make a huge success of it.

Eventually, we read in the trade paper the *Morning Advertiser* that Charrington's and Fuller's had completed a pubs swap deal, and the Moss Hall Tavern was one of those pubs; it would reopen as a Fuller's managed house. I was furious, as someone at Charrington's must have known of this deal at the time we were carrying out our time-consuming research and attending interviews. The whole wasted exercise further strengthened my resolve never to become a big brewery tenant.

These uncertain weeks always started with me signing on each Monday at 11.30 am at the local Jobcentre, known then as the labour exchange, on Battersea Park Road, and run by the euphemistically called Department of Employment, although it was only for the benefit of the unemployed. I would run there in my tracksuit and, clutching my dole card, would join the long queue. One day, the young woman at the counter said it was time I went for an interview with the Professional and Executive Recruitment Division in Lavender Hill, so I jogged there to register as an unemployed professional executive. When I declared myself untrained, unqualified and not particularly keen on taking a job, I was told there were few employers in the area that would be prepared to grant me an interview for anything unless I wanted a job as either a waiter or a cook in a fast-food restaurant. I thought how fortunate I was that I had no ambition to work for anyone ever again and was spurred on to find that elusive site.

One day, in February 1979, I ran from Lavender Hill along the River Thames down to Blackfriars Bridge, and from there I decided to return home along the A3 via Kennington and Stockwell to

How the Duke of York became a Goose

Clapham. While I was running around the decidedly seedy and run-down nether regions of Elephant and Castle, I had to stop at traffic lights under a railway bridge. Before I could cross the road, I spied a boarded-up building on the opposite side that had clearly once been a pub. There was something about it that appealed to me and during the five miles or so on the run home, I decided to make further enquiries.

Straight from my bath, I rang round local planners, police and rating authorities and eventually discovered the property was owned by the City of London Corporation, which had leased it to Truman's Brewery as a pub, the Duke of York. It had been on the market for several months but no one had shown any interest in it. This wasn't surprising, owing to its location under a huge iron railway bridge at the junction of two busy roads and surrounded by restricted parking. I rang the Corporation at its headquarters in the Guildhall and was put through to the surveyors' department, where I spoke to Raymond Wicks. We arranged to inspect the pub the following day.

I remember seeing Raymond's friendly, clean-cut face as I walked from Borough Underground station towards Southwark Bridge Road. After much fumbling with dozens of keys, he eventually found the correct one and we pushed open the boarded-up door and could see absolutely nothing. The mains electricity had been cut off months before and the security hoarding was so effective there wasn't a chink of light. Fortunately, Raymond had brought a torch that he shone around and I saw a small room with a circular central bar with a couple of mock Tudor partitions dividing the space. The false ceiling had mock Tudor beams that had never quite joined up and it was dripping water onto a carpet that was soggy with mould.

Raymond said all the lead had been ripped off the roof a while ago and all three floors were saturated with water. He was surprised the ceilings hadn't come down. The smell of damp and stale air permeated the whole building and it was far colder and damper inside than it was on the windswept and rainy streets of a February morning in Elephant and Castle.

As we picked our way over the piles of broken glass and furniture,

Raymond shone his torch into an old food cabinet to reveal the almost intact skeleton of a rat that had clearly given up the uneven struggle to find any food. I asked Raymond if we could venture down to the cellar, but neither of us could find the right key, so we kicked open a likely looking door and descended a rickety old staircase. Pipes and wiring dangled from the ceiling and the whole place was a sea of broken wooden crates, empty beer kegs, smashed bottles, general rubble and filth. Undeterred, I was excited at seeing by torchlight the sheer size of the cellar and its excellent ceiling height of around 7 ft.

Two thoughts occurred to me. First, if Truman had given up the lease, then the City Corporation would presumably lease the pub to me as a free house, which meant I could do whatever I liked with it and sell whatever beer I wanted to, rather than be tied to Truman's beers, as had previously been the case. Second, if the pub could become a free house, then why not brew my own beer right here in the huge cellar? I was, after all, an experienced brewer!

It was something I'd never considered doing before but the idea came to me as a flash of inspiration, or perhaps divine intervention, as I stood with Raymond in that dripping, dank cellar. Tremendously excited, I slapped him on the back and said, 'That's it, I know exactly what I'm going to do here. Let's go and find a pub up the road where I can tell you all about it.'

We stumbled upstairs, locked the corrugated iron security hoarding, and headed off to The Ship, a Young's pub, to thaw out. We ignored the strange glances we got from people as we walked to the bar, covered in cobwebs and dirt and with the torch still on as we'd forgotten to turn it off. I babbled on to Raymond with all my spontaneous thoughts about starting a brewery in the cellar and running the pub as a free house. To my surprise, Raymond thought it was a good idea. He told me the pub had been on the market for several months and before Truman's closed it, they'd leased it to three different tenants over the past five years. Each one had given up as the business failed around them. Truman's didn't want to renew the lease and the City Corporation was keen to find someone who would try something completely new and different in running the pub.

After a couple of hours, Raymond and I agreed I would produce a feasibility study and work out a level of rent I thought would be acceptable. He went back to his boss and told him he had found an out-of-work brewer who had come up with the novel idea of how the premises could be developed. As soon as I got home, I rang Louise to say I thought I'd found what we were looking for and that I wanted to start a brewery. In her usual sensible but supportive way, she said, 'Well, that's fine. Just get on and show me how it's going to work and how we're going to pay for it.'

With that encouragement, I phoned the Inland Revenue (now HM Revenue & Customs), whose local office was conveniently based some 200 yards from the pub. I was put through to an officer, who listened attentively to my proposal. I had to assure him it would only be a small brewery and nothing the size of Courage, Watney or Whitbread, which were the long-established, big breweries they usually dealt with. I told him that in the mid-19th century there were some 40,000 pubs in Britain that brewed their own beer on the premises, but by 1979 this number had dwindled to just four in the whole country. All the others had either ceased brewing or had been swallowed up by big brewers. The excise officer I spoke to said I'd have to leave the matter with him.

I then rang the local council's planning department and explained my proposal to them. They said they didn't know if it would be acceptable from the planning point of view and asked if they could go away and think about it. I received similar responses from the rating authority, the fire department, the licensing justices, the environmental health officer, the district surveyor, the borough engineer and even the trade effluent officer. Everybody I could think of was taken by surprise and at a loss about what to do as there were no contemporary precedents.

By the time Louise returned home that evening, I'd called most of the local authorities and could report to her that, while there had been much sucking of air through teeth, no one had actually vetoed my initial proposal. Encouraged by this, we sat down to work out how much we thought the project might cost. We rapidly came to the conclusion that whether it cost £2,000 or £20,000, it was an academic exercise as we didn't have any money of our own to invest. But I went to bed full of optimism that we'd finally found the right opportunity and I lay awake pondering how we were going to make it work.

While I worked on the plans and feasibility study, I phoned round many of my old contacts and friends in the brewing and leisure industry and told them of my plan to run a pub that brewed its own beer. The general opinion was that it was a good idea and highly original but there was no way it would work on a site as small as the Duke of York. These prophets of doom made me even more determined than ever to succeed. I was on my own – with the full support of Louise. She always maintained to our friends and family, 'David is the ideas man.' I looked at the figures and could see that if some things went wrong, we could still make the project pay. I didn't think we were taking such an enormous risk because in our hearts we both felt sure it would work. Although the figures were only estimates, they were based on ten years of hard-won experience in the brewing and leisure industries.

On Monday 26 March 1979, I signed on at the Jobcentre, not in my usual tracksuit but in a jacket and tie, which attracted even odder looks than usual. But I had to sign on before going to the Guildhall for an interview about the lease on the Duke of York. My feasibility study was to form the basis of my negotiations with the Corporation and had been dispatched a few days earlier. By that time, Louise and I were more than ever convinced that the future lay in the development of the pub as a free house with its own brewery in the cellar.

We had set our hearts on this unique project and I waited to be summoned to the office of the City surveyor with considerable trepidation. Most of the interview was spent discussing the level of rent and the finer points of the lease. It was only towards the end of the interview that I realised they must have made up their minds to offer me the pub, subject to a reasonable level of rent, which we agreed at £7,250 a year for a ten-year lease, with a five-year rent review. It was only on the Tube home, with the Northern Line rattling to Clapham South, that I realised my months of unemployment would soon be at an end and we really would have the opportunity to start, develop and run our own business from scratch.

My main concern was how best to scale down the production equipment needed to create a new brewery in a room measuring no more than around 8 ft x 10 ft. The principles of brewing are virtually the same regardless of scale but trying to fit a complete brewery into such a restricted space, coupled with the fact that it would be located directly under the gents' urinals, would be a challenge. After a lot of research and many phone calls, I decided the best course of action would be to ask a new company called Brewpubs to supply the equipment at a cheap capital cost and I would then pay them a franchise fee on what was produced.

I met Roger Booth of Brewpubs, who had already supplied his kit to a couple of other pubs, one of which was run by an old trade customer friend, Richard Vernon, from my days at Theakston's. Louise and I visited Richard on one of our trips north at his pub near Clitheroe. We were impressed with his Brewpub kit, though I was alarmed to see that his Customs & Excise licence cost £1,575. This seemed an extortionate figure and I felt that if the licence alone cost that much, I would never be able to afford to brew, as the kit alone would cost around £3,500. Richard howled with laughter and, blaming my poor eyesight, explained the licence cost £15.75 – I'd failed to see the decimal point.

While I was up north, I took my plans to show Paul Theakston, who was running Theakston's Brewery at Masham. He warmly endorsed our proposals and said using Brewpubs, even with the franchise fee, seemed the best way of starting up, especially as the equipment was cheap. Two other contacts from the world of brewing whose advice I sought were Claude Arkell at Donnington Brewery near Stow-on-the-Wold and Peter Austin, the former head brewer at Hull Brewery. Peter had come out of retirement to launch the Ringwood Brewery in Hampshire. The enthusiasm and moral support of these experienced brewers was just the encouragement I needed to pull the deal together.

Louise and I wanted the decor of the bar to be something truly traditional, such as a new bar down the length of one wall, exposed floorboards, church pews for seating, oak trestle tables and brass wall lights and certainly no fruit machines, carpets, droopy red lampshades or green Draylon button-backed banquette seating. I wanted a proper bar fitter to produce a Dickensian-style bar and back-fitting together with the food servery.

As most of my previous developments had been more to do with disco and live entertainment pubs, I'd never built a 'traditional' bar. I mentioned this one evening when I was having supper with Louise's brother Charlie and his wife Debbie. They suggested I should speak to her brother, Peter Hare-Scott, who was an area manager with St George's Taverns, the managed house division of Watney's. Peter and I met for lunch and I explained my dilemma. He felt the sort of place I'd described had just been developed by him in the refurbishment of the Clarence in Whitehall. He was right, although I think they had gone a little over the top, with serving wenches in Dickensian-style costume while liberal amounts of sawdust scattered over the floor made it either slippery or caused spilt beer and scraps of food to congeal into lumps. Peter felt the best person to talk to about creating the sort of ambience Louise and I envisaged would be a young bar fitter he knew called Richard Barker-Harland, who was in partnership with David du Boulay of du Boulay Construction.

When I arrived the following week at du Boulay's address, I found Richard and his wife in a two-room flat adjacent to the workshop. He was in bed sweating profusely with a vicious bout of flu. He was nevertheless able to show a tremendous enthusiasm for all my plans and said he understood exactly what I wanted. 'It's just what I enjoy doing,' he said. 'Leave it to me.'

With the wheels in motion regarding the brewing equipment, building work and bar decor, I felt I could concentrate on dealing with the many local authorities in Southwark and Greater London, as well as thinking about where all the money might come from. Customs & Excise had checked the few remaining brewpubs in the country and were satisfied their stringent regulations would be adhered to at the Goose, so I applied for my brewing licence, remembering to put a clear decimal point on the cheque for £15.75.

I learned from helpful officials at Southwark Council that financial assistance could sometimes be given to new businesses starting up in this run-down inner-city area, provided they were involved in manufacturing and creating jobs. I duly met with the council's employment and industrial development officer, whose first question was, 'How many jobs is your new manufacturing business going to create, Mr Bruce?' I replied, 'Well, at least one, as I shall be coming off the dole, and if the project works I hope to provide at least a further eight full-time jobs.'

It took nearly a year, after filling in innumerable forms and exchanging letters, before it was agreed that the council would grant a 12-month rent-free period. It was a helpful gesture but in view of the time and effort it had taken it didn't seem worthwhile, as I'd needed the money upfront and not as a retrospective payment several months after the pub had started trading.

I was horrified one morning to receive a letter from the City of London Corporation saying they would have to withdraw their offer of a lease as, under some ancient covenant, the Duke of York couldn't be leased to a private individual but only to a company. The City's solicitor wouldn't budge and declared that if a suitable company couldn't be substituted for Louise and me by 5 pm then he would no longer consider our application. Frantic phone calls followed, as a result of which we were able to buy an off-the-shelf company, Wetherland Ltd, from our solicitors, but we couldn't use this company until we'd paid for it in cash. There was more panic, as we didn't have the required £100 between us. So, just before the banks shut that afternoon, Louise plucked up the courage to ask her boss at BUPA, Jerry Williams, if he could lend her £100, which he kindly agreed to do. I rushed to the Guildhall with my new, incorporated company certificate just before it closed.

While all this frenetic activity was going on, I continued to add the final touches to the feasibility study that had already been returned with a negative response from my old manager at the Midland Bank in Masham. His comments included 'If brewing in a pub is such a good idea, why are there only four pubs in the country still doing it?' and 'If it is such a good idea, why hasn't someone else thought of it?' These were less than encouraging comments from the 'listening bank' (the bank's nickname in its advertising at the time), and a friend suggested I might get a more sympathetic hearing from his manager, Dick Putland, at Lloyds Bank in Southampton Row. Dick and I hit it off immediately. He was positive and enthusiastic about supporting the project, which looked like costing around £20,000. Dick's main concern was not so much whether it would work, in view of my experience of brewing and running pubs, but how well secured any loan from the bank would be, bearing in mind the experiences of the previous licensees of this short leasehold property.

He refused to take a first charge on the lease, as he quite rightly felt that a short ten-year lease on a premises, linked with the continual failure by my predecessors, was probably worthless as security for my bank loan. Therefore, reluctantly, I said I'd try to persuade Louise to join me in giving the bank a second charge on our house in Clapham. Fortunately, property values in that area of south London had soared since we bought it three years earlier and Louise agreed that she'd be prepared to risk a proportion of the increase in value of our house for the bank to take as a charge. As a result and thanks to Dick Putland's vision, 50 per cent of our funding requirements were met when we agreed the bank could take a second charge for £10,000 on our home. However, this wasn't agreed until we'd been warned by Dick that the bank prided itself on its reputation for calling in charges given as security against loans should the business fail. The threat of losing your home is an excellent way of concentrating the mind and, from the bank's point of view, it sorts out the committed entrepreneur from the rest.

Now that the bank loan was safely under our belts, I felt confident I could approach one or two of the big brewers for free trade loans to help cover the cost of our funding requirements. After many meetings with trade representatives from both breweries, where my feasibility study had been dissected, ridiculed and generally pulled to pieces, I was fortunate in securing two free trade loans, £7,000 from Charrington's and £4,000 from Shepherd Neame. Both loans were at 5 per cent, which was tremendous value bearing in mind that the bank base rate was then 16 per cent and I was borrowing at 3 per cent over base, so the loans were cheap money in comparison to my 19 per cent bank interest rate. In return, all the brewers wanted was for me to buy their lagers, bottled beers, wines and spirits, which suited me as in any event I would have had to go to a brewery for those items.

In that exciting last week of April 1979, I had managed to bring together all the finance required for the project, 100 per cent of it borrowed. This included the £100 to buy the company that had by then changed its name from Wetherland Ltd to Bruce's Brewery (Southwark) Ltd.

One evening my sister Pippa, who was the PR manager at the Savoy Hotel, asked me if I'd given any thought to what we might name the pub and whether we were considering having any logos, slogans and mottos. I had to confess I'd given no thought at all to the marketing and public relations side of the business. I ran through a variety of names that I thought might be appropriate, especially one I'd once spotted on a pub at Mickley near Ripon that had closed. It was the Goose & Firkin, and it seemed absolutely right for the kind of operation I envisaged. The goose would help portray the wholesome Dickensian-style food I'd provide while a nine-gallon firkin cask would be most fitting for my little brewery.

Pippa arranged for me to meet Jamie Nimmo, who was a rising star in the creative department of D'Arcy Masius MacManus, the advertising agency where she'd once worked. Jamie and I met for a pint in a pub near his office in Regent Street and agreed to design a suitable logo of a goose drinking from a firkin, which could be used on T-shirts and signwriting, including an etched mirror that Richard Barker-Harland was proposing to have made and fitted above the fireplace. The mirror also featured for the first time the Latin motto devised by my cousin Michael Kaye, 'Usque ad mortem bibendum!' ('Drink until you die!').

I was able to collect the keys to the premises on 24 April, when Raymond Wicks and I carried out an inventory of the sparse fixtures and fittings that had not been damaged by vandals or water from the leaking roof. Now I had official access, Louise and I could spend our evenings and weekends clearing out a lot of the junk and rubble and start to mark with chalk precisely where we wanted everything in the bar to be placed. We could only get the feel of the premises by standing and waving our arms around, which could not be gained by studying plans in an office.

A builder friend, Michael Sperling, and I spent a lot of time talking about this side of the development, which required a lot of structural work, as well as encouraging him to persuade his subcontractors to keep down the formidable costs of plumbing and wiring. This behind-the-scenes activity, which customers never see, was extremely time consuming. The roof in particular needed a lot of attention and could only be seen by passengers on trains that rumbled within feet of the rusty guttering.

One evening, as Louise and I stood armed with our respective pieces of chalk, it occurred to us that we'd given no thought as to how we'd furnish the pub. We'd felt that church pews and refectory tables would be the most suitable but we had no idea where we could get suitably sized pews. The following Saturday, while pursuing our favourite hobby of trailing round junk shops to look for a bargain or two, we mentioned our dilemma to the owner of a second-hand furniture shop, who said he'd be able to find us some suitable pews for the pub.

When we returned from a backpacking holiday in the Greek islands, there was a great pile of letters from people who had answered our advertisement in the *Morning Advertiser* for a management couple. The next few weeks were spent interviewing a huge cross-section of hopeful applicants. As I'd be spending most of my time underground brewing the beer, someone would have to be responsible for running the pub. There were two or three possible candidates but in the final judgement, Louise and I were unanimous in agreeing that the best couple were Tint and Alistair Watson, who were running a pub in Padstow.

They were both larger-than-life characters. Alistair closely resembled Mr Pickwick and he would certainly look the part behind the bar. Tint was a first-rate cook with plenty of catering experience. I rang them one evening to say they were just the couple we were looking for only to be told that, while they'd liked everything they had seen, they couldn't face returning to London from Cornwall. On reflection, it might have been better if the interview hadn't taken place underneath the leaking roof of what would become the manager's bedroom as train after train went rumbling by the window. We were devastated, as there was no one else we felt was right for the job. But just three days later, Alistair phoned to say that he and Tint had been chewing the fat and, despite rumbling trains and leaking roofs, decided the job was just too exciting to turn down.

One of the most frustrating events during our early days of setting up was a strike at British Telecom, especially as it was well before mobile phones. This meant there was no telephone at the pub and no chance of having a line installed until the dispute was over. I had to spend precious time running all round the area desperately trying to find public phone boxes that weren't vandalised in order to communicate with the outside world as the project started to hot up. The week before the builder started, Dick Putland asked if he could inspect the site in which his bank was about to make a hefty investment. I remember the astonishment in his voice when I suggested he should turn up with wellies, a warm coat and a torch for a meeting on a warm June afternoon. Fortunately, he was undeterred and remained cheerful and enthusiastic, even after picking his way over the damp mess and rubble.

On Monday 11 June, the builders moved in and we started to spend the bank's money. We'd received firm estimates from Michael Sperling and Richard Barker-Harland and it was clear from the day that building work started that we'd be hard pressed to keep within my £20,000 budget. I decided to phone round a few friends to explain my predicament in the hope they'd join us in the evenings and weekends to carry out a bit of voluntary labouring and save a few bob on the builders' costs. Louise's cousin and her stepbrother, plus a student lodger, were in charge of removing the bitumen and glue from the old lino on the floorboards. One of their friends joined this labouring gang and there was much laughter when someone asked him to pop to the hardware shop round the corner and buy a tin of 'elbow grease', much to the shopkeeper's amusement.

I was conscious that whatever money I'd managed to raise would probably not be enough, and I was keen to receive what had already been agreed. I spent a lot of time in call boxes ringing up people at Charrington's, asking where the £7,000 cheque might be. During one of these conversations, I was informed that their official view was that, while the pub might work, it would be overtrading if it ever did more than £2,000 a week, which was a little over my own best estimate. Little did any of us realise at that stage that the pub would never take less than £4,000 a week. In hindsight, it reinforced my feeling that you should never listen to 'the experts' and certainly not if they're from a big brewer.

Mike Pope, a lecturer in art and design at South London Polytechnic, dropped in one day and asked if I needed any help with painting the outside or general signwriting. When I confessed I hadn't considered the matter, Mike kindly offered his services along with some of his students, and we agreed to paint the pub's exterior a dark emerald green and cover as much of the outside as possible with signwriting.

My suggestions on both green paint for the exterior and the name Goose & Firkin had both been overruled by the so-called experts in the brewing industry. Green was deemed to be an unlucky colour, so there were scarcely any green-painted pubs in the country and none in London. I'm not certain if it was perversity or sheer bloody-mindedness, but green was what I wanted. Now, I could do what I wanted, but I would go on to find that many of the things I proposed and which were unprecedented at the time have now become the norm. But it was Mike Pope who deserves the credit for the much-admired wooden carved hanging sign depicting the Goose & Firkin. By the end of the first week of building work, the pub had been virtually gutted and resembled a shell on each floor. It was the point of no return, as there was nothing left of the old pub.

Although I wasn't planning to open the Goose for another month or so, I was already contemplating opening a second pub. When I heard that two sites were due to be leased by Grosvenor Estates in Mayfair, I couldn't resist the temptation of arranging to view both the Mason's Arms and the Carpenter's Arms. On a Monday morning at 7 am, I saw the builders starting to work and went to meet the Grosvenor Estates agent at both pubs. They were in a smart area of Mayfair and I felt somewhat conspicuous in my scruffy labourer's clothes. I was looked down upon with amused disdain by the agent, who had agreed to show me around. As I was leaving the second pub, a large, chauffeur-driven car pulled up and six smartly dressed men in dark suits got out and prepared to enter the pub. I exclaimed, 'My goodness, it's either the mafia or the big brewers', to which the obvious leader of the group replied, 'You're wrong on both counts. We're from Young's Brewery and my name is John Young. Who are you?'

I explained what I was doing at the former Duke of York and John Young, the Wandsworth brewery's chair, and his entire board were so intrigued that we arranged for them to visit the Goose later that morning. Showing them round and in particular where the brewery was being created out of the rubble in a corner of the cellar under the gents' urinal, I felt they couldn't believe what they were seeing or hearing, although they remained politely enthusiastic. It was from that first meeting that I developed a close affiliation with John Young and his team.

I was keen to acquire the lease of the Carpenter's Arms, which had a cellar big enough to brew in, and so we set about preparing a feasibility study for the pub, even though the Goose had yet to open. But a month later Grosvenor Estates wrote to me and said that while my proposals and levels of rent were acceptable to them, they were reluctant to grant me the lease as my concept was unproven. They added that they were concerned about being party to a joint failure of reviving the ancient practice of pubs brewing their own beer on the premises. 'I'll show them,' I thought as I threw their letter in the wastepaper bin.

The project at the Goose was gathering pace. Each day started at around 5 am, when I got up to do my paperwork and attempted to keep control over the many tasks and costs that were arising. I seldom went to bed before midnight and there was no time to stop for weekends or other distractions. By the end of June, Tint and Alistair Watson had moved into the top floor of the pub, even though it hadn't been decorated. It was essential they started to assume responsibility for the pub side such as staff recruitment, finding food suppliers and pianists, leaving me free to concentrate on the overall development of the site and, in particular, the brewery.

At 6 am on Thursday 5 July 1979, my 31st birthday, Roger Booth and I started to brew the first beer at Bruce's Brewery in Southwark. We'd worked out the recipe together, based on my hope that what we produced would taste something along the lines of Fuller's and Young's, London's two independent family brewers. It would be at least a week before we would know what it tasted like for the customer. All went smoothly but it was hard to concentrate on brewing with the new equipment as there were constant interruptions from well-wishers and the curious who could not only smell the beer being brewed but could also see the steam rising from the central light well that acted as a chimney in the middle of the building above the cellar.

After all the months of unemployment followed by weeks of research and development, the first major hurdle in opening our first business had been overcome and we had beer bubbling away and waiting to be sold. However, looking at the bar upstairs, I realised there was still a long way to go before we could sell the beer to the public. Richard Barker-Harland and two of his carpenters were having to moonlight as they were busy on another job so they had to work on our bar and back-fitting between 4 am and 7 am before going to their 'normal' day's work. They would pull my leg when I turned up to start work as 'late' as 6 am in the brewery.

The Watsons were busy recruiting bar and catering staff and a miscellany of pub pianists. Louise and I wanted to meet and listen to the pianists before engaging a couple of regulars. One Saturday evening, we encountered Crazy Jimmy playing in a back-street boozer near Waterloo Bridge. He was brilliant and we managed to poach him immediately for the Goose, which was conveniently close to where he worked as a nightwatchman at the South London Polytechnic, where our signwriter Mike Pope also worked.

By the second Monday in July, I felt things had progressed so well that we could almost open that week, so I announced that morning that in 48 hours, the Goose would open. As usual, everyone assumed I was joking and just carried on with their work until it became obvious I was serious and whatever they were doing would have to be finished by Wednesday 18 July. If not, the work would have to be completed after the pub had started trading.

The money had almost run out and it was essential that we started trading to generate some cash and start to pay off the rest of my outstanding bills from the subcontractors. A number of them had begun to get a little nervous as word got out that neither Louise nor I had any more cash of our own. Our ability to pay depended entirely on the pub proving to be a success. This helped to concentrate minds and some 30 of us worked through the night on the Tuesday prior to our Wednesday 18 July opening.

My neighbour, Mike Vaughan-Fowler, dropped in on his way home to Clapham on Tuesday evening and was still there in the early hours of the morning. He'd been detailed by Louise to hang all the curtains round the windows as she'd only just finished making them earlier that evening. Everyone was involved: wife, friends, hired hands, relatives and volunteers. There was no escape for all those wonderful people, who worked right through the night to complete the job.

As Wednesday arrived, at 11 am, we opened the doors of the Goose & Firkin to the public, with paint still drying on the radiators. Within minutes, people started to drift in and for the first time ever I heard a complete stranger ask for 'a pint of Bruce's Bitter, please'. Standing there in my white overalls and wellies, I waited in trepidation as he took the first sip. It was great watching him smack his lips, announce his approval and hand over a £1 note, marking the first pint of my beer ever sold for money. As a train rumbled overhead, I thought at last our train had left the station, too. What a wonderful feeling that was.

Lessons and learnings

🍺 **Lesson 2: Build a trusted support network**

I couldn't have achieved any of my ambitions without the unwavering, loyal support of my wife through all the good and the bad times. Also, my close friends in the brewing industry offered invaluable advice and enthusiastic support for my initiative. Start to build contacts and a circle of friends and advisors and share your plans (as well as your doubts) with them so you can benefit from their advice.

🍺 **Lesson 6: Control the cash**

Starting a business with absolutely no personal financial resources at all is certainly not easy. Borrow as much as you can from banks, family and friends but try to hang on to all your equity, as that's where the value in your business will eventually be. Equity is gold dust.

🍺 **Lesson 9: Look after yourself and your family**

Keep fit to enhance your energy and maintain a razor-sharp brain in order to tackle the many obstacles you'll encounter all along the way. Make time to relax with family and friends to avoid becoming a complete workaholic and to help keep stress at bay. At this time, running, which had always helped me to stay fit, also helped me to find my first Firkin pub.

From early days to Old Peculier

1958–1972

Now that I've shared the story of the Goose & Firkin, let me rewind back to the beginning. From an early age, I've wanted to do something special with my life. I was a firm believer in fate and determined to make the most of every opportunity that came my way. By my late twenties, I was convinced that all my many and varied experiences to date were leading to something positive and it wouldn't be long before I'd start my own business.

I'd been very happy at my prep school, Cheltenham College Junior School, and ended up as a house prefect. From around the age of nine, I gained the nickname Jumbo as I was quite a chubby little chap. I resolved to lose my puppy fat by running. I did this at least twice a week, barefoot and in thick corduroy shorts that flapped around below my knees due to my mother's policy with all my clothes that one day 'I would grow into them'. I would run five miles, which was 40 times round the 220-yard grass running track, on Wednesday and Saturday evenings during the summer term. Not only did this rapidly lose some weight but it also nurtured my love of running.

When I wasn't running, I was cycling on my Raleigh bike. It had taken me four years to save the £25 it cost, and it became one of my most treasured possessions. I used to cycle happily up to 100 miles a day and one of my most memorable summer holidays was cycling, aged 16, around the chateaux of the Loire in Brittany.

It was while I was at prep school that I realised how incredibly inept I was when it came to any form of logical thought, and simple arithmetic in particular. I just couldn't fathom out how, if one was travelling in a train at 65 miles per hour and there were 100 telegraph poles, each one spaced 20 yards apart, how many fractions of a second would elapse between passing each one. And, quite frankly, I didn't care. I feel that could be the root cause of many of my successes and failures: unless I really cared about a project and was fully committed, I didn't apply myself. Sometimes, if I couldn't answer an exam question, I'd just write 'Don't know, don't care'!

My father, having been the headmaster of Bishop Cotton School in Simla, India, spent hours giving me extra coaching, especially in maths and Latin, in the hope I wouldn't let him down and fail my common entrance exam for the senior school. Even with his expert teaching, I still failed to grasp the basic rudiments of maths and only managed to pass the exam by a two per cent margin.

My first two terms at Cheltenham were enjoyable but uneventful, apart from setting new records for the junior half-mile and one-mile track events, both of which I achieved while my father was watching proudly on sports day. Just six weeks later, while I was on holiday with an uncle and aunt in Yorkshire, my aunt received a phone call to say my father had died suddenly, aged 46, from a heart attack. This was a devastating blow for a 13-year-old schoolboy and its effects, both good and bad, would alter the course of my life forever.

I vividly remember cycling to pay my last respects to my father in the chapel of rest at Leatherhead Crematorium, and I also recall a parish church packed full of mourners and rows of wreaths and flowers laid out at the crematorium. My father and I had always been good friends but it's only from the early teens that a boy can start to really share interests with his father, and this was going to be denied to me. Everything I was going to miss about him became apparent as I listened to the various eulogies made by the many strangers during his memorial service in the newly dedicated OBE Chapel in St Paul's Cathedral in the City of London.

Within a few months of his death, it became clear that my mother and I would have to leave our home, which was provided as part of his job as principal of the Queen Elizabeth Training College for disabled people. My father's career had been spent in the British Army, teaching, or running a college, and he'd never had to invest in a house of his own. This meant we had no family asset to sell and almost no money in the bank to help buy our first one. His total estate came to around £5,000, and my mother spent £3,000 buying a three-bedroom cottage near Cheltenham so she could be near my boarding school. I feared I'd be taken away from school after just two terms as my mother couldn't afford the fees. Fortunately, Humphrey Whitbread, a governor of Queen Elizabeth's, wrote to my mother saying he'd heard about our sad news and financial plight, and would she mind if he paid for my education out of his charitable education trust? At least my education was secure, but that still left the family with very little income to live on. Humphrey Whitbread was a member of the great brewing dynasty, so this was my early brush with brewing.

At the age of 44, my mother decided to train as a teacher and started a course at Cheltenham Technical College. We found ourselves doing our homework together, which was a novel experience. Once she'd qualified, she became a teacher at the Star Centre for Youth at Ullenwood, near Cheltenham, where she taught domestic science and home management to severely disabled young adults.

At school, my resentment of authority grew when the headmaster told me one day that athletics and cross-country running were too individualistic and I should become more involved in team sports. My final term was marked by my keen disappointment at not being made a prefect or captain of the athletics or cross-country teams, especially as I'd been awarded my colours for longer than anyone else.

Sitting my maths O-level and failing for the fifth time was a humiliating experience. I was also conscious of my family's impecunious state and that most of the other boys at school had fathers to guide them in their future careers. I remember the demeaning feeling as other boys were leaving at the end of term with their school trunks in the backs of their fathers' Jaguars and Rovers while I was waiting by the bus stop, having dragged my trunk along the pavement on a roller skate, as they swept by.

Careers guidance at school had been negligible, and the only suggestion I ever received was that I might make it as a policeman as I was 'good with people'. Instead, I applied for university but knew I would stand no chance of being accepted due to my lack of O-level maths. All my applications were duly rejected by return and it became clear I needed some form of qualification, so I started to look around for a job that would train me in general business management. I failed to be accepted for Unilever's prestigious management training programme but was accepted by Shell-Mex and Courage, Barclay & Simonds. I decided to join Courage for no other reason than I thought a career in pubs and breweries would be more enjoyable than petrol stations and oil refineries.

On the day I started my first job, my landlady brought me a cup of tea at 4.30 am. This was followed by a huge, greasy breakfast before I was dispatched into the crisp, wintry air to catch the first trolleybus of the morning from Tilehurst into Reading town centre. It was then just a short walk along Bridge Street until I reached the Courage brewery, which was ablaze with light as the night shift was coming to an end at 6 am.

I reported to the brewery foreman, who gave me a clean, white boiler suit and wellington boots and told me to report to the malt store at the top of the tower brewery. My days as a brewer were about to begin. The next six months were spent covering all aspects of beer production, and I received a thorough practical training, although reporting for the 6 am shift after an evening in London wasn't always easy. There were many occasions when I went straight from the milk train at the station to the brewery.

Milling, mashing, boiling, cooling, bottling, kegging, canning, laboratory analysis and quality control were all included, and at the end of six months I'd enjoyed an exceptionally good grounding in how to make beer. I wasn't happy socially while working in Reading which, unless you were at the university, had little to offer an 18-year-old who usually had to be in bed early before the 4.30

am alarm for the morning shift. The 10 pm to 6 am shift also did nothing to improve my social life. It was with some relief that I was transferred to Bristol for the next part of my training, which included transport, distribution and hotel management with Anchor Hotels and Taverns. My most notable achievement while I was working in the transport department was to misunderstand the Bristol dialect and send 200 dozen bottles to the British Legion Club in Bermondsey, London, rather than two dozen bottles to the British Legion Club at Burnham-on-Sea, Somerset.

I took my first flat in Bristol on Clifton Road, just behind the University Union. I shared the flat with Johnny Jessop, who'd been a friend from age nine at prep school, and Bob Loosley, Johnny's colleague in the sales office of Robinson's Waxed Papers at Fishponds. My first monthly pay cheque for the princely sum of £40 after tax went on a pair of contact lenses, which meant I no longer had to peer through a pair of glasses with thick, milk-bottle-bottom lenses. An entire pay cheque after moving to Bristol was lavished on a Morris Minor convertible: £40 included the piece of string that held on the front bumper. I proudly arrived for work one morning in my acquisition but was refused entry to the staff car park by the commissionaire, who felt such a scruffy and dilapidated vehicle would bring disrepute to the brewery.

It was good to be working normal office hours for the first time and my social life picked up enormously. I made many friends there who are still close friends today, especially Bob Loosley, who eventually became best man at my wedding and godfather to my first daughter, Rebecca. Bob also owned a Morris Minor convertible before he graduated to the dizzy heights of a 'frog-eyed' Austin Healey Sprite. We used to have great excursions with our two cars in convoy as we headed off over the new Severn Bridge to camp in the Brecon Beacons over the border in Wales.

Those early days in Bristol proved to be short, as I was soon transferred to London, where I began one of the most interesting periods of my training, learning about wines and spirits with Charles Kinloch and Saccone & Speed. Based in Park Royal in north-west

London, I covered many miles, belting up and down the A4, well before the M4 was built, passing through Hungerford, little knowing I would live there one day. I made more on my mileage allowance in my little car than I did earning a salary. Apart from being educated about fine wines, I was also interested to learn about the bulk generic wines that were delivered from Spain, Germany and France by huge road tankers then tested and conditioned in tanks prior to bottling. The spirits side of the business was learned in bonded warehouses at Gainsford Street in the old Docklands area behind the Courage Brewery at Horsleydown near Tower Bridge, and it was there that I picked up the skill to blend whiskies.

When I returned to Reading, I was sent to work in various accounts departments, where my crass inability to fathom maths made life a struggle.

It was while I was working in the tied trade department that the time came for me to serve my first pint, which was about the only job in the brewery I hadn't yet done. The Jack of Both Sides at Cemetery Junction in Reading was the appointed venue, and it was with some trepidation that I pulled my first pint of draught Guinness for a large Irishman on a Friday night. I just managed to get the right level of frothy head in the glass and give the correct change. The latter point was my biggest fear given mental arithmetic was not my strongest point. Trying to remember orders for large rounds, understanding the strong Irish accent and adding up the rounds correctly before working out the change demanded supreme powers of concentration. The worst thing was having three separate mechanical tills: one for drinks, one for tobacco and one for food. Trying to sort out payment for a mixed order was the ultimate challenge and the more the customers shouted, the harder it became. By the second night, I'd got the hang of how to serve a pint correctly and work out how to use the tills. However, my shift ended after only ten minutes. An almighty punch-up had started between about 20 burly Irish labourers, who were throwing bar stools, tables and glasses at each other. The manager shouted at me to lie on the floor behind the bar while the various missiles were flying over the heads of us frightened bar staff. Eventually, four vans full of police arrived and arrested all the fighters, leaving no customers in the bar, so the pub was closed for the rest of that evening.

The final part of my training was devoted to free trade sales. My area of responsibility covered Portsmouth and its environs, where I visited working men's clubs and naval establishments where Courage had long-established trade. During one of the free trade visits, I had to go with a keg fitter to the Royal Military Academy at Sandhurst to repair a faulty keg line. I was wearing my Courage overalls complete with an embroidered golden cockerel badge. There were howls of laughter when the bar opened at lunchtime and two or three chaps I'd been at school with came into the officers' mess and found me, a true artisan, crawling around behind the bar in my overalls.

I successfully finished my two years of management training and was transferred to the industrial management office in Bristol. I'd expressed an interest in personnel management and found the economics, industrial psychology and sociology particularly interesting. I'd thought of becoming a member of the Institute of Personnel Management, which as far as I could tell was the only professional qualification in the world that didn't require maths O-level as a prerequisite. I embarked on a correspondence course but abandoned it after a few months as I just couldn't study in the evenings after a hard day's work.

When I returned to Bristol, I moved back into the flat on Clifton Road. I bought an old TR3 sports car for £120 for fun, but there was a snag: the job was terribly boring. I went to stay for the weekend with the uncle and aunt in Yorkshire who'd had the unfortunate task eight years earlier of telling me my father had died. While I was there, I heard that Theakston's Brewery in Masham, near Ripon, was looking for someone to help Paul Theakston run the brewery. Paul's father Frank had died and his uncle Thomas had retired. I borrowed my uncle's Land Rover and rumbled across the North Yorkshire moors and into Wensleydale to meet Paul Theakston. We immediately got on and I learned that, at the age of 23, he had the formidable task of keeping the brewery going. He was looking for a contemporary with general brewery experience to share the running of the brewery,

18 tenanted pubs and some 50 or so free trade outlets in the Yorkshire Dales.

I was delighted to be offered the job as brewer and sales manager, especially as just a few weeks earlier, Courage had told me that, until I was in my thirties, it would be unlikely for me to be considered responsible enough for any junior management position such as looking after a dozen or so pubs. At Theakston's, at the age of 21, I had the opportunity to not only look after 18 pubs but also a whole brewery. Courage didn't try to persuade me to stay when I handed in my notice, so I packed my old school trunk and boarded the train to York. My uncle met me at the station and drove me to the King's Head in Masham's Market Square, where I settled into a tiny room on the top floor.

David with his team at Theakston's Brewery, 1970

Six months later, I heard there was a cottage on the opposite side of the Market Square that was available to rent, and Paul felt it would be fun if he moved out of his mother's house. So the two young brewers moved into the cottage, which soon acquired the nickname

Downwind – the worst place to be after a night supping Old Peculier. Stuck in the wilds of North Yorkshire, there were few eligible young ladies to pursue so the local bachelors used to take it in turns to meet girls off the train from London at York station on Friday evenings, and many hilarious weekends ensued. I also spent my leisure time exploring the beautiful countryside of the Yorkshire Dales or sailing with Paul in his dinghy off the coast at Scarborough and Whitby.

I'd brew about 40 barrels of beer (36 gallons in a barrel or 288 pints) two or three days a week and spend the rest of the time visiting the Theakston's pubs in my Triumph Herald convertible and attempting to promote sales of the beers to free trade pubs. I was also responsible for general admin and the wine and spirits department. I had to be jack of all trades: brewing, driving the Bedford three-ton dray or serving behind the bar at a local fell race, in which I would often also participate.

In the early 1970s, CAMRA was starting to knock the big brewers for cutting back on the production of traditionally brewed real ales in favour of keg beer that's chilled, carbonated, filtered and pasteurised. The most notorious brewery was Watney's, with its Red Barrel and the advertising slogan of Watney's Red Revolution. Gradually, as a result of CAMRA's campaigning, interest in real ale grew and so did the reputation of Theakston's beers. As a result, we became increasingly busy.

It soon became apparent that Paul and I needed an accountant as, although his prowess at maths was far greater than mine, we did need more financial information. An accountant was duly appointed and not long after he started, Paul and I were horrified to learn that the brewery was making virtually no profit at all. We also appointed our first free trade salesman as it was essential that sales were increased to rescue the high level of cost per barrel. Sales and marketing grew in importance and Paul and I had fun trying to devise a new beer with the help of an advertising agency in Leeds. We thought their suggestion of Double Barrel might be highly appropriate, especially as Paul and I seemed to be the only two people in Wensleydale who didn't spend our leisure time shooting grouse. However, within days of approving the name, we received solicitors' letters from Allied

Breweries, saying they felt the name infringed on their clients' Double Diamond trademark, and from Watney's, who were equally concerned about the impact on the name Red Barrel. So, our new beer never came to fruition but it did mark the first time my activities drew the attention of the big brewers.

One day, Paul told me his cousin Michael Theakston had been made redundant after a career making coal-mining pit props, and he wished to join the brewery. From then on, my days at Theakston's were numbered. I was also hearing rumours that, as the brewery was doing so well, other young members of the family would soon be joining, including Michael's three sons and Paul's brother John. This led me to ask if I could buy shares in the business, but I was told firmly by Michael they'd never entertain anyone owning shares unless they were called Theakston. This was my first realisation that nepotism is fine as long as you're a beneficiary, but it's grossly unfair to a loyal hard worker who's denied access to sharing in the fortunes of a business he's helping to make a success.

One Sunday afternoon, coming home after watching the Three Peaks Race, with Paul's Norwegian ex-girlfriend Trine sitting on my lap in the passenger seat (in the days before seat belts were fitted), we were in a head-on collision with another car. Simon Staveley, a good friend, was at the wheel. I had severe cuts to my eyeballs from the windscreen, which smashed on impact. There were six of us in the car and Simon broke his leg severely. We were all rushed by ambulance for the hour's journey to the nearest hospital in Northallerton. I thought I'd never see again as my eyes were swathed in bandages. To my great relief, when the doctor untied them I realised I could see after all. The doctor thought my sight was saved by my contact lenses, both of which were broken by the windscreen glass hitting them, but they acted as a shield for my eyeballs.

As so often happens with me, fate decreed that good should come out of this near disaster. Six weeks later, I attended a wedding wearing my replacement lenses for the first time. This was a painful experience and my eyes were bloodshot and streaming with tears when a gorgeous blonde girl came over and compassionately asked if there was anything she could do to help. She introduced herself as Louise, and we were inseparable for the rest of the day. We even altered the place settings for the dinner that evening so we could sit together. On our seventh subsequent meeting, we became engaged to be married.

I started house-hunting and found a cottage for us to live in after our wedding in Copt Hewick, near Ripon, which was a terraced, two-up, two-down for £3,500. I had to borrow the £500 deposit from my mother.

One day, I found a note on the doormat asking me to go to Michael Theakston's house in Harrogate. I had a bad feeling that all might not be well and my fears were justified. Michael explained that in view of all the other young Theakstons who'd be joining the brewery in the coming few years, he thought I'd always be pushed sideways and ultimately downwards. He repeated his remark that because I wasn't a Theakston there would be no chance of becoming a shareholder. With great regret, I agreed to leave with the princely sum of £1,000 in compensation and the use of the company car for three months. I stopped at the first phone box and rang Louise in London to tell her that her fiancé had just lost his job and ask if she wanted to call off the engagement. To my great relief, she said no, but from that phone call Louise would embark on a life as the wife of a man whose entrepreneurial career was about to begin.

Lessons and learnings

🍺 **Lesson 1: Follow your instincts and demonstrate your motivation to succeed**

If you really wish to become one, there are no barriers to becoming an entrepreneur. My schooldays were generally lacklustre and I failed university entrance but realised I needed a trade or a training, so I became a management trainee and learned how to brew.

🍺 **Lesson 3: Be brave, ambitious and determined to overcome all obstacles**

When my father died when I was only 13, I had to grow up quickly and learn to be independent and self-sufficient, both being traits shown from an early age by successful entrepreneurs.

🍺 **Lesson 4: Seize opportunities as they arise**

When I experienced being on the wrong side of nepotism, I left the family-owned company and vowed to start my own business rather than work in someone else's. Sometimes being forced into a position you didn't choose can make you more resourceful and help you to think in different ways.

Learning the hard way with punch-ups and pythons

1973–1978

As I didn't have a job, I had plenty of time to get our first home ready for my bride, although it was so small there was little to alter or decorate. The rest of my time was spent helping Louise plan our wedding and, since her mother had died at the same young age as my father, 46, she had to carry out most of the arrangements herself.

People were surprised to hear I was no longer at Theakston's, especially as the company appeared to be doing so well. The most important thing for me, as I was taking on a mortgage and a marriage, was to obtain some form of income as soon as possible. I was driving home from Harrogate one day and called in on an old friend, John Owen, who by the age of 28 had built a chain of discotheques and nightclubs throughout the north of England. He'd occasionally drive to Masham in his white convertible Rolls-Royce and we'd have a pub lunch during which he'd extol the virtues of being an entrepreneur. John proved that from humble beginnings he'd built a business and a small fortune and had enjoyed a lot of fun along the way.

John was sympathetic to my predicament and agreed I must secure work quickly as a result of my new commitments. He was busy preparing his business for its impending sale to Mecca and offered me the job of assistant catering manager to improve the food sales of his operations. I explained I knew little about cooking but he stressed that however little I knew it must be more than some of his nightclub managers, so I got the job. I busied myself for the next few months gaining experience not only in how northern nightclubs operate but also in how hard it is to persuade people to eat in a discotheque when all they really want to do is drink and dance.

I nearly came to grief when I was responsible for the opening of a smart new restaurant at Harrogate's Intercon nightclub. I was putting the final touches to the grand opening when the chef rang to say he'd just been offered another job and wouldn't be coming back. He assured me that all the food supplies had been delivered and I'd have nothing to worry about if I took on his role for the evening. I had no alternative but to agree. Everything was going smoothly until I realised the 500 chicken pieces he'd ordered all needed roasting. I'd instructed him to buy pre-cooked chicken that we could just pop into the deep-fat fryer prior to serving. The problem was that we only had fryers and no ovens, and panic ensued. Louise offered to come and relieve me as chef while I phoned round Harrogate to find a catering establishment with a couple of spare ovens free on a Saturday evening.

Like an episode of *Fawlty Towers*, I spent the next few hours dashing through the kitchen window and up and down the fire escape with trays of chicken that I drove to a restaurant on the other side of town, then brought the cooked ones back ready for Louise to serve to an unsuspecting public. The evening proved to be a huge success with many compliments for the high standard of catering but it was an experience I wouldn't want to repeat in a hurry.

The sale of John Owen's Intercon Group to Mecca went ahead and in came the hard men from Britain's top leisure company. My interview was more like an inquisition, but I was offered the job of assistant catering manager at the Nottingham Palais. The prospect didn't enthral me as it would mean moving house and working until 3 am six nights a week. I didn't feel it would be a good start to our marriage. Out of work again, I was introduced to two property developers in Bradford. I arrived outside a launderette in Duckworth Lane and parked my two-door, beaten-up brown Ford Cortina behind two shiny red Jensen Interceptors.

I went up to meet them and spent a hilarious couple of hours that I'd hardly call an interview and they decided I'd be appointed managing director of a new company, Twin City Investments, named after the two cities Sheffield and Leeds. I'd be given, and not have to buy, 20 per cent of the equity. My brief was to buy and develop sites suitable for discotheques and nightclubs in the hope we could emulate John Owen's success. My salary of £4,000 a year was twice what I'd been earning at Theakston's less than a year earlier and I certainly had no complaints about the Fiat 124 Sport Coupé they gave me in place of my Cortina.

Unfortunately, only a few months later, along with many other property companies and secondary banks, the great property crash of 1973/74 dramatically affected our plans. I was asked for my car keys back and told not to bother to come in again. As I headed off along Duckworth Lane on the bus, I bore no hard feelings but wasn't looking forward to telling Louise that her new husband was out of work yet again.

Louise hadn't been particularly happy living in Yorkshire. As mentioned earlier, she'd launched her own catering company, Crumpets, with a friend, Di Milligan, but it didn't look as if it would provide sufficient income for one person, let alone two. Some evenings I'd returned from Bradford to find Louise lying on a night storage heater trying to keep warm and she was missing having a proper job.

One of our friends, Richard Whiteley, who'd go on to become the first host of TV's popular *Countdown* programme, phoned to say he'd seen an advertisement in the *Daily Telegraph* placed by Charram Ltd, a London pub and disco company, for an area manager. I applied for the job and was asked to go to London for an interview. We realised it was important to visit the outlets run by the company, so Louise and I zig-zagged across the country from Manchester and Newcastle down to London and Brighton. It proved worthwhile because some of the other applicants for the job hadn't bothered to visit a single outlet owned by the company, whereas I'd produced a detailed trading report on each outlet. When the MD, Peter Salussolia, asked for my opinion of the Cocked Hat in Scunthorpe, I was able to reply,

'It was closed,' and this answer proved I'd visited all the units.

I was offered the job and Louise and I started house-hunting in London and soon found a small two-up, two-down terraced house just off Lavender Hill in Battersea for £13,500. I'd been happy working in Yorkshire as I love the countryside and have Yorkshire blood in my veins on my mother's side, so moving to London was a daunting prospect. My new place of work was above Flanagan's Fish Restaurant on Kensington High Street. When Louise dropped me there on my first morning, I had no idea what I was letting myself in for, but at least it was some form of employment. And, as we were in London, Louise would have a better chance of finding an interesting and, we hoped, well-paid job.

My responsibilities covered a dozen or so large London pubs, some with live entertainment, three discotheques and two cabaret clubs. The outlets were primarily pubs that Bass Charrington had leased to Charram and included such well-known venues as the Duke of Richmond in Earl's Court, the Trafalgar in the King's Road, Chelsea, and the Clarence in Piccadilly. Outside London there were pubs and discos in South Wales, Brighton, Leicester, Manchester and Newcastle. They added up to long, hard days in a tough business with late nights and lots of driving, always more than 1,000 miles per week.

One night there was great excitement in the small street where we lived, when two police cars arrived with flashing lights and officers told me the Volunteer pub in Barking had gone up in flames. The records showed I was the nearest member of the management team. As a result, my black mafia-style Renault was escorted across London at high speed to attend the scene.

I had a mercy dash through the night on a second occasion when I was phoned at 10 pm one Friday to say there had been a major punch-up at the Black Bull in Lewisham High Street. Most of the police vehicles and ambulances had gone by the time I arrived after zooming round the South Circular, and there was little I could do. I well remember my disgust at finding half an ear embedded in the pub's front window, through which one of the bouncers had thrown a customer. The remaining piece of ear was removed from its glass resting place, popped into an ice bucket and dispatched by a police car to the local casualty department in the hope the owner might appreciate its recovery.

Worse was to follow. One evening, Louise and I were having supper with some friends when the manager of our Newcastle pub phoned to say there had been a murder on the premises. As I was the joint licensee, I abandoned the supper party and set off for Newcastle at a rate of knots and was stopped by the police on the A1 near Bedale in Yorkshire for speeding. I was subsequently awarded my first endorsement when I failed to convince the magistrates I was only hurrying in order to attend the scene of a murder. When I reached the pub in Newcastle at around 1 am, there was a heavy police guard on the door and all the customers had been taken away for questioning in a convoy of coaches. The only evidence that a murder had been committed was a chalk outline on the dancefloor where the victim had been found with a knife in their back. It was only discovered when the DJ had put on a slow record and the crowd had left the dance floor to buy more drinks and exposed the corpse. It transpired he was a victim of an inter-gang feud but from that night the trade was ruined and I had to close the venue forever.

Back at head office in London, there were rumours that Peter Salussolia was planning to leave the company. Charrington, who had leased most of the London pubs to Charram, were disappointed with the company's performance and announced they'd soon be putting in some of their own employees prior to reabsorbing most of the pubs into their own estate. When it became clear that my days at Charram were numbered, I wrote to the Star Group in Leeds saying how impressed I was with their Scamps discotheques and Hofbräuhaus Bierkellers and wondering if they had any suitable vacancies. I was subsequently called to Leeds for an interview and offered the job of regional manager for the north.

Louise had settled into an excellent job as PA to the sales director of Total Oil and we were enjoying living in our terraced house in Battersea. It was with much trepidation that I came home from Leeds to announce I'd been offered a job in the north of England. Louise, philosophical as ever, felt that a job in the north would be better than no job in London but she wouldn't entertain the thought of returning to live in Yorkshire. I remember the awful sinking feeling when the taxi arrived early one Monday morning to take me, complete with packed suitcase, to King's Cross to catch the train to Leeds. When I'd said goodbye to Louise, standing in her dressing gown on the front doorstep, both of us trying not to show our true feelings, I felt I was going off to war. And in a way, I was.

In Leeds, I was shown to the basement car park, where I was dismayed to find that my company car was a brown, four-year-old Ford Cortina with no radio and a heater that didn't work. I'd soon be travelling 1,200 to 1,500 miles a week on Britain's northern motorways in this beaten-up vehicle. Being away from home three or four nights a week, staying in seedy hotels and working until at least 2 am, often at weekends, forced me to drive at breakneck speed through the night to get home for the occasional day with Louise over a weekend.

After six months of this tyranny, I could no longer put up with the management style of the Star Group. Candy Whiteley, who was then married to Richard Whiteley, mentioned one day that she'd done some marketing work for a firm in London called Leisure Sales Development (LSD). I met the four directors and our objectives seemed compatible. I'd resigned from Star Group and needed a job, yet again. They were keen to develop a new pub company and broaden their experience of leisure retailing. On paper, it looked a good fit. As I was meant to be an expert on running pubs, I persuaded them to let me have a minority stake in a new company, LSD Entertainment. I had 44 per cent of the equity and the four of them held the remaining 56 per cent. I couldn't believe my luck. After a few miserable months with the Star Group, I was now in London with a large stake in a new company. There was just one problem – no money, as usual. In order to buy my stake I needed to find £5,400, which we didn't have.

Louise was working for Vic Amos, the sales director of Total Oil, and she explained our dilemma to him. Vic said he'd mention our problem to a friend in Yorkshire, Malcolm Sykes. I rang Malcolm out of the blue and couldn't believe my luck when he agreed to lend us the money for five years, interest free. Time was of the essence, as Charrington's had agreed to grant LSD the tenancy of the Artesian pub in Notting Hill. However, I was told bluntly that if I didn't have my 44 per cent investment banked by the end of the week, they'd go ahead without me. I thought this was a bit harsh as I'd be a key member of the team and it turned out to be an early warning signal that my three years with LSD would not have a happy ending. Fortunately, Malcolm sent the cheque without delay and they didn't have the opportunity to exclude me from the project before it had even started.

With my experience of running pubs, clubs, restaurants and breweries, I came up with a raft of ideas to develop the Artesian. It would be an understatement to say I was disappointed to hear one of the directors say the opportunities for the company were so great that he, and not me, would be managing director and he wanted me to be the resident pub manager and licensee. As I'd then put in my £5,400, I wasn't in a position to argue. Louise had patiently waited for my job in Leeds to come to an end in the hope I might spend some time at home with her and was now told I'd be staying in the manager's flat above a pub in Notting Hill. She gamely agreed there was no alternative and the hands-on experience would hold me in good stead for the future. For the second time in a year, I packed my suitcase and left Louise at home, only to return five days later with bags full of dirty washing for my two nights off each week. As no company car was provided, we'd bought a Fiat 500 to enable me to travel to and from the pub.

The Artesian was a rough, tough, busy Irish pub and it was with some trepidation that I accepted Charrington's challenge to clean it up. My prime objective when I became the resident manager was to introduce new staff, preferably young and female, reasonable food at lunchtimes instead of curled-at-the-edge sandwiches and pickled eggs, and to broaden entertainment from the regular ceilidh band. This wasn't as easy as I'd hoped, due to the bad name the pub had in the area for spontaneous punch-ups, the first of which I would soon experience.

It was the long, hot summer of 1976, and the police from Harrow Road nick, reputedly the toughest police station in London, warned me that relations between the Irish and West Indians would become more overheated than usual in the warm weather and I'd have to be exceptionally vigilant to stop any aggravation. The first big punch-up I had to tackle was on a sultry Friday night when two West Indians started fighting after arguing over who should pull one of the prostitutes who frequented the pub. When I clambered over the bar top, scattering glasses as I went, the fight was well under way and I had to step between them to try to keep them apart. This served to turn their attention to me, resulting in them attacking me. One of them picked up a glass, broke it on the edge of a table and lunged at me with the jagged remnants. Instinctively, I raised my arm to protect my face and the next second blood was gushing from the arm. Several regulars now joined in the fray to protect me and attempt to stop the other two fighting. By the time the police arrived, there was a right old mêlée going on and several customers, in addition to the pugilists, were bundled into police vans to spend the night at Harrow Road nick.

The next few days were relatively quiet as everyone kept their heads down, but trouble flared again the following Saturday when some drunken Scots upset Irish locals who tended to monopolise the pool table. I heard a tremendous crash of breaking glass and, running into the public bar, I saw the windows and frames had been removed by the pool table that was now lying upside down on the pavement. It had been heaved through the window by the Scots as their way of demonstrating to their fellow Celts how they felt about not being made welcome round the pool table. Another serious incident involving the pool table ended in a customer being stabbed, resulting in a near-fatal stomach wound needing 90 stitches and, eventually, a trial at the Old Bailey at which I had to be a witness.

The Notting Hill Carnival is normally a happy, multicultural musical event spread over the August Bank Holiday weekend, but it erupted in violence that hot summer of 1976 when I was managing the Artesian. The pub was right in the middle of the carnival and, as previous years had been relatively peaceful, I saw no reason not to open as usual. I hadn't anticipated the huge procession of floats and dancers coming past the doors of the Artesian. As each procession came past, the doors were flung open and hundreds of revellers swept in and cleared boxes of bottles and cans from the shelves. We couldn't take their money fast enough. Everyone was good humoured in spite of the crush.

Around 7 pm on the Saturday, the police came to warn me that trouble was flaring in various parts of the neighbourhood and I should shut the doors and not allow in any more customers. An hour later, I saw around 100 police officers in full riot gear with batons gathered outside the pub. I could hear the shouts of the troublemakers as they headed towards the police, who moved off up Chepstow Road to confront them. Then I heard police sirens and the tinkling of glass and, running out of the pub, I could see about 50 yards away that a gang of youths had commandeered a Rover police car and turned it over before setting fire to it. I kept the doors of the pub locked and the customers inside stayed much longer than they intended to avoid the risk of walking home – a great excuse for a lock-in! On Sunday, I walked to the bank to put the not-inconsiderable weekend's takings into the night deposit box.

The Artesian wasn't only a round of violent incidents. I'd learned a lot with Charram about the importance of live entertainment in London pubs and was determined to introduce the best acts I could find. As well as the ceilidh band for Irish customers at weekends, there was usually a DJ playing disco music, topless dancers, drag artists or striptease.

When strippers weren't stripping, the topless go-go dancers were gyrating to a pounding beat. A great favourite was a schoolteacher in Croydon by day, a topless go-go dancer complete with a python by night. She would arrive in her MG Sports convertible with a huge German shepherd dog in the passenger seat and the snake coiled in a laundry basket on the back seat. The 8 ft-long python used to slither all over her while she was performing her topless act and it provided a steamy new dimension to the show. One night, I heard screaming and shouting from the music room. While she had been having a well-earned rest, the python had slithered out of its basket and wriggled among the feet of the audience until it wrapped itself around the legs of a woman who almost had a fit on the spot. To soothe everyone's frayed nerves, large brandies all round were issued.

The pub was doing well but my relationship with my fellow directors at LSD was not. They announced that, as the pub was trading so well, they felt it was unfair that they should have such a small stake as 14 per cent each, making up their collective 56 per cent shareholding compared to my 44 per cent. They'd decided that each of the five of us should have a 20 per cent shareholding, reducing my stake by some 24 per cent. When I asked what would happen if I didn't agree, I was told I'd be made redundant. I was compelled to agree with their proposal as I didn't want to be out of work yet again. Some months later, I realised the way they'd structured the new shareholdings hadn't been fully understood by either me or my solicitor. Too late, we realised that the four of them had 20 per cent each of the A shareholdings (voting shares) and my 20 per cent were non-voting B shares. The chair, having gained my reluctant agreement to this arrangement, finally appointed me as managing director of LSD Entertainment and suggested we should try to expand the company, with Andy McDonald as the resident manager at the Artesian. This left me free to find and develop new sites.

I'd proved to Charrington's that I could turn round one of their problem pubs and was asked to take a look at the Peacock in Freemasons Road, Canning Town, in east London. This was a large pub with a huge public bar and entertainment-cum-cabaret room, but it had clearly seen better days before the decline of Docklands several years earlier. It was overshadowed by high-rise tower blocks.

The surrounding area had seen better times and it was a hard task trying to drag the customers back. Entertainment was along the lines of the Artesian but I soon discovered the penchant East End ladies had for male strip shows. Such was the interest that all the tickets were sold well before the first evening. Some 200 ladies in their best bibs and tuckers had gathered for a hen night in the cabaret room. One night, there was nearly a riot when the male stripper failed to turn up and 200 women all started chanting for me to be his replacement. I wasn't tempted!

Meanwhile, the Artesian was trading well and I turned my attention to finding a third site, in spite of the disappointingly low turnover at the Peacock. I'd secured two Charrington tenancies and decided to see what Watney's could offer. Within a few weeks, we'd taken over another run-down, rough pub, the Larkhall in Larkhall Lane, Clapham. An advertisement for management staff had produced only one applicant, so he got the job. He'd been a professional boxer, as his squashed nose and cauliflower ear proved, and he was clearly a man to be reckoned with. It came as no surprise when he suggested staging London's first topless girls' boxing tournament in the pub, an idea that received widespread publicity. The evening was a great success and the girls really did box topless while wearing men's-size boxing gloves.

During one of the bouts, I noticed through the window the braided hats of three senior police officers, and the next morning I was told by the chief superintendent at Clapham nick that if I were to persist with live entertainment, I'd have to get a music and dancing licence from the Greater London Council. I duly got the licence after many expensive improvements had been made to the pub to comply with environmental, health and fire regulations. As a result, I could legally stage a wide range of live entertainment but the costs of converting the Larkhall, together with its relatively low turnover, meant the Peacock and the Larkhall almost negated the profits generated by the Artesian.

After two and a half years and taking on three pubs, the profitability of LSD Entertainment was negligible. However hard I tried, I couldn't improve the turnover of the latter two pubs. Relations with my fellow directors deteriorated as all four of them started to advise me on how to sort out the management and turnover problems, of which none of them had any experience. I did my best to reassure them but the interference got worse. I used to go home at night thoroughly dejected and my mood rubbed off on Louise, who was becoming exasperated by my tales of discontent with the other directors. It became clear that the only way to escape the problems was to resign and let the others sort out the pubs with their own academic and unproven theories.

I made a thorough search of the head office to find all my letters of appointment and contracts, then handed in my resignation. I was told they'd only accept my resignation if I worked my three months' notice. The catch was that I wouldn't be paid, due to the company's lack of profits. I decided that if they weren't going to pay me, I'd leave, and I cleared my desk, at the same time requesting the return of my investment in the company of £4,400. They refused on the grounds that just because I was leaving LSD's employment, I didn't need to cease to be a shareholder. If I wasn't receiving any salary, I needed that capital sum to live on. Louise mentioned the problem to her latest boss, Jerry Williams, at BUPA. He suggested we needed a corporate lawyer to advise us and introduced us to Jill Sewell, who was working for Alexander Rubens in the City of London. She scoured all the legal documents and agreements I'd brought from the LSD offices and felt my best line of attack was that my investment had been secured by a debenture. As a debenture holder, Jill said, I could threaten to appoint an official receiver to LSD and close it down if they refused to repay my debenture.

A deadline of noon was agreed, and at one minute to 12, I was given a cheque for the full amount. I phoned Jill and Louise to let them know the triumphant news and went to the nearest branch of the Halifax Building Society to pay the cheque in. A few days later, the blood in my veins turned to water when the Halifax phoned to say the cheque had been made out for pence, not pounds. Furious, I stormed into the offices of LSD and demanded a replacement cheque for the proper amount, which I was given on the spot.

As Louise and I celebrated, we agreed that even though I was out of work yet again, whatever happened in the future, I wouldn't work for anyone ever again. The time had come for me to control my own destiny.

Lessons and learnings

🍺 **Lesson 2: Build a trusted support network**
As a result of my time with LSD Entertainment, I learned to always use a good lawyer. They then introduced me to a brilliant accountant. Keep your professional advisors closely in the loop as your business develops.

5

The Goose spreads its wings

1979

By the end of the first week of trading at the Goose, we'd taken more than £4,000, just over twice our estimate of turnover predicted in the feasibility study. I promptly ordered new equipment from Brewpubs that would increase the capacity of the brewery from three barrels a week to 20 barrels, which would enable us to not only cope with the extraordinary demand but also add one or more different Bruce's beers.

When I was told it would take up to three months to build the new equipment, I rang Peter Austin at the Ringwood Brewery in Hampshire and asked him if he'd like to brew my beer under licence until the new kit arrived. He was delighted to lend a helping hand as he was only in his second year of production, and suddenly picking up an order for 20 barrels of beer a week was a great fillip to his business. As I didn't want to lose my credibility as 'the local brewer', I arranged for Ringwood to deliver either early in the morning or at weekends. This temporary measure got us out of a jam and enabled us to guarantee supplies and maintain the customers' initial curiosity and interest at such a vital time in early trading at the pub.

Whenever time permitted, I conducted spontaneous brewery tours and up to a dozen of us would walk through the door marked 'Ladies' and then down to the brewery, where I'd attempt to explain my craft. Much amusement was caused when I pointed out the tiny can of Boots' home brew kit that had been put in a red wooden box with a glass front that carried the message 'In case of emergency, break glass'.

There were always groups keen to look round the brewery and on one of these occasions, when I was waxing lyrical about the importance of cleanliness at all times, I invited some visitors to look inside the brewing copper where I added hops to the boiling brew. The copper was located next to the brewhouse at the bottom of a large light well that ran up through the centre of the building. When I peered in myself, I saw that there were at least half a dozen cigarette butts lying in the bottom of my highly polished vat. I was a non-smoker and couldn't understand how the butts had got there.

It was only when the incident was repeated another couple of times during the next few weeks that I realised what was happening. As men were standing at the urinal in the gents' loo on the floor above, they were pushing their cigarette ends through a ventilation grill, little knowing what lay beneath. The problem was easily solved by blocking the grill. We ended up with a smellier gents' WC and had to improve the ventilation with an extractor fan, but anything was better than having fag ends in the beer.

One of the first official groups I showed round the brewery came from the Society for the Preservation of Beers from the Wood. The SPBW attempted to persuade brewers to keep their beer in wooden casks in preference to stainless-steel ones. It was ironic that, when they came to the Goose to inspect what they presumed would be an authentic, traditional small brewery, they were confronted by rows of gleaming polypropylene fermenting vessels and stainless-steel storage tanks. A unique piece of equipment was a pair of Louise's tights that I used to strain the hops. I used one leg for one brew and the second leg for the next. One day, a leg full of hops was spotted hanging half out of the dustbin on the pavement outside. With the inevitable small changes in flavour with small-batch brewing, this soon led to some wag asking me if I used clean or dirty tights as a hop filter!

While the SPBW was a small organisation, CAMRA, formed in 1971, had quickly become highly influential, with its vocal efforts to reverse the trend towards filtered, pasteurised and artificially carbonated keg beers. I soon found myself cornered by earnest CAMRA members, including one who told me he'd been appointed my official brewery liaison officer and I should discuss all matters concerning the brewery with him. This high-handed attitude didn't endear me to him, and soon CAMRA publications were giving the Goose some bad publicity. The nub of their complaint was that my beer was not truly real ale because I used malt extract.

CAMRA's claim that my beer wasn't real ale upset me. The problem with small-scale brewing is lack of space. I didn't have room in my tiny brewery for the necessary malt store, mill, auger, hot liquor (water) tank and the mash tun where I'd normally mix the malted barley with hot liquor to produce my own malt extract. As far as I was concerned, my beer was very real and the customers certainly seemed to be enjoying it. These early encounters with CAMRA were to plague me off and on for years to come. Apart from snide comments in their monthly paper *What's Brewing*, CAMRA also produced the annual *Good Beer Guide*. While the Goose did appear in the guide, it was listed as a pub brewing its own beer but the only traditionally brewed ales mentioned were those from Charrington and Shepherd Neame, not any of my Bruce's malt extract beers.

If CAMRA was an outside influence, we had internal ones, too. One involved Alistair's pet parrot which, unlike the famous Monty Python bird, was far from deceased. Alistair phoned me at home one Saturday to say something awful had happened and could I get to the pub as fast as possible. When I arrived in his office, I found him sitting ashen faced, surrounded by a pile of tiny pieces of coloured paper and spindly coils of metal thread. I looked bemused until Alistair explained that his parrot had escaped from its cage just outside the kitchen window. It had flown through the open window and into the office while Alistair had popped to the loo in the middle of counting the busy Friday night's takings. When he returned, he found the parrot spitting out bits of paper and silvery thread and

Alistair realised to his horror that the bird had rapidly consumed several piles of banknotes.

We checked the till rolls and sifted through the debris to discover the parrot must have eaten several hundred pounds' worth of banknotes. He was clearly a discerning parrot, as he'd eaten only the high-denomination notes, such as the mauve £20, brown £10 and blue £5, and hadn't started on the lower-value green £1 ones. We put the parrot back in his cage and phoned our insurance company and the bank to let them know of this extraordinary occurrence. Fortunately, we received full compensation for our insurance claim, probably on the grounds that we must have been telling the truth as no one could possibly make up such a bizarre story.

The first few months following the opening were chaotic, and I seemed to leap from handling one crisis to another, either the beer running out or not being able to accommodate all the customers in the pub, which resulted in queues on the pavement outside both doors.

By the end of August, things were still going well at the Goose, and Andy McDonald, with whom I had worked at LSD Entertainment, joined as a part-time bookkeeper, which meant I didn't have to concern myself with processing paperwork and paying the wages. He was amazed the pub had taken off so brilliantly, although the opening had cost more than we'd anticipated. Nevertheless, he assured me there was plenty of money in the bank to replace our little Citroën Dyane with a flashy sports coupé. I had spotted a brand-new silver Lancia HPE at a garage in Waterloo, and I enjoyed collecting it one Friday afternoon after first taking Dick Putland to lunch to thank him for making it all possible.

I found as many excuses as possible to promote the Goose & Firkin. The new car came in handy when Louise drove me round Hyde Park Corner one September afternoon with me dressed as a goose, sticking my head out of the sunroof and honking at passers-by, exhorting them to visit the pub as we made our way to the first *Sunday Times* Fun Run in Hyde Park. I had hired a goose costume with webbed feet and a rubber mask complete with a huge orange beak.

What I hadn't appreciated until I'd been running for a mile or so was that the costume was made of nylon. The exertion of running on a hot day meant I was dripping with sweat inside the costume. Undeterred, I battled on with the fundraising prank, even though I spent most of the run with children and onlookers saying 'Oh, there's a duck' and replying in a muffled voice through the rubber beak, 'I'm not a duck, I'm a goose from the Goose & Firkin. Why not come and visit us at the Elephant and Castle?' By the end of the race, I was hoarse, soaked with perspiration and completely exhausted but I felt the publicity had been worthwhile.

The Firkin fun run flyers

One result was that a group of Morris dancers had seen me and thought the Goose might be a good place for them to display their arcane rituals at Sunday lunchtimes. The pub soon had a reputation as a good place to watch Morris dancing. To underscore the pleasure, we installed an East End-style shellfish stall on the pavement, where customers could enjoy cockles, whelks and winkles washed down with my beer.

In October, I set about hunting for a site for the next Firkin. In spite of the stress, it had been great fun developing and opening the Goose, and I hoped to have the opportunity to repeat that experience. I was also spurred on by the doomsters who'd initially said the entire project would fail. They were now admitting they might have been wrong, but I should count myself lucky to have had one success while never risking another one. As always, my mantra was 'Never listen to the experts' and I was excited to read in the *Morning Advertiser* that Flanagan's Black Bull in Lewisham High Street was due to be leased. The leaseholders were none other than the City of London Corporation, my existing landlords at the Goose & Firkin. Charrington's Brewery had given up the lease on the premises. When I phoned the Guildhall to find out who was handling the property, I was pleased to be put through to my friend Raymond Wicks, who'd been responsible for letting me loose on the former Duke of York.

I collected Raymond in my shiny new Lancia and we drove to Flanagan's Black Bull. In common with the Duke of York, it had been closed and boarded up, even at first-floor level. It was a rough area and I remembered the pub from when I'd been the area manager for Charram. Flanagan's was one of the dozen or so pubs I had to supervise and, in those days, when it was a busy disco and go-go dancer venue, it attracted all the roughs and toughs of south-east London for miles around. The pub had been shut down by the police for under-age drinking, drug-taking and general unruliness. The story went that the manager was seen one Saturday night being chased down the high street at one in the morning followed by two local hoods who kept stopping to take careful aim at the fleeing figure with their crossbows. Fortunately, none of the bolts struck their target.

Armed with torches rather than crossbows, Raymond and I unlocked the boarded-up front door and crept cautiously into the darkness as the electricity had been cut off. The pub looked a complete wreck and the carpet was so soiled with spilt beer and dirt that it looked and felt like sticky linoleum as all the fabric had worn away. The place stank of damp and as we picked our way further into the building, a revolting stench of decomposed flesh became stronger. It was only when Raymond shone his torch under a bench seat that we found the remains of the pub cat, which had obviously been shut in when the place was boarded up. On the walls by the dance floor were posters advertising which strippers and topless go-go dancers had performed during the pub's final week of trading. The only object that seemed to remain intact was the DJ booth, which, as I remembered from Charram's company policy, was surrounded by bulletproof glass. This was designed to protect the DJ from flying bottles and glasses if he played a record the customers didn't like.

Flanagan's Black Bull was a long and narrow pub, and the only windows faced on to Lewisham High Street. Even if the lights had worked and the windows and doors weren't boarded up, it would still have been a dark pub, and this caused me concern. However, with the same flash of divine inspiration that had occurred when I decided to brew in the cellar of the Goose & Firkin, this time it was even more obvious: I would locate the brewhouse on the ground floor at the end of the bar. This would act as a focal point for the whole pub and add considerable light and interest to an otherwise poky area. I knew immediately it would be ideal as my next site and was dismayed when Raymond said he'd received innumerable phone calls from as far away as Lancashire, and this time he thought there would be much more competition for the lease.

I spent a couple of weeks working on feasibility studies with Andy McDonald and had several site meetings with Michael Sperling, David du Boulay and Richard Barker-Harland. As a result, I calculated that I could afford an annual rent of £11,250. Tenders had to be submitted by noon on a certain date and I had plenty of time to catch the Underground from Clapham South to Bank, where it was just a short walk to the Guildhall. What I hadn't allowed for was the train to be stuck at Kennington for close to an hour because of a signal failure, and when I finally arrived at Bank station, there were only eight minutes left before the noon deadline. I'd never run so fast in my life and just managed to hand in my tender at 10 seconds to noon.

As I wasn't certain my tender would be accepted, I continued with my search for a second pub where I could brew. I met Alan Hall, sales director at Ind Coope Taylor Walker, the London arm of Allied Breweries, and outlined my proposals to him. He introduced me to the group's managing director, Michael Griffiths. I explained that I was keen to apply my concept to other pubs and wondered if they had any suitably run-down outlets I could look at. A few days later, they suggested I look at the Seven Stars and Half Moon in Goldhawk Road, Hammersmith. This turned out to be a large Victorian pub near a busy roundabout. It had plenty of room to brew within the bar area. With my team of builders, bar fitters, surveyors and camp followers, we clambered around the Seven Stars and Half Moon and all warmed to the idea of applying the Firkin magic to the pub. Alan Hall and Michael Griffiths were delighted with our proposal and I became enthused at the prospect of developing not only that pub but also being let loose on other pubs owned by Allied Breweries in London.

I was disappointed to hear from Alan and Michael that, while their board had approved my ideas, the Transport and General Workers' Union said it couldn't believe they'd deliver more beer to the Seven Stars and Half Moon if I brewed on the premises. The union was concerned its draymen would lose their productivity bonus, which was based on how much beer they delivered to each pub on their round. They couldn't appreciate – as I'd proved at the Goose & Firkin – that by brewing my own beer, I could increase the total barrelage of beer sales in a pub from, say, 200 barrels a year to around 1,000 by attracting more customers, many of whom would drink products other than mine.

Following that disappointment, I was delighted to hear a couple of weeks later from Raymond Wicks that my offer for Flanagan's Black Bull had been accepted. It hadn't been the highest offer but the City of London Corporation were impressed by what I'd achieved at the old Duke of York and were happy for me to lease another of their properties. Within a few days of being granted the lease, I'd arranged meetings with district surveyors, borough engineers, environmental health officers and licensing police, all of whom expressed amazement that I was prepared to have another go in Lewisham High Street, an area infamous for roughness, especially following the National Front riots a few years earlier. My feet hardly touched the ground and I spent my time whizzing between Lewisham and Elephant and Castle, jumping in and out of building site clothes, brewing clothes and suits for meetings with bankers.

In the middle of this mayhem and much to my surprise, I was asked to be the guest speaker for MBA students at the London Business School, where I was asked to describe from first-hand experience what it's like to start a business from scratch. Media interest continued and the more publicity we got, whether on television or in the national press, the busier the Goose & Firkin became. The experience fed my appetite to open my next pub, if only to give the customers who couldn't get into the Goose somewhere else to try.

Just when I was at my busiest and running from one meeting to the next, Neil Watson, my brewer at the Goose, was knocked off his motorbike while he was collecting yeast from the Courage Brewery at Horselydown, resulting in a badly broken leg. The unfortunate Neil had left a brew boiling in the copper for an hour with newly added hops while he nipped out to collect the yeast. When he didn't return, no one thought to go down to the brewhouse. As a result, the beer evaporated and the powerful electric heaters burned out when they no longer had any liquid to heat. This meant I had to brew again at the Goose while I was attempting to keep all the other plates spinning as well as getting ready for the busy Christmas trade.

The Firkin Saga

Lessons and learnings

🍺 **Lesson 8: Encourage and nurture free PR, even if it entails fancy dress**
Take any opportunity for free PR. Not everyone will want to dress up as a goose to attract attention in a fun run (though it worked for me), but think laterally to create your own PR chances.

A Fox, a Frog and battles with bureaucracy

1980–1981

After Christmas, I resumed work on getting Flanagan's Black Bull into some sort of shape. I discovered at the rear of the pub an area that had clearly been a beer garden but was now just a dump for rubbish and scrap several feet high. I thought this could be a major attraction – one of the few beer gardens in London. With my design and development partners, Richard Barker-Harland, David du Boulay and Michael Sperling, we put together a complete scheme that, when the costings were done, would cost approximately £70,000. This was money we didn't have and so once again it was off to see Dick Putland at Lloyds Bank.

We'd proved we could fill a pub to capacity and, on the strength of the success of the Goose & Firkin in its first few months, Dick lent us £50,000 secured against the lease of the Black Bull. Once again, backed by our successful free trade barrelage figures at the Goose, we secured £20,000 from Charrington's, whose lager and bottled beer would be sold at the new venture. However, with the negative comments of our professional advisors about how lucky we'd been at the Goose and that we were unlikely to repeat this success, we decided to operate the second pub as a separate legal concern. We formed a new limited company, Bruce's Brewery (Lewisham) Ltd, with its own funding to protect the Goose from any possible financial contamination.

The formula for creating a new company for each new pub was repeated from then on, as I wanted to avoid the domino effect of one of the new ventures failing. However, it proved to be an accounting nightmare by the time we had several pubs up and running. Each one had a different year end and they required separate records for bookkeeping, wages and auditing. But the pain was worth the comfort of knowing that one bad apple wouldn't ruin the barrel, if you'll excuse the pun.

I was brewing at the Goose one day in the absence of Neil Watson, who was still laid up with his broken leg, when the local HM Customs & Excise Officer mentioned that his nephew, Martin Pyle, had just left school and was keen to start some practical work experience in south-east London. He wondered if I'd take him on as a trainee brewer. As a result, I began to teach Martin brewing skills at the Goose. As Neil's leg improved, he took over responsibility for Martin and all production matters, freeing me up to concentrate on developing the second pub. As part of my keep-fit regime, I started to run from my home in Clapham to the new pub in Lewisham, a 12-mile round trip, all along London's busy South Circular road. This helped me combat the stress of growing the fledgling Firkin business.

Stress was never far away. The Goose continued to trade exceptionally well. All the coverage in the media attracted more custom but had other unexpected results. One day, I received a phone call from a man at HM Customs & Excise's licensed premises valuation department, who told me he'd been following our progress with interest. He asked to meet urgently and duly arrived armed with a file full of the pub's history and, most importantly, its most recent resurrection. He explained that the rating of licensed premises was based on the barrelage of products sold and had nothing to do with the shop frontage or square footage, as is the case with other retail outlets. He calculated, after reading the many press articles on our success, that the rates should go from zero, which it was while unoccupied after our predecessor had failed, to ten times what it had been prior to its closing down. It was a classic case of bureaucracy attempting to stifle successful private enterprise. To my horror, I found there was no right to appeal and I was hit with an unexpected and very substantial retrospective rate demand.

There were times when I needed to get away from the seven-day-a-week pressure of running a busy pub and developing new outlets. In February 1980, Louise and I became the proud owners of a small cottage in the Black Mountains of South Wales. We'd enjoyed camping in the Brecon Beacons for many years, and one day we spotted a cottage high on a mountainside overlooking Llangorse Lake and the Beacons. It was isolated and desolate but with sensational views.

It was an investment in sanity, with superb walking and running country on our doorstep. This is where much of the planning of the Firkin business was undertaken.

Back in London and regardless of the relentless pressures of work, I always tried to attend the weekly training nights of Thames Hare and Hounds, the world's longest-established cross-country running club, just off the A3 between Wimbledon Common and Richmond Park. My Uncle Dick, who'd alerted me to the job at Theakston's Brewery many years earlier, had been a member since 1936, when he'd narrowly missed being selected to run for Great Britain in the Berlin Olympic Games.

Training runs on a Wednesday could last for up to two hours, regardless of weather or season. After an especially long run one evening, we were all taking a shower, and I found the equally tired and muddy runner next to me was enthusing the assembled company about a pub he'd discovered in south London where the owner had come up with the bright idea of brewing his own beer in the cellar. I pricked up my ears and listened while he went on and on about what an amazing and fun place it was and perhaps we should all go there after the next Wednesday training run.

I seized the opportunity to slip into the conversation and say that I'd probably be there in any case. Only then did my neighbour realise that the pub he was encouraging us to visit was run by the lathered, naked man standing in the shower next to him. In the pub afterwards, my fellow runner Antony Fletcher fixed a date when we could meet for lunch as he said the Goose was such a brilliant idea that he'd like to become an investor. At this stage, I had no idea what an important influence Antony would have in the future development of the Firkin Group.

We met at the Boot and Flogger, a wine bar in the back streets near Southwark Bridge. We enjoyed a lively lunch and I explained how the Goose had come about and what I was hoping to do in the future. Apart from being keen runners, we had a shared delight in beer and breweries and it was wonderful to meet such an enthusiast for my new venture. Further meetings took place, and the conversation usually revolved around Antony wanting to buy equity if not in the Goose then in the new venture in Lewisham. I explained that, as a result of all my experiences over the past decade, I felt that equity was gold dust and shouldn't be given up lightly, even if I had no alternative means of raising finance. I remembered Michael McDonald, the original importer of Carlsberg lager to Britain, saying to me when we were discussing various ways of funding the new business that in his experience, 'You can only sell your equity once.'

Our next-door neighbour Robert Bourne, who'd offered the services of the brewing and leisure analyst at the stockbrokers where he worked, Fielding Newson Smith, mentioned one day that his brother Richard was writing a book called *Londoners* and wondered if I'd be interested in featuring in it. I was flattered and agreed to meet Richard. As a result of a few interviews, I was delighted to appear for the first time in a hardback book (published in 1981) that featured a wide variety of people doing unusual things in London. I was the only one, of course, who spent most of his working life in a subterranean brewery in south London.

Within months of starting our new venture, we'd created an extraordinarily successful business and had built genuine loyalty and goodwill from our customers. This was demonstrated by the pilgrimage many of them made from miles away just to drink our beer and have fun at the Goose. In recognition of this loyalty, we decided to form a club our customers could join for a membership fee of £5, which would enable them to receive a quarterly newsletter, discounts off polypins – small, take-home plastic barrels of ale – T-shirts, car stickers, badges and other Firkin memorabilia that we'd created. Unwittingly, we started what today would be called a database, but then we didn't even have a computer to mail all our members and it was a hard administrative slog to type the information into lists.

A special T-shirt was commissioned, the front of which featured the Goose & Firkin logo in colour surrounded by the words 'I'm a Firkin boozer'. On the back, which may have caused some concern to the female members, we had the truism, 'I'm in the Firkin Club!'

Rules of Membership for the Firkin Club

1. SUPPORT wholeheartedly the brewing and imbibing of Bruce's Beers at any, or all, of our Firkin pubs.
2. PROVE that it has been known, however rarely, for you to buy a round of drinks.
3. INDICATE clearly that from time to time you can raise a smile or even laugh when within a fully licensed environment.
4. SAMPLE and comment honestly upon (spittoons provided) all new beers which may from time to time be inflicted upon you.
5. NURTURE the fact and instruct both your friends that there does exist in Britain at least five public houses NOT owned by the national brewers.
6. ATTEND one of the Firkin pubs at least monthly and let it be witnessed (or wet-nursed) that you hold aloft a glass of Bruce's Beers in solemn salutation to the ever vigilant Firkin Fauna.
7. CRINGE on seeing the very words "Hearty Pub Grub" usually advertising 'spot the filling' sandwiches, 'soup in the basket' or rolls that make your gums bleed.
8. ALLOW yourself, on application, to be personally vetted by the Master Brewer.
9. ABHOR droopy red lampshades, green dralon button-back banquette seating, flock wall paper and swirly patterned carpets.
10. LEARN to hate (if you don't already) fruit machines, juke boxes and space invaders.
11. OBJECT not to the fact that the word member may from time to time be substituted by the word nuisance at the Master Brewer's discretion, i.e. a Firkin member becomes . . . .

Firkin Club membership rules

The Goose continued to thrive and the design and development for the second pub was proceeding smoothly. I decided to switch from the Brewpub system and asked Peter Austin at Ringwood Brewery if he'd design and provide the kit for the second venture. The five-barrel brewery with its tiny, bright orange mill and 12-foot auger leading to the mash tun, made a wonderful spectacle. The *Daily Mail* reported soon after we opened that it was one of only three breweries in Europe where customers could actually see their beer being brewed. The other two were in Munich and Prague. And so Lewisham joined two of the great brewing capitals of Europe.

We furnished the pub with old church pews from a junk shop. We made refectory tables to match and within eight weeks of moving on site the pub was ready to open. I wanted to call the pub the Duck & Firkin, following the use of goose at the first pub. There was much agonising between me, Louise and anyone prepared to listen, and in the end it was decided to pursue the 'f' alliteration. We looked for an animal beginning with 'f' rather than another member of the fowl family. The word fox sprang to mind and could be associated with a goose as there were several pubs called the Fox & Goose. However, the real reason for not calling it the Duck & Firkin was the obvious spoonerism that would inevitably occur!

Jamie Nimmo, who'd produced the graphics for the Goose, was commissioned to provide similar artwork for the Fox & Firkin. I remember arguing with him, when I saw his first draft, that foxes didn't have small white tips to their tails and I removed the tips from the finished artwork. There was much grovelling from me when a stuffed fox was delivered for display on the bar and I saw that a fox really does have a white tip to its tail, but it was too late to alter Jamie's artwork.

Early on the morning scheduled for the opening, the police told me I couldn't go ahead because the resident manager I'd appointed had declared on his job application and the justices' licence application that he had no police convictions. I was horrified to be told by the licensing sergeant that my new manager had a criminal record for assaulting a police officer and causing grievous bodily harm, one of the most serious convictions you could have if you wanted to manage licensed premises under close police scrutiny. It was only after I'd given personal undertakings for his good conduct as his co-licensee that the licence was granted later that morning and we were able to open.

And so, on 7 May 1980, the Fox & Firkin, London's second brewpub in more than a century, opened, and again we were mobbed with customers from the first evening on. As well as the state-of-the-art brewery, I decided this second pub would have high-quality food. I insisted there should be a 15 ft-long food servery staffed by a professional chef wearing chef's whites complete with a tall white hat. The standard of the food quickly gained a high reputation, especially at lunchtimes, but we had to take food off in the evenings as the pub was too crowded for staff or customers to carry food around. The insistence on high standards of catering resulted in my gaining the reputation of the man who brought smoked salmon sandwiches to Lewisham High Street.

David brewing with his first 'full mash' brewery at the Fox & Firkin

With the brewery in sight of customers and the long bar and food serveries, I still wanted to break up the space a little more. When Richard Barker-Harland said he'd found an old church pulpit in a junk shop in Fulham, it seemed the ideal way of creating the diversion I was looking for and it provided an additional focal point. The first Sunday after opening, the vicar of Lewisham came in after morning service in his parish church just up the road. After enjoying a pint of beer, he could see I was having a problem emptying the pub at 2 pm, which was the Sunday closing time. He kindly offered to go up into the pulpit and start one of his sermons, which he guaranteed would empty the place far faster than all my shouting.

Unfortunately, after a few months, the pulpit had become abused by some of the customers and one night we came close to disaster when around a dozen Millwall football supporters, who had come to drink copious amounts of Hürlimann Swiss lager – nicknamed 'hooligan lager' in their honour – started to make the pulpit rock and sway and almost fall onto two large tables of happy drinkers who were oblivious to the danger. Sadly, after that near disaster, we had to remove access to the pulpit.

Following the success of the piano player and singing evenings at the Goose, it was essential to provide similar entertainment at the Fox. We were lucky to find a local school teacher, Mike Hayes, together with an ardent CAMRA supporter, Dave Cousins, who was a wizard at playing the spoons. Mike and Dave rarely missed a Friday or Saturday evening and the pub gained a tremendous reputation for its singalong nights. Customers were provided with song sheets so they could join in all the verses. There was a wide variety of songs, including hits from the two world wars.

Such was the success of these weekend evenings that it wasn't long before I was summoned to the local police station. The chief superintendent had received complaints of overcrowding at the Fox, and singing by the public wasn't permitted without a Greater London Council music and dancing licence. I was formally cautioned for these misdemeanours. For the next few weeks, we had to use bouncers to keep the crowds out and restrict the numbers to keep within the limits for licensed premises. But we found it impossible to stop the crowds singing, even though we stopped issuing them with song sheets.

A few weeks later, the chief superintendent inspected the pub to make sure I was complying with his requirements. He found all the customers simply humming to the piano and spoons players, a performance that didn't require a licence. Following his visit, we soon returned to our old ways and never had any further complaints from the police.

One Saturday morning, after clearing up following the Friday night revelries, I went down to the cellar to rack one of my latest brews into the storage tanks, only to find the cellar was flooded to waist height due to a blocked drain. Luckily, all the beer dispense tanks were bolted tight shut but the drain had to be unblocked straight away. I stripped down to my underpants and waded through the evil-smelling water. As I approached the drain's location, the movement caused an electrical cable to drop into the water. I thought that would be the end of me but fortunately the fuse had already blown all the wall sockets and the water wasn't live. Eventually, we were able to unblock the drain and the water subsided, although it left a disgusting smell and mess everywhere that took several days to clear up.

I then discovered to my horror that some of my beers were starting to taste sour and vinegary and some fruity flavours had crept in that resembled bananas and blackcurrants. These may sound delicious to the uninitiated but to a brewer they mean that a yeast infection is starting to develop. I consulted brewing chemists, including the Brewing Research Foundation, and eventually the cause of the infection was put down to two possible reasons. First, as access to the brewery was through a door connecting the bar, every time someone went in or out of the brewery, impure and smoky air from the bar wafted into what should be a sterile environment. Second, since milling the malted barley prior to mashing was in close proximity to the open-top fermenting vessels, the malt dust was probably infecting the beer.

As a result, the door from the bar was moved and the fermenting vessels were fitted with lids. The problem was eventually solved but only after pouring thousands of gallons of beer down the drain with the loss of raw materials and labour. Fortunately, we were able to reclaim the duty from Customs & Excise. A far more serious problem was that we kept running out of beer, which upset the customers. Ironically, some customers were upset as they'd grown accustomed to the banana and blackcurrant flavours created by the infections which, fortunately, had now been cured.

No sooner had we won the customers round again than we had

a problem with Thames Water, who had the habit of switching the water supply to Lewisham between two sources without any warning. The pH value or acidity of water is critical in the brewing process as it allows the brewer to obtain the maximum benefit of mashing the malted barley with hot water, and it was quite unacceptable for the mains water to change dramatically without warning. The matter was further aggravated when a water main burst as a result of nearby roadworks. Once it had been repaired, the main was sluiced with neat chlorine to kill any bugs that might have got into the water supply. I was innocently filling my hot water tank just as the heavily chlorinated water was passing through Lewisham and, as a result, my next two brews stank of chlorine and had to be poured down the drain under the supervision of an inspector from Customs & Excise. It wasn't a good start for the first few months of brewing in Lewisham.

When you consider Lewisham's reputation, along with the surrounding neighbourhoods of south-east London – Bromley, New Cross and Peckham – I was pleasantly surprised to have my prejudices crushed, as we had exceptionally pleasant customers at the Fox & Firkin. I followed my reputation as the man who brought smoked salmon sandwiches to Lewisham High Street and further surprised my clientele by providing string quartets dressed in formal black ties to play classical and baroque music for the punters. This was in marked contrast to the honky-tonk piano and spoons evenings. The most controversial evening was when my uncle, John Shearman, of the Kipling Society, hosted readings from the works of Rudyard Kipling, an event that was surprisingly well supported.

As soon as the pub was open, we were able to tackle landscaping the pile of rubbish and junk at the back of the premises. I came to the conclusion that, rather than removing all the mess, it would be better to use it as part of the landscaping, which is why the beer garden at the Fox had such high, raised flower beds with all the scrap and rubble dumped underneath them. A garden pool was dug and a small fountain installed to keep the water circulating so the goldfish in the pool stayed alive. The statue that provided the fountain was based on the Manneken Pis statue in Brussels, which is a depiction of a small boy peeing into the water. I hadn't bargained for some of the customers feeling encouraged to follow the action by urinating into the water, which was not good for the goldfish, and they had to be removed. We were unable to restrain some of the customers from their disgusting practices and the pool had to be filled in. This wasn't such a bad move as it provided additional space for more seats and tables in the beer garden.

I was sitting with the staff in the garden one afternoon between shifts and we discussed whether to put a slogan on the back of the T-shirts that initially had only the Fox logo on the front. None of us could think of a clever way of incorporating the words Fox and Firkin until one of Andy McDonald's friends exclaimed in his broad Irish accent, 'Oh, for fock's sake, this is a complete waste of time,' and with one voice we cried, 'That's *it* – for Fox sake, buy me a Firkin pint.' As soon as the T-shirts with that slogan on the back went on sale, they became much sought after and from then on each new Firkin pub had to have its own slogan.

While I was attempting to keep an eye on the Goose and the Fox, I was also looking around for a third opportunity. I was keen to prove my critics wrong again. I was running as much as possible between home and the two pubs and would run to Lewisham and back at least twice a week as part of my training for the first London Marathon, which was due to take place in April 1981.

I was sufficiently encouraged by the continuing success of the Goose and the first few months of trading at the Fox to approach the City of London Corporation to suggest extending the lease of the Goose to 15 years. This would give me greater collateral to borrow and finance further expansion. As I anticipated expanding the Firkin concept, I took up an offer from Peter Austin at Ringwood Brewery to take on one of his brewers, Tim Kirby, who wanted to move to London. Tim was able to help brew with Neil at the Goose and Martin at the Fox, freeing me up to concentrate on fundraising and finding new sites.

As I'd funded the first two pubs entirely from bank debt and free trade loans, I felt it would be prudent to take on some institutional funding in return for a small percentage of the equity, if only I could find a small merchant bank or venture capitalist who'd put a sensible value on my equity. Earlier discussions regarding selling some of my equity had been swiftly dismissed by me when a) someone had wanted to invest only £5,000 for 25 per cent of the equity; and b) someone else wanted to be appointed as chair 'to provide leadership to my new venture', as if I needed any such help!

Various meetings were held around the City but I felt that either the chemistry was wrong between us or the numbers simply didn't stack up when putting a value on my equity. Thank goodness I didn't ever sell it too cheaply! On the positive front, I continued to receive favourable press coverage. An article by Barry Akers in *Marketing Week* had cartoons by Ken Pyne, whose work appeared regularly in the *Times* and *Private Eye*. Through Barry, I met Ken and enticed him down to the depths of Lewisham one Saturday lunchtime. Ken has been drawing brilliant, bespoke cartoons for me ever since.

As the sole proprietor of two businesses, I was confronted by bureaucratic problems almost by the minute. One such gem was being advised by the local trading standards officer for Lewisham that while I had a price list on display it was not sufficiently clearly displayed and I was therefore contravening the Price Marking (Food and Drinks on Licensed Premises) Act 1979. It was an offence I was able to rectify simply by providing a slightly larger printed version of the existing price list. As I borrowed money and risked everything to develop a private enterprise, I reflected that I was constantly being observed by an army of civil servants and local authority bureaucrats, many of whom seemed hell-bent on pointing out innumerable violations of obscure rules and regulations in an effort to impede my progress.

Soon after my shocking contravention of the price list legislation, I was given details of freehold licensed premises in west London that were being sold by Allied Breweries. At last I had the opportunity to not only expand my idea of reopening pubs abandoned by the big brewers, but also buy my first freehold free house. The only snag was that, as usual, I didn't have any money to buy the freehold let alone redevelop the premises and install a brewery.

Then I remembered all the miles I'd run and lunches and dinners I'd shared with Antony Fletcher, who was constantly pressing me to let him invest in one of my pubs. Could this now be the opportunity for him to show me the colour of his money? I contacted Antony and he'd lost none of his enthusiasm to get involved in one of my ventures, so we arranged to inspect the premises under offer. The Tavistock Hotel was at the end of a cul-de-sac in one of the seedier parts of Notting Hill. It had eventually been closed by Allied Breweries after the tenant had gone bust. In addition, several closure notices had been served on the freeholder by local authorities. The borough engineer had served notice due to a major structural crack down one wall. The district surveyor reported extensive woodworm in all the joists. There was an improvement notice under the Health & Safety Act for more offences than you could list on three sides of paper. There was a similarly long list under the food hygiene regulations and further closure notices under environmental health and offices, shops and railway premises acts.

Antony was undeterred by the gloomy list of closure orders and remained keen to get involved in some way in the acquisition and subsequent development of the pub. Time was short, as we had to make our offer by the beginning of July, which gave us only a couple of weeks to strike a deal. It was agreed that an offer to buy the freehold of the dilapidated premises would be made for £96,650. The freehold would be owned by Antony, who would then grant a lease to my third company, Bruce's Brewery (Portobello) Ltd, to develop and run the premises. There would be an option for Bruce's Brewery to buy the freehold from Antony after three years at a sum no less than £200,000, which would at least double the value of Antony's investment and enable Bruce's Brewery to acquire its first freehold free house, which by then would have three years of trading under its belt. It was agreed to sweeten the deal with Ind Coope Taylor Walker, the London division of Allied Breweries, by offering to buy 500 barrels of its beer between the Goose, the Fox and the new premises that we hoped would soon be known as the Frog & Firkin. In this way, we planned to deter any competitive bids.

By September, our detailed structural surveys had been completed and we agreed terms with Allied Breweries for both the purchase of the freehold of the Tavistock and the free trade beer agreement for the other two pubs. An enormous schedule of work was drawn up, incorporating not only sorting out the many breaches of statutory regulations but also the complete renovation of the premises and creating a basement brewery. I agreed to spend in excess of £60,000 on the redevelopment, which was part of the deal with Antony. Countless meetings followed with Antony and his incredibly diligent lawyers and we were eventually able to acquire the freehold of the property. Richard Barker-Harland from du Boulay Construction started work on the Herculean task of redeveloping the site. Soon after moving in, the builders appeared to have virtually gutted the place, in particular at ground level, where all the floors and joists had to be removed due to the extensive woodworm and rot.

At a site meeting one morning, we were interrupted by a loud cry and found that David Budd, the finance director of du Boulay Construction, had jumped, as there were no floorboards, into the cellar via the cellar flaps in the pavement, had landed awkwardly and broken his leg. This was especially unfortunate as all the workers on site had assumed he was joking and offered no sympathy until he turned up the next day in a full plaster cast and hobbling on crutches.

While Antony had enabled us to buy the Tavistock Hotel, I was still courting other investors. I was mentioned in an article in *Venture Capital Report* as a small business start-up seeking equity finance. As a result, I was overwhelmed with enquiries from hopeful investors who fancied owning a part of a fast-expanding chain of small breweries. As always, they were far too greedy and wanted too big a stake of the equity for too little investment.

One of my many meetings with brewery bosses turned out to be an embarrassment. One morning, the chair of Shepherd Neame asked if he could come and see me at the Goose. I assumed he either wanted to give me an even bigger free trade loan in return for selling more of his beer or, better still, he might have some pubs I could buy from him. I agreed to see him with a warm glow of anticipation. However, Bobby

Neame had neither of these possibilities in mind and was looking angry when he came into the office at the Goose. He demanded to know why a 36-gallon cask had been returned to his brewery as being unfit for sale when in fact it was full of water. He'd been alerted to this by his local Customs & Excise officer. It's customary that if any beer goes off and is returned as unsaleable then the brewer can destroy the beer under the supervision of Customs & Excise and reclaim the duty before giving a credit note to the customer. It's a long-standing fiddle in the pub trade for some publicans to send back their slops as bad beer and claim a credit note for beer that should be drinkable. But on this occasion, it wasn't even beer but pure water. Luckily for me, I was able to explain that I put the water in the barrel while I was using it as a buffer tank while cleaning out the cellar tanks and casks in the Goose one weekend while Neil was on holiday. Stupidly, I hadn't emptied the water from the cask before it was returned to Shepherd Neame. The draymen had put the cask full of water on their dray assuming it was bad beer being sent back for credit.

As the work on the Tavistock progressed and the smelly mess from the previous licensee's collection of dogs, cats, guinea pigs, pigeons and ferrets was removed from the area of the cellar where we planned to install the brewery, we turned our attention to the brewing equipment. As a special project, I'd entrusted the design and development of our third brewery to our new employee, Tim Kirby. We'd used equipment from Brewpubs at the Goose and Peter Austin's kit at the Fox, but this time we decided to design and manufacture the entire brewery ourselves. Through Tim, we met John and Jim Welch of J A Welch & Sons of Stratford, east London. We got on so well with this team that we decided not only to use them to build the brewery for the Frog & Firkin but also to create a new company to design and build breweries for other start-ups. One snowy January evening, John Welch had a flash of inspiration for the name of this new company. He said that if we took the first syllable of each of our two surnames, it would create an appropriate name for a brewery equipment manufacturing company: Bruwel Ltd. We'd launched our own business less than two years previously and now Louise and I were not only about to open our third pub and brewery but also had a 50 per cent stake in a brewery manufacturing company. Our little empire was expanding.

While the funding for the development of the Frog & Firkin would come from Bruce's Brewery, as usual we had no money, so once again we approached Dick Putland at Lloyds Bank. Dick came up trumps again and was happy to lend us the difference between the new free trade loans from Allied Breweries of £27,000 for the 500 barrels of beer we'd promised them and the £60,000 we were investing in the premises. Our expansion so far had been entirely funded by Lloyds Bank and free trade loans from big brewers and yet we still owned 100 per cent of our three own businesses, even though Antony was involved in the freehold acquisition of the Frog's premises.

These arrangements didn't slow my relentless drive for additional institutional finance and as a result I was nurturing Colin Mitchell, the legendary brewing analyst in the corporate finance department of Buckmaster and Moore. Following an onsite meeting in Notting Hill, I removed my grubby sweater and jeans and squeezed into my suit for my first corporate lunch of 1981 in Colin's boardroom at the Stock Exchange. Later that day, I had to switch back from suit to informal garb to meet the beer expert and writer Michael Jackson, who wanted to sample my beers at the Fox. Michael enjoyed a worldwide reputation as a beer judge/writer and it was with some trepidation that I watched him sample a line-up of my various beers. It was a slow Tuesday evening in January, the pub was ominously quiet and I confess that none of the beers were at their best. Michael was polite but clearly not overwhelmed with enthusiasm after his tasting session. His opinions weren't as good as I'd hoped and they were at odds with the volumes of the beers enjoyed by punters.

There were some management changes during the Christmas period – not unusual in the licensed trade – and we were recruiting and changing staff. I recruited Roger Howard and Tricia Bannister to take over at the Fox, while Roger Hill was employed to manage the Frog. By the beginning of February, the old pet room in the cellar had been turned into a pristine shell of gleaming white, fungicidal paint and the brewing kit duly arrived on the back of a lorry from J A Welch.

No one had thought how we'd be able to squeeze it into such a tiny area. Eventually, and with Customs & Excise waiting to measure and gauge the fermenting vessels, we had to remove the entire window and surrounding brickwork to ease in all the plant for our new brewery. On Tuesday 17 February 1981, the Tavistock Hotel was relaunched as Bruce's (Portobello) Brewery Company at the Frog & Firkin.

The brewer and his brewster, Louise

That same morning, an enormous package landed with a thud on my doormat. It contained the plans for yet another pub that had been sent to me by Keith Hallett, an architect in Bristol. He wondered if I'd consider putting one of my breweries into his latest development, the Grade II-listed former Wool Hall in Bristol. Would our fourth pub be located outside London?

Meanwhile, the opening party for the Frog & Firkin, advertised in both the Goose and the Fox together with Antony's friends and our fellow runners of the Thames Hare and Hounds, packed the first night. It was absolutely rammed to the extent that people were so close together they couldn't even reach for matches or lighters to light the cigarettes between their lips. It all boded well for another successful Firkin.

Lessons and learnings

🍺 **Lesson 2: Build a trusted support network**
Seek professional advice whenever necessary, as I did with the Brewing Research Foundation when I experienced production problems. As the company grew, I also needed to consult advisors relating to corporate finance and legal matters. Although these costs may seem a lot, in many cases these advisors can save you money – and from disaster.

🍺 **Lesson 4: Seize opportunities as they arise**
I took a chance to diversify when I set up Bruwel Ltd to manufacture turnkey breweries for subsequent brewing entrepreneurs. It was a different way of using my expertise and passing it on to others, as well as expanding my trade. Keep looking for ways to use your knowledge and contacts to enhance your business.

🍺 **Lesson 7: Inspire and educate others and put something back into your community**
Engage closely with your customers and keep them involved with all aspects of your business. The way I did this was with the Firkin Club, which provided members with a wide variety of fun merchandise to wear and use.

7

Fun runs, a busted nose and seeing red in Bristol

1981–1982

The Frog & Firkin exceeded all our most optimistic hopes and expectations but just when I felt absolutely nothing could go wrong, bureaucracy came crashing down once more. Within a month of our successful opening, we were served with an unbelievable hailstorm of notices from the Royal Borough of Kensington and Chelsea under the Health and Safety at Work Act 1974, the Offices, Shops and Railway Premises Act 1963, the Food Hygiene (General) Regulations 1970, the Food and Drugs Act 1955, the Public Health Acts 1936, 1937 and 1961, the Water Act 1973, and the Control of Pollution Act 1974. They were mainly raised by a lady from the local environmental health office. Her biggest concern was not the contraventions of these sundry acts but in particular the glass panel in the floor through which customers could look down on the brewery and watch the brewers at work.

My efforts to prove the strength of the panel involved persuading the chief superintendent from Notting Hill police station to jump from a table on to the panel, which was brave of him, bearing in mind he weighed more than 20 stone and valued his manhood. But the only way we could satisfy the environmental health officer was by asking the technical advisory service at Pilkington Glass, the manufacturer of the panel, to write an affidavit that stated the permissible distributed loading weight for a piece of reinforced glass the size of our viewing panel would be 20,000 newtons per square metre, which the officer had to accept was correct. We were also able to satisfy her with the sparkling white walls and ceiling of the brewery and beer cellar areas of the basement. These had been fumigated professionally to try to remove all the pungent animal smells left by our predecessor's dozens of furry pets and birds.

Soon after we opened, there was a serious fire in one of the nearby buildings. Five fire engines turned up with a turntable ladder. As soon as the fire was put out, some 50 thirsty firefighters descended on the bar during what would otherwise have been a quiet Monday lunchtime. They slaked their thirsts with copious pints of Bruce's Bullfrog Bitter, Froghopper and Portobello Porter and then departed. But in their well-refreshed state, three of them left their shiny yellow helmets behind. We rang the fire station several times but the helmets were never recovered and inadvertently started what became a legendary collection of hats accumulated over the years, including a few of what looked like brightly coloured tea cosies. Complete strangers would come in and leave all manner of bizarre headwear with strict instructions that they should join the collection above the bar. It was one of the firefighters who, after several hours of gallant firefighting, had coined the phrase 'If you've got a croak in your throat, hop into the frog', which in turn led to the Frog & Firkin slogan 'For Frog'ods sake buy me a Firkin pint'. This remarkable strangulation of the English language was soon adorning the back of T-shirts throughout the civilised and, more particularly, uncivilised world.

With three Firkin pubs successfully up and running, it was necessary during the spring of 1981 to recruit new members of the team to support the three pub managers and the three brewers. Andy McDonald, who ran the group's finance and administration, persuaded Louise to give up the two top bedrooms of our house in order that they could be turned into offices. He recruited Maria to help with accounting and wages. This was fine until Maria's new boyfriend collected her from work in all weathers on his motorbike. In spite of our protestations, he'd trudge from the front door along the hall and up four flights of stairs in his oily leathers, often scraping his crash helmet along the wallpaper all the way up the stairs and then down again. It was just one of the corner-cutting exercises we had to endure as we tried to expand the company on a shoestring, as we weren't yet in a position to afford the rent of a proper office.

On the production side, we appointed Stephanie Harding as production director. We'd been impressed by her ability to help us sort out a number of quality problems at the Fox. She brought with her considerable experience from her time at the Brewing Research Foundation, where she was responsible for the propagation of yeast at the National Collection of Yeast Cultures in Norwich. The appointment also enabled Tim Kirby to put more time into dealing with enquiries from potential Bruwel customers. In March 1981, we received our first order for a ten-barrel brewery with three fermenting vessels from the Red Kite Brewery at Tregaron in Dyfed, Wales, for £12,425. This was followed a month later by a further order for a second ten-barrel brewery from Dave Roberts, who was about to start the Pilgrim Brewery at Redhill in Surrey. Both he and Kieran Healy from Wales started their training at the Fox and the Frog breweries in order that they'd be fully conversant with how to use their kit by the time it was delivered. It was gratifying to know that my Firkin adventure was inspiring others to venture forth with their own brewing operations.

While all this was happening in London, I started travelling to Bristol during March 1982 to pursue the possible development of the Old Wool Hall in St Thomas Street. It had taken a lot of negotiating but the deal to open what would become the Fleece & Firkin had finally been agreed. Keith Hallett and Colin Harvey, architects well known to the City of Bristol Corporation, would acquire a 125-year lease on the Wool Hall from the City Corporation and Bruce's Brewery (Bristol) Ltd would own 20 per cent of that head lease while the Wool Hall Company in turn would own 20 per cent of Bruce's Brewery.

For obscure legal reasons, however, Bruce's Brewery (Bristol) Ltd could not itself own part of the lease in the Wool Hall Company so a new company, Fleece Ewe & Runne Ltd, was created to represent the 20 per cent of Bruce's Brewery (Bristol) Ltd in the lease. You can always rely on lawyers to complicate a perfectly simple deal. By the time the lawyers had finished, Bruce's Brewery (Bristol) Ltd had been granted a sub-lease by the Wool Hall Company with a rent of £15,000 a year. But all the legal ramifications took ages to sort out before we could begin thinking about the tortuous process of trying to obtain both planning permission and a justices' licence for the empty premises. It was clear we faced a Herculean task but any misgivings were set aside by my determination to create another Firkin success, albeit outside London.

Back in London, I was finishing my rigorous training for the first London Marathon on 29 March 1981. On the appointed day, 7,500 runners set off around the streets of the capital from Greenwich in the south-east, over Tower Bridge, around Docklands and ending up outside Buckingham Palace. There were more than a dozen runners from Thames Hare and Hounds, where I had done much of my training and road work with Andy Stevens, and we all finished the race. I came 2,152nd and recorded a personal time of three hours and 16 minutes. I was pleased as I really didn't know if I'd even finish the distance of 26 miles 385 yards. My sister Pippa and Louise provided the support team and, apart from seeing me off at the start and being there at the finish, they popped up in a variety of places during the race. I was especially pleased to see John and Jim Welch flying the flag for Bruwel in the far eastern section of the marathon route.

As the first anniversary of the opening of the Fox & Firkin drew close, I received a notification of a rate increase from the regional property valuer on behalf of Inland Revenue. I should have expected this, as the same had happened with the Goose. The valuer said that since the Fox had traded so much better since opening in May 1980 than it had as the Black Bull, he'd decided to increase the gross value of the rates from £3,000 a year to £10,800. In effect, he was tripling the rates, a direct penalty on the success of our efforts. Several months of arbitration followed, at the end of which the valuation office conceded they'd been overzealous and the rates were increased by 25 per cent and not the threefold amount that was originally demanded. This bureaucratic process absorbed precious management time which could've been put to more productive use in growing the business and creating more new jobs in previously closed-down buildings.

To aggravate my already frayed nerves, just a few weeks later, even more bureaucracy made a further attempt to derail our progress. The Greater London Council's department of architecture and civic design served notice on me under the London Building Acts (Amendment) Act of 1939 section 35 Licensing Act 1964, saying it had been brought to their attention that I intended to carry out further alterations to the Fox & Firkin. This was simply not true as I'd redeveloped the premises only a year earlier with their full consent. I concluded it was a rival licensee in Lewisham who wanted to stir up trouble and slow our inexorable success. We were not to be thwarted.

As part of the first year celebrations for the Fox in May 1981, I'd decided to donate the sponsorship money I'd raised in running the London Marathon to the Mayor of Lewisham's local community charities. I hadn't realised the first anniversary party during the evening coincided with local elections. The National Front held a march and turned out in their full regalia complete with leather jackets and swastikas accompanied by skinheads daubed with Union Jacks. What should have been an evening of celebration turned out to be the exact opposite. The National Front marchers trickled into the pub all evening and by the time I was ready to present the cheque to the mayor, there were around 50 NF supporters in the pub shouting 'Sieg Heil' with Hitler-style stiff-armed salutes. The mayor was blind and asked me what the noise was. I tried to reassure him it was just the natural exuberance of the crowd that had gathered to watch the ceremony. I identified the leader of the group and summoned up the courage to approach him and plead with him to quieten down his fellow marchers. I was thinking that this mean-looking, tattoo-covered skinhead was coming round to my way of thinking when, with no warning, he headbutted me from about six inches away. The blow was so hard that my nose exploded and blood gushed everywhere. It was difficult to host an evening with the local mayor with blood pouring down my brand-new white T-shirt.

An almighty punch-up then broke out. Many of my loyal customers were upset at the way their 'guv'nor' had been treated and were beginning to lay into the National Front supporters. I managed to shout to Louise, who'd witnessed the scenes, to call the police. They arrived promptly and helped to stop the fighting before too much damage was done and several of the troublemakers were arrested and taken away. It wasn't the best way to celebrate the first anniversary at the Fox.

My smashed face was repaired and once again I threw myself into the Bristol project. When I wasn't at the Wool Hall, I was promoting the London Firkins, which were attracting considerable publicity, including a large spread in the London *Evening Standard* written by the business editor. While this publicity helped to secure the Firkins a trendy following and reinforced the existing customers' love of the pubs, it had its downside as it tended to flush out unwanted attention from time-wasters and people wanting to buy a slice of Firkin magic.

The brewing industry continued to be fascinated by the Firkin concept of brewing on the premises. I was showing one of the main board directors of Allied Breweries around the pubs and he turned to me and said in slow and measured tones, 'You know, David, the reason why I think your pubs are so busy and successful when so many of mine aren't is because of the professional standard of amateurism that seems to pervade your entire organisation.' My first reaction was to be affronted by his remark but on reflection I think he showed acute insight. I vowed from that day to maintain this 'professional standard of amateurism' and to make it the hallmark of the Firkin culture.

The Allied director was correct in saying that no other pub run by a big brewer could replicate the Firkin experience. And long may it continue, I thought. As I became more expert at developing the Firkin concept, I consciously nurtured an ethos with customers and staff of being an enthusiastic amateur taking on the might of the big brewers. It was a David and Goliath syndrome in the same way that Richard Branson and Freddie Laker took on British Airways, beating the establishment at their own game.

Towards the end of May, my spirits were high even though my nose was still very sore. I headed off to Paris with Louise to run in the Paris Marathon. This was a great experience, starting in the Bois de Boulogne and running for 42 kilometres past all the famous sights in Paris and finishing directly under the Eiffel Tower. I completed the run in three hours and 12 minutes, slightly faster than my London

Marathon time, in spite of the wet cobbles on the streets and the fact that I insisted on wearing a blue beret for the whole race that became heavy and sodden with the rain. In addition, while waving the flag for good-old Blighty, my Union Jack shorts ran themselves in more ways than one as the dye dripped, giving me red, white and blue streaky legs, much to the amusement of the French onlookers.

A gang of runners from Thames Hare and Hounds was also in Paris and we had a celebratory meal that night where, for some extraordinary reason, I drank only red wine as part of my rehydration following the day's exertions. Medical evidence states that you can lose up to two gallons of fluid during a marathon and it's highly recommended to replace that fluid with water rather than French wine. It wasn't surprising that the following morning I woke with the world's worst hangover.

During the summer, as well as my Bristol activities, I intensified my search for possible Firkin sites closer to home. Then, in August, the City of London Corporation came to our assistance yet again when the lease of the Old Ivy House in Goswell Road became available. It was another Charrington's pub and the brewery had decided not to renew the lease on the tied house. I was sceptical about whether City Corporation would lease a third pub to a small private company like ours, bearing in mind our lack of a strong covenant. But despite my pessimism, we were offered a ten-year lease at a rent of £18,750 a year. This would become our fourth pub and would be called the Pheasant & Firkin. The premises were in quite good condition and the bar was in effect ready to trade and the proposed investment was mainly in the tiny cellar in which I insisted on placing a correspondingly tiny brewery. Little was I to know what the builders would find hidden in the cellar.

Things were hotting up everywhere with inevitable problems arising. In Bristol, John Littler from Cartwrights, the licensing solicitors, had started the licensing process for the new brewery and pub on the ground floor of the Old Wool Hall. He immediately faced opposition not only from most of the local licensees but also from the Courage Brewery just 200 yards away, where I'd worked during my brewery management training course. Such irony!

Word of the Firkins was spreading worldwide. In September 1981 I had a visit from Charlie Papazian, president of the American Homebrewers Association based in Boulder, Colorado. He was keen to see how commercial brewing could be carried out in a small space within a pub. He was followed by Hans Hopf from the Hopf Weissbierbrauerei at Meisbach, south of Munich. He expressed interest in becoming our agent in West Germany for Bruwel, as he could see brewing in both Gasthofs and bars could be equally successful in his own country. Apart from the interest from abroad, customers' word-of-mouth recommendations, which were always free, spread the message of our success across London and there was no need to spend any money on advertising or PR.

Our ever-patient bank manager, Dick Putland, went to both the proposed Bristol site and the new Pheasant & Firkin during the autumn. He agreed to fund both the new developments as long as he could have a charge based on the leases of the three trading Firkins being revalued to ensure we'd have sufficient collateral on the whole estate in case, to quote him, 'we went down like a pack of cards or the domino effect'.

We needed just £20,000 for the Pheasant, as the City of London Corporation wanted to keep the premises open following the departure of Charrington's tenant. We decided simply to refurbish the bar and domestic accommodation and treat the more costly development of the brewery in the cellar as a second stage once we'd created sufficient cash flow and profit from the bar to justify the expense. On 12 November 1981, the Pheasant & Firkin opened with beer transferred in casks from the Frog. The opening invitation was two redeemable coupons. Each one was worth a pint of Bruce's Pheasant Bitter when the bearer announced to the bar staff and all the assembled company that he or she was truly a 'Firkin Pheasant Plucker'.

The week that the Pheasant opened was also the first time I visited the burned-out shell of a boarded-up railway station at Denmark Hill in south-east London. I'd been approached by Jeremy Bennett on behalf of the Southwark Environment Trust, which was attempting to persuade British Rail not to raze the premises to the ground following a disastrous fire. I was flattered I'd been recommended to Jeremy by a fellow local resident in Denmark Hill, Terry Jones of *Monty Python's Flying Circus* fame. Terry used to drink at the Goose on his way home from working with John Cleese and the rest of the Python team, and he'd been singing the praises of my beer and food. One day, Terry had left a note for me behind the bar at the Goose saying, 'Love your beer and if you'd like to brew it at Denmark Hill railway station, ring me on this number.'

Jeremy needed to find an alternative use for the premises that would provide income by way of rent to the British Rail Property Board. After an initial site meeting at Denmark Hill, I agreed to have a beer with Jeremy Bennett at the Fox and work out a plan. On that particular evening, there happened to be a string quartet dressed in full black-tie regalia playing classical pieces in the middle of the bar while the customers, quite uncharacteristically, stood or sat and listened in rapture to the superb music. I don't know if this convinced Jeremy I was capable of performing miracles and if I could bring classical music to a pub in Lewisham High Street, I could save the Denmark Hill railway station from destruction. I agreed that I'd be interested in taking matters a stage further with the restoration of the station and creating a Firkin pub.

By November, Bruwel had built a third complete ten-barrel plant for the Leith Brewery just outside Edinburgh. We also needed more assistance on the production side and Rory Garden and Colin Summers were appointed as brewers. Both had graduated from Heriot-Watt University in Edinburgh with a BSc in brewing science. We now had three highly qualified brewers on the team, with Stephanie from the Brewing Research Foundation. Much to my astonishment, neither Rory nor Colin had ever set foot inside a brewery or brewed a pint of beer during their three-year brewing course. However, we would soon change that!

By the end of the year, the Firkin team was looking stable and strong. We had four Firkin pubs trading successfully and it was an unwelcome setback when I received a letter from the environmental health officer saying that blue asbestos had been discovered in a sample of pipe lagging taken from the basement at the Pheasant, precisely where I was hoping to install the brewery. I was introduced to a new piece of legislation that hadn't crossed my path before: the Asbestos Regulations 1969 Act, as enforced by the Health & Safety Executive. Asbestos is a serious health risk and specialist contractors have to be appointed, complete with a mobile decontamination unit with a lurid skull and crossbones on it. The unit removes the offending substance from the premises, which have to be closed while the work is carried out. This wasn't the best way to encourage people to visit the newly opened pub but there was no alternative. The Pheasant closed in early January 1982 but when it reopened two months later, we'd installed the new brewery complete with a large glass panel in order that customers could see their beer being brewed.

The first few months of 1982 were dominated by innumerable trips to Bristol both by car and train to attend site meetings where things were moving apace at the Wool Hall under the direction of Richard Barker-Harland. Richard was finding it difficult to work with the architect, Keith Hallett, who was my business partner in the project. Keith had firm ideas of his own, in particular when it came to agreeing the colours for woodwork and columns in the building. In the four Firkin pubs in London we'd used an abundance of green and that had become our corporate livery. As a result, Richard had painted everything green at the Wool Hall. We were both furious to discover that, instead of tackling us about our choice of colour, Keith had brought in his own decorators one night and repainted everything dark red. Richard responded by bringing back his own decorators one evening and returning the colour to green. There was a furious row at the next site meeting but eventually a compromise was reached and both red and green were used.

Richard was brilliant in planning the look and feel of the Firkin pubs and his enthusiasm and dedication to any project were wholehearted. For example, one Sunday evening, as he put his dog out for its final pee, he saw large snowflakes falling. He lived an hour south of Bristol and heard that roads might be impassable by the morning. So, he jumped into his small Renault van and drove to the Bristol site. He opened the large double doors of the Wool Hall, drove into the building and bunked down for the night in a sleeping bag in the back of the van. It was typical of Richard to ensure he was the first person at work on Monday morning when less dedicated souls were trickling in up to four hours late due to the few feet of snow that had fallen overnight.

The sheer scale of the development in Bristol was devouring cash. We decided to install a ten-barrel brewery, twice the size of the other pubs, with a bar 40 ft long and 20 draught beer engines. Everything was on a bigger scale and correspondingly expensive and it wasn't surprising that the old building was soaking up money. We'd negotiated only a £75,000 loan from Lloyds Bank and the money was proving to be insufficient to meet our costs.

Nevertheless, we managed to open the Fleece & Firkin on 10 March 1982. The opening was made memorable by Richard Barker-Harland, who borrowed a friend's horse box and filled it with a flock of sheep. The sheep were herded into the pub in the middle of the opening ceremony, much to the chagrin of the local environmental health officer who asked, as the 30 or 40 sheep rampaged among the guests, dropping poo all over the flagged floors, whether this would be a regular occurrence. It was manna from heaven for the local TV station and gave us extensive coverage.

In spite of our disagreements, Keith Hallett had excelled himself with a number of clever touches, one of which was a stuffed sheep sitting on top of the back-fitting behind the bar, wearing Wellington boots and a cloth cap while resting a pint of beer on a firkin. Above the door, a large clock was attached to a circular track around which a herd of sheep would move and, as the clock struck, they would bleat out the number of hours. This wonderful timepiece, when amplified, was a showstopper, until the mechanism was eventually sabotaged in the interests of peace and quiet. The use of puns was extensive. The main door announced the Public Baa and slogans were predictably puerile, including 'Ewe Mutton forget Bruce's', 'Sheep shape and Bristol fashion' and, our masterstroke of tortured English, 'For flock's sake wool ewe baa me a Firkin pint'. However wince-making the puns, they helped give the pub its own distinctive and eccentric character. As well as the notorious Dogbolter, which had been brewed in London since 1981, we also brewed Bruce's Bristol Bitter, a stout called Black Sheep, and Bootlace Bitter in honour of the BBC TV series *Shoestring*, which was filmed in Bristol.

The Fleece & Firkin was the first experience of a pub opening for Sally Smith, who had joined the team in January. She was employed to help Louise with the increasing amount of paperwork generated by applications for new licences and new projects. I was under no illusion that the Fleece was on the wrong side of Bristol Bridge and the river and wasn't on the usual pubgoers' circuit. Clifton's students and business people in the city centre would need a lot of persuading to cross the river into our back street. Sally and I distributed leaflets several times to raise awareness and encourage foot traffic to sample the delights of our new pub.

Eight weeks after launching the Fleece, we were at last in a position to open the brewery in the basement of the Pheasant & Firkin in Goswell Road following the tortuous removal of the blue asbestos in the cellar. On 18 May 1981, we launched our fifth Bruce's Brewery and, in honour of our close proximity to the Barbican Centre, we introduced Bruce's Barbican Bitter. As a result of our experience with the environmental health officer at the Frog concerning the safety of the glass panel in the floor, we installed an even bigger one at the Pheasant that took up the whole of one section of the public bar. The glass covered almost the whole area of the brewery beneath and it provided much interest to customers and brewers alike. There was no opportunity for the brewers to slack as there was nowhere for them to hide.

It was good to have the brewery up and running, but there were problems looming in Bristol. I'd received innumerable reports that the management at the Fleece left much to be desired. I was beginning to wonder if I'd bitten off more than I could chew. Running pubs in London was easier: they were more accessible and it was a market I knew well. A 240-mile round trip every time I wanted to check on the Fleece was becoming a bore and very time consuming.

It was therefore with some relief that I was able to head off to Boulder, Colorado, in June 1982 at the request of Charlie Papazian, president of the American Homebrewers' Association, to be the keynote speaker at their annual conference. Louise joined me on this much-needed and exciting trip and, as I had just opened the Frog & Firkin, I dressed up as Kermit the Frog and froghopped my way up onto the stage. The title of my talk was 'The English Brewpub and the Resurgence of the Small, Local Brewery in England and America'. At the time there were no brewpubs in the whole of North America, due to the continuing federal restrictions imposed during the Prohibition era in the 1930s. Following that, Louise and I decided to take a break and spend ten days driving across the Rocky Mountains to Los Angeles via the Grand Canyon and Las Vegas.

I had a hectic schedule of activities but still tried to keep up with training for the Bristol Marathon that was due to take place on the last Sunday in July. There was a mix of talent in the team, ranging from experienced runners from Thames Hare and Hounds to Martin Rose, the pub pianist, who'd never run more than five miles before. When the starting pistol was fired, Martin had to stub out his cigarette with his running shoe before he could join the race.

It was an exceptionally hot morning and the course went from the Unicorn Hotel in the city centre all the way out to Avonmouth via Shirehampton. About halfway round I started to develop a painful blister that was caused by wearing a new pair of running shoes. I'd broken the cardinal sin of any marathon runner of racing with shoes that hadn't been well worn. The blister came back to haunt me and, 24 hours later, I was lying in bed at 3 am with my foot feeling as if it was about to explode. Louise bundled me into the car and took me to A&E at St George's Hospital in Tooting, where the foot was X-rayed as the doctors feared I'd broken a bone during the race. It turned out that the blister had gone badly septic, which resulted in a course of antibiotics and no running for at least a fortnight. In retrospect, it was a well-earned rest from pounding the streets.

Lessons and learnings

🍺 **Lesson 4: Seize opportunities as they arise**

Once my business became better known, I seized opportunities to open a brewery in Bristol and help to open breweries in France and North America. Also, by being asked to speak at various conferences and MBA courses, one opportunity always seemed to lead to another. By following up a note left behind the bar one day, I seized the opportunity to develop my most beautiful pub ever, the Phoenix & Firkin. Once you start to take advantage of opportunities you'll gain more confidence to follow those that take you to new areas of business.

🍺 **Lesson 5: Delegate as soon and as often as possible**

As soon as your new business is trading satisfactorily, delegate as many responsibilities as you can and try to employ specialists who are either cleverer or generally better than you. In my case that meant qualified brewers, experienced pub managers and qualified accountants.

Booming pubs, a tax threat and brewing a Barbarian

1982

In August 1982, I got the first real corporate shock of my business career. Our solicitors, Bishop and Sewell, were worried that, as the business was visibly doing well, Louise and I might be incurring significant tax problems. They suggested we should seek top-level advice from major accountants. We consulted John Power, a senior tax partner at Touche Ross. Before he could assess our situation, he asked one of his corporate finance and special projects partners, Mike Middlemas, to produce a report on the progress of the Firkin pub business, now in its third year of trading. It came as a bolt from the blue when he declared that, rather than having immediate tax problems, the actual profitability of the company was sadly lacking and, in spite of our high sales, there was a danger of us going bust. Drastic remedial action was needed immediately, we were told. So much for my professional amateurism ethos – this was a time when genuine professional help was needed, although I never lost the feeling that the friendly, anarchic and enthusiastic approach to the business was part of the Firkin's success.

We'd been kidding ourselves that because all the pub breweries, with the possible exception of Bristol, were heaving with customers and Bruwel was continuing to build complete turnkey breweries for other people, business was booming. The problem was that we didn't really know what was going on as we had no proper management or financial systems in place to cope with our success.

The report made several key recommendations. The most pressing issues were to appoint a professionally qualified finance director and significantly reduce the group's overdraft by selling the Fleece in Bristol. We'd already spent too much time and money on the Fleece. This was in part due to the age of the building and its distraction from the main core business in London, which was beginning to suffer from neglect. It was agreed that we'd advertise in *Accountancy Age* for a suitable candidate. Mike Middlemas was so concerned at the perilous state of affairs within our group of companies that he asked Louise, Andy McDonald and me to visit him at his farm in Hampshire during his holiday in order that he could alert us personally to the severity of the situation, as he felt time wasn't on our side.

Within days of the Touche Ross report being published, a further blow arrived in the form of a letter from a Bass Brewery solicitor threatening us with an injunction if we didn't change the name of Bruce's Barbican Bitter, which was brewed at the Pheasant. Bass claimed the public might be confused between our cask-conditioned draught beer and their bottled, non-alcoholic Barbican. We were dismayed that we'd rattled the cage of one of the big brewers but Andy McDonald responded in verse and Bass, in fairness, replied in a similar vein. The doggerel was framed and hung for all to see in the Pheasant. But the outcome was a foregone conclusion, as we weren't in a position to take on the might of Bass in a legal battle. We changed the name of our beer to Bruce's Barbarian Bitter, with artwork incorporating both rugby players and other sporting folk. Ironically, sales increased when one of our beers was no longer named after Europe's biggest arts centre, which was just down the road.

In the midst of trying to find a new finance director, stemming the businesses' losses and trying to pull Bristol out of a hole, I received a phone call from John Nichol of Fleurets, the licensed property agents, saying that Watney's had just failed with their application to re-licence the Balloon Tavern in Lots Road, Chelsea. John asked if I might be interested in taking on the lease if I were successful in re-licensing their pub for them. The full licence had lapsed when Watney's had shut the pub and allowed the British Sub-Aqua Club to use the building as a meeting venue. When I asked John if it might be possible to view the building, he said, 'What about this evening?'

Louise and I dropped everything and I asked Antony Fletcher to join us. We agreed to meet John Nichol that evening for a tour of the building. Predictably, it was closed and boarded up, and we needed torches to find our way around, even though it was a glorious autumn evening. The pub was built in a semicircle on the corner of Lots Road opposite an enormous scrap metal yard that would become – though it's hard to believe – the upmarket Chelsea Harbour development. The pub was as dilapidated as we'd come to expect with all our acquisitions but it had the advantage of an enormous cellar where we could place a brewery. We retired to the Duke of Cumberland, a Young's pub at Parsons Green, where we decided over a few pints of Young's Special to pursue Watney's for the lease of their unlicensed freehold premises in Chelsea.

We suggested Antony might be interested in helping us finance not only what would eventually become the Ferret & Firkin but also become involved in the redevelopment of the fire-gutted Denmark Hill railway station site, to be called the Phoenix & Firkin, where both planning and preliminary costs were beginning to sound alarm bells.

Bruwel continued to make progress with its first export sale to Hans Hopf's wheat beer brewery in Bavaria. It was a complete 4.1 hectolitre plant with hot liquor back, mash tun, copper, hop back and two fermenters at a cost of £10,527. On the strength of this, we appointed Hans to be our agent for Bruwel in Germany and he actively started to attempt to find other customers. At the same time, to strengthen our presence in that vast brewing country, I became involved with the German brewing trade association, Brauring.

As Christmas 1982 approached, I started to make discreet enquiries with national and regional brewers to see if one of them might like to buy the Fleece & Firkin. I wanted to avoid putting the pub on the open market and had several meetings with Keith Hallett and his partners to see if their architectural practice might like to diversify into brewing and running a pub. My discussions weren't successful.

During my many visits to Bristol, aware of the continuing loss of stock and general lack of profitability, it amazed me that the pub seemed to be busy and was taking around £8,000 a week. But, despite the large numbers of people visiting the pub, they didn't seem to drink very much and were inclined to order halves rather than full pints, which were the norm in London. They made their half pints last for a long time, whereas in London, drinkers were clamouring for more pints. I never did fathom why Bristol boozers stood holding their halves and formed a nice crowd but never really put their hands in their pockets.

Plans for the Lots Road site for the Ferret & Firkin were proceeding well and John Nichol had negotiated an amazingly good deal with Watney's. If we were successful in gaining a new justices' licence for the premises, we'd pay Watney's only £7,500 a year for a 15-year lease. This showed what a depressed area of Chelsea this was in 1983, in which we planned to invest more than £100,000. Ironically, Watney's was plagiarising my idea of pubs brewing their own beer and had installed brewing kit in the Orange Brewery in Pimlico. One of their surveyors let me know that Watney's was looking for other opportunities and I was happy to share my experiences with him in return for Watney's tremendous support in developing the Balloon Tavern.

It was a shocking blow to learn that Dick Putland was leaving the Southampton Row branch of Lloyds Bank, as he'd been such a wonderful supporter of the Firkin project from the very beginning. Dick told me off the record that he'd been considered by his bosses to be 'too entrepreneurial in his lending attitudes' and was being transferred to head office for a non-lending role. He'd be replaced by a colleague whose main claim to fame was that he didn't like lending money to anyone unless they could prove they didn't need it. This didn't bode well.

Our disappointment at Dick Putland's departure was offset on 14 December 1982 by Bruce's Brewery's launch of the world's first commercial beer brand in home brew kit format. Dogbolter 24-pint home brew kits costing £3.50 each were a significant step forward in spreading our reputation as brewers, pub operators and now home brew kit providers. A Ken Pyne cartoon featured in the 'Bruce-proof instructions' and the slogan on the label, 'I'd make me a pint of Dogbolter if I were you – I get aggressive when I'm sober!', made it an instant media and trade success. We challenged everyone who bought a kit to bring in the result of their brewing to compare it in a blind tasting with the version brewed in one of our pubs. Plenty of people took up the challenge and there was often only a negligible difference. This proved what a good kit Stephanie Harding had devised with our maltsters, EDME, who had produced the hopped malt extract from their malted barley and mash tuns in Suffolk.

My gifted amateur reputation secured me the illustrious position of keynote speaker at the London Business School lecturing MBA students on the fine art of starting a business with no money, trying to grow it with no money and rapidly having to cope with ever-increasing demand – but still with no money. I was becoming quite an expert on the subject, but only by learning the hard way. Such invitations spurred me on and helped me believe I wasn't such a clot after all, despite my complete inability to pass maths O-level.

Lessons and learnings

🍺 **Lesson 6: Control the cash**
Just because your sales figures are looking good, it doesn't necessarily mean you're making a profit, hence the need for a qualified accountant to be your finance director. My pubs were packed to the rafters, so I thought I was making a fortune by overtrading, but it took a financial expert to turn my sales into positive cash flow.

9

Making tracks at Denmark Hill while the Balloon is going up

1983

I started the New Year in 1983 resolved to adopt the recommendations of the Touche Ross report. It was most urgent to dispose of the Fleece & Firkin in Bristol to reduce borrowings, ease cash flow and free up time to develop new London outlets. One day, I was showing the managing director of Halls of Oxford, part of Allied Breweries, around the Fleece, as he was thinking of installing mini-breweries in some of his managed houses, particularly in Oxford and Plymouth, and he was assessing whether to use Bruwel as the supplier of equipment. I not only proudly showed him round the Fleece's brewery and extolled its virtues but also dropped heavy hints that if he wanted to start a new venture with brewpubs, he could do no better than buying the Fleece and using it as his flagship outlet. Ironically, he never bought any Bruwel equipment, but he did eventually buy the Fleece.

Later that month, the new Lloyds bank manager summoned me to the bank early one morning. Living up to his gloomy reputation, he told me that until I sold the Fleece, the bank wouldn't lend me any more money. This would delay the opening of both the Ferret & Firkin in Chelsea and the Phoenix & Firkin at Denmark Hill. Both pubs were moving ahead apace but they needed bank funding to complete.

I hadn't told the new bank manager that everyone I'd approached regarding the possible sale of the Fleece had been negative in their responses. I'd been very hacked off to read a report from one prospective buyer, who described the Fleece as 'a single bar, back-street boozer on the wrong side of Bristol city centre'. This wasn't exactly the way I wished it to be seen. I'd developed what I saw as an exciting destination venue free house with its own brewery and one of the longest bars and greatest number of hand pumps in Britain. But beauty is in the eye of the beholder, especially when you're selling.

Once again, I decided to explore the opportunity of selling equity to a venture capitalist. Even they seemed more preferable partners than the now very unhelpful attitude shown by Lloyds Bank. Venture capitalists – or vulture capitalists, as I called them – had a reputation of being more open minded with entrepreneurs who wanted to expand their businesses with development capital.

We took Mike Middlemas's advice and pursued the recruitment of a professional chartered accountant who'd be appointed as finance director. Much of January was spent interviewing candidates, and we finally chose Chris Fawcett who, quite by chance, had also worked for Courage, but on the financial side rather than brewing and general management. He was made fully aware of the predicament we were in following three years of buoyant sales, very little financial control and massively undercapitalised from day one. Chris threw himself into his role with enormous vigour. A few days after he started, he brought a cheque to my office for just over £1,000 from Southwark Council. I racked my brains and finally remembered that way back, before the Goose opened in 1979, I'd applied to Southwark Development Corporation for a grant. I met the criteria, as I was starting a new manufacturing business in an inner-city area and would create a number of new jobs, including mine. A vast number of forms had been filled in and no doubt many meetings were held but, hey presto, nearly four years after I really needed the money, my application was granted and the cheque finally arrived. We banked the money with gusto.

Work on developing the Balloon Tavern was progressing well and

John Littler, the Bristol-based lawyer from Cartwrights, was chasing the licence application. Much to my amusement, the main reason why the licensing justices had refused to grant Watney's a licence for their own freehold premises was that there were already sufficient grotty Watney's pubs in the area and they didn't want yet another one. I doubt the ruling was expressed in quite those terms.

While the campaign to obtain a new licence was gaining momentum, I was spending a lot of time with Jeremy Bennett of the Camberwell Society and Southwark Environment Trust. We were working with lawyers for British Rail on the complex legalities of trying to put a pub and brewery across four fully operational railway lines beneath the dangerous structure of a burned-out station. By March we'd agreed terms and signed the lease for 41 years at £15,000 a year. However, there was a nasty little clause that British Rail refused to remove, which stipulated that they could terminate the lease immediately at any time for operational reasons. This was non-negotiable and the only solution was for us to take out a separate insurance policy in the unlikely event of 'operational events' occurring. The insurance would protect our capital investment and the loss of profits for the remainder of the lease.

The complex terms of the lease included the financial commitment of the various parties interested in the restoration of the historic building that the Poet Laureate and train lover Sir John Betjeman had once described as 'A neat Victorian building well worthy of preservation and quite out of the ordinary... all roads lead to Denmark Hill.' The financial commitments incorporated in the lease were:

- Southwark Environment Trust: £32,000
- Historic Buildings Council: £56,000
- British Rail: £76,000
- Greater London Council: £20,000
- Bruce's Brewery (Denmark Hill) Ltd: £120,000.

Little did any of my co-investors know that I had no money to contribute until I either sold the Fleece & Firkin and/or changed banks.

March 1983 marked the first anniversary of the opening of the

Fleece but, as all it had done so far was to lose me money, I found it hard to generate much enthusiasm for a celebratory party. I was also becoming increasingly despondent that I'd ever be able to sell the pub at any price. This would adversely affect my ability to borrow money and continue with development of the successful Firkin pubs in London along with the two new ventures, the Ferret and the Phoenix, that were undergoing applications for new justices' licences.

To cope with the pressures, I spent at least every other weekend at our cottage in Wales. Buried in a bolthole, we could really relax, go for long walks and cross-country runs and enjoy cosy evenings by two enormous log fires as we gathered our strength for the next round of growing the business in London.

As a result of my keynote address to the American home brewers in Boulder, Colorado, the previous year, Charlie Papazian came to see us on his next trip to London and I took him to the Goose, Fox, Pheasant and Frog along with the two proposed new sites for the Ferret and Phoenix. He told me that since my visit to the US, several brewpubs had opened. The first was Bill Owen's in Hayward, California, known as Buffalo Bill's Brewpub, where he brewed 'the world's bitterest beer – Alimony Ale'! Charlie was also my guest at the monthly lunch for members of SLOBA, the Small London Brewers' Association, where I had the pleasure of introducing him to Patrick Fitzpatrick, the owner of Godson's Brewery at Old Ford, east London, as 'Pricktrack Pissf***trick'. Charlie fell for it, thinking it was a wild Celtic name.

Out of SLOBA came the formation of SIBA, the Small Independent Brewers' Association. Peter Austin was appointed the chair and Louise the secretary, and its membership grew rapidly as other small breweries sprang up across the UK. Peter and I had decided to form SIBA as we'd each been rejected when we applied to join both the Incorporated Brewers' Guild and the Brewers' Society.

Although Harrington Griffiths, the secretary of the Incorporated Brewers' Guild, had always been most courteous and helpful when I'd contacted him on a variety of points, my application to join the Brewers' Society met with the claim that, although I was a fully licensed and indeed legally incorporated commercial brewer, I was 'too small and too new' to join the venerable society, which represented virtually 99 per cent of Britain's national and independent brewers.

I replied that, around two centuries ago, people called John Courage, Ben Truman and Samuel Whitbread had also started brewing in their respective pubs and that they too were then small and new, and look what had happened to them. The reply from the official spokesperson was, 'Ah yes, but that was then and this is now.'

The logo of Dogbolter is only blurred when you are sober!

By April, we'd been granted a provisional justices' licence for the Balloon Tavern. We succeeded where Watney's had failed, and I was able to sign a lease for a rent of £7,500 a year with an undertaking that I'd sell at least 300 barrels of lager and other products bought from Watney's. These would supplement Bruce's range of beers brewed on the premises and to be named as Stoat (as in stout), Ferret Ale (as in 'Every Ferret Ale has a happy ending') and for the non-drinker or Watney's fan, Weasel Water, together with our notorious and ever-popular strong ale, Dogbolter. Another typically Brucey slogan was 'Bruce's beer – you'll pre-Ferret to any other!' Jamie Nimmo, who'd devised all the corporate logos, produced a wonderful new one for Dogbolter that showed a blurred dog's head and two blurred bones in the shape of a skull and crossbones. The image, we made clear, would only appear blurred if the customer was sober and after a few drinks all the blurred lines of the dog and crossbones would appear as a clear single line.

The granting of the provisional licence for the Ferret & Firkin meant that the justices would grant a full licence with the provision that I complied in every way with all the local regulations and the plans submitted and approved by the justices. In April we started to spend the £60,000 we'd allocated to the project, fully aware that Lloyds Bank had said no further support would be available until we sold the Fleece. We were in a conundrum as we didn't want to be in breach of contract with Watney's, who'd just granted us the lease. The fabric of the building was in a far worse state than we'd imagined and soon the chartered surveyor appointed by Antony Fletcher to inspect the Frog & Firkin two years earlier was employed by Bruce's Brewery (World's End) Ltd to represent our interests against the army of surveyors and engineers appointed by Watney's. The biggest problem was that the whole of the ground floor was supported by joists all the ends of which were completely rotten to some 4 ft or 5 ft in from the exterior walls. The building had become riddled with damp due to the proximity of the River Thames less than 100 yards away. In the end, Richard Barker-Harland and I persuaded all the experts not to spend a fortune on a new set of joists and floor for the pub but to build a new wall 4–5 feet in from the outside wall that would support the dry sections of joists. The solution saved tens of thousands of pounds, which in any case we didn't have.

Bovis, the contractors nominated by British Rail, were starting work on restoring the exterior of the station at Denmark Hill, and they attempted to persuade me to work with them on developing the pub interior and brewery. Every time we had a discussion on costs, their estimates were about three times more than I'd been used to with

Richard Barker-Harland of du Boulay Construction. I continued to resist Bovis's approaches without demotivating them as they worked on the external structures.

At about this time, I encountered a major problem with Watney's. I'd told them I wished to change the name of the Balloon Tavern to the Ferret & Firkin but was told by the business development manager that it had been taken to board level and the directors insisted I should incorporate the word balloon in the new name. This was due to the premises' historic association with early balloon ascents on the very spot in Cremorne Gardens where the pub had been built. I'd already instructed Jamie Nimmo to devise a simple logo of a ferret alongside the usual firkin, but now I had an external and unwanted influence on my freedom to call my pubs whatever I liked. This was my first experience of renting a premises from one of the big brewers. I was mindful of the fact that they were prepared to allow me to brew my own beer in their Chelsea freehold and operate it as a free house on the condition I bought lager from them.

Long and convoluted discussions followed about how to incorporate the balloon name alongside the ferret. Eventually it was agreed that the Ferret & Firkin in the Balloon would satisfy the Watney's board, but it didn't scan quite right for me. I felt the pub's location close to Chelsea Creek should be acknowledged in the name and it was finally agreed that our sixth pub would be the Ferret & Firkin in the Balloon up the Creek. Andy McDonald said it would be the longest pub name in the world and warrant us a place in the 1983 *Guinness Book of Records*. Jamie Nimmo devised a highly original logo of a ferret wearing a Biggles-style flying helmet and scarf and holding a foaming pint of Ferret Ale while suspended below a hot-air balloon using a firkin cask instead of a basket.

I was conscious I'd embarked on another enormous capital development programme with neither the blessing of Lloyds Bank nor securing any outside equity finance. One of my customers, who worked in the City, suggested Barings Bank and, with some trepidation, I squeezed into my only suit and went to a meeting in the boardroom of one of the world's oldest merchant banks, dating from 1762. I described with much enthusiasm all the breweries and pubs I'd opened in the past four years and then the epitome of a Hooray Henry announced in a cut-glass voice, 'Well, this is all very interesting, Mr Bruce, but we're bankers, don't y'know, and we don't usually talk about brewing beer and pubs, we usually only talk about money. I don't think yours is the sort of business in which we would enjoy being investors.' Feeling I was some sort of vulgar oik, I quickly removed my odious presence from the bank's hallowed premises. I'd be churlish not to admit a degree of schadenfreude in 1995 when Barings Bank was bankrupted by Nick Leeson, a rogue trader in Singapore, and sold for £1 to the Dutch bank ING.

I continued to try to cultivate Halls of Oxford in the hope that, as their enthusiasm for brewing in pubs continued to grow, so might their interest in buying the Fleece. Tint and Alistair Watson, whom I'd dispatched to Bristol to take over the management of the Fleece, and who'd been brilliant at running the Goose, failed to make a success of the Fleece and wanted to return to London. Bristol continued to be a thorn in my side.

As well as Charlie Papazian, I was inundated by other Americans who wanted either to start their own bar with a brewery or an independent microbrewery. Bruwel was busy with enquiries from China to Alaska and they were keeping Stephanie Harding and her team busy showing potential customers the kits on offer. We dispatched an export order of four modified cellar storage tanks to the first brewpub in Canada, the Troller in Vancouver. Bruwel was now an international manufacturing company and Hans Hopf was campaigning hard in Germany while I developed my contacts with Brauring to strengthen my reputation as a pioneer of small breweries.

Lessons and learnings

🍺 **Lesson 2: Build a trusted support network**
Team up with fellow entrepreneurs with whom you can bounce around ideas and share many of the problems that arise – it's lonely at the top! I enjoyed meeting regularly with fellow start-up brewers, which led to the creation of the Small London Brewers' Association and then the national Small Independent Brewers' Association.

10

Battles with bureaucrats and other lowlifes

1983

The terms of the lease with British Rail and Southwark Environment Trust were agreed, so we could start the tortuous process of trying to obtain a justices' licence for the Phoenix & Firkin. Under the archaic laws of the licensing acts, the first stage was to gain a Certificate of Non-Objection to the granting of a new justices' licence by a subcommittee of the local licensing justices. If we were successful, we could then make a similar application to the main committee of licensing justices. Only when we'd jumped through all these hoops could we then approach the licensing justices themselves with an application for a new licence.

On 7 June, John Littler and the rest of my team of professional advisors arrived at the Crown Court at Newington Causeway. To help fight our corner, I was accompanied by an expert witness who'd surveyed all the other licensed properties in the area, and an independent professional market researcher.

When we arrived at the court, we were greeted by coachloads of licensees from nearly all the pubs in the area who were objecting to our gaining a licence. The pack was led by Charrington's Brewery, who owned the freehold of most of the pubs where the tenants were opposing us. I was alarmed to discover that Charrington would pick up the legal costs for the licensees as well as the local Licensed

Victuallers' Association. This was ironic, as the Denmark Hill site had already been offered to Charrington, Courage and Whitbread before I was approached. The big brewers had all turned it down, saying the station would never work as a pub. Such was their fear of my successes that they now wanted to stop me from having any more.

There were several adjournments, but I was finally awarded a provisional licence for the Phoenix. It was won in spite of widespread opposition, with Charrington hiring one of the top licensing barristers to oppose us, but John Littler continued his 100 per cent success rate of gaining new licences for Bruce's Brewery. We attempted to prove to the justices that, in spite of the opposition, what we proposed would satisfy a need in the area for interesting own-brewed beers and imaginative food in a unique setting. One of my witnesses, a young doctor at King's College Hospital, announced under oath that he and his colleagues were certain to use the pub as it was within emergency bleeper distance of the hospital. One of the justices solemnly replied, 'In that case, remind me not to be taken as a patient into King's College Hospital after lunch, in case you have been drinking there prior to operating on me.' A titter of laughter ran round the sombre courtroom.

I was also attempting to finish the redevelopment of the Ferret & Firkin in time for the next meeting of the justices on 29 June, when they could grant me a licence. As all the building work was being carried out on the strength of a provisional licence, the pub had to be inspected before 29 June by the various authorities to make sure I'd complied with all my undertakings. On the Friday before the justices were due to consider my application, I arranged to meet the environmental health officer and the fire officer to prove we were ready to open subject to a final inspection by the justices themselves. All went smoothly with the health officer but the fire officer arrived and spread out a set of plans we'd never seen before. In addition, there was a thick file of statutory notices, again all new to us. The fire officer then started to inspect the premises armed with the paperwork. As his face grew increasingly perplexed, he asked Richard Barker-Harland and me why we hadn't carried out any of the work that had been notified to Watney's two years earlier when the brewery had made its unsuccessful application to re-licence the site. Richard and I looked at each other in amazement as this was the first we'd heard about such demands being made to Watney's.

We told him we didn't know about these proposals and he said that wasn't his problem and we had until Tuesday morning to put in place all his recommendations or our application for the licence would be adjourned until at least September, when the justices next convened. There was no point in venting our anger at Watney's. We had to complete all the recommended work, which even the fire officer admitted was impossible. He made a note on his file that we'd failed his inspection, which was passed automatically to the clerk to the justices.

Richard rang round every contact he knew in the building trade and flooded the pub with labourers who worked round the clock all weekend. By 10 am on Monday morning, the fire officer returned and agreed that all his recommendations had been successfully complied with. When the licensing justices turned up in a minibus one hour after he'd left and given his approval, they still had the note made by the clerk the previous Friday that we'd failed the fire inspection. I pleaded with them to ring the fire officer when they returned to the courthouse and they reluctantly agreed to do so. They also said in passing that they didn't think the premises were ready to open as paint was still drying and furniture wasn't in position. I assured them it would be by the time we opened on Tuesday, but they said they didn't have time to return and re-inspect the following day and planned to reject my application and adjourn the case until September. That would have meant economic doom for the Firkin Group.

Richard and I agreed we'd work through the day and following night with an army of helpers to get everything ship-shape. I then arranged for a photographer to film all aspects of the premises at 5 am the following morning. When we attended court at 9 am, we were able to produce colour photos of the completed premises, ready for opening. The photographer swore an affidavit that he'd taken the photos at 5 am that morning and what the justices were looking at was genuine. We stood nervously in the witness box at Knightsbridge Magistrates Court as the magistrates said this was all very irregular. Our lawyer, John Littler, came to our rescue and managed to persuade the court that, subject to the various undertakings and affidavits that had been sworn, the premises did now comply with all the statutory regulations and the licence should be granted. The magistrates adjourned for a nail-biting half hour, then returned and approved our application, although clearly under duress. Once again, we'd crept under the wire by the skin of our teeth and avoided disaster.

The following day, Tuesday 29 June, the Ferret & Firkin finally opened under Andy McDonald's management. In his new role as managing director of the Firkin Group, he wanted our latest flagship to run brilliantly from day one under his direction. This left Chris Fawcett in the office to look after finance and admin, while Andy was free to try to make money out of our latest venture. We had a brilliant opening party, the first since the Fleece had opened in Bristol. Among the guests, I was especially happy to see the entire board of Halls of Oxford, who seemed to be showing interest in possibly buying the Fleece. I made sure they had a memorable evening.

Following the last-minute drama of trying to persuade the justices to grant the final order for our licence, I didn't need our manager at Lloyds Bank to phone the next day and say he'd read in the *Evening Standard* that, contrary to his instructions, we'd opened a new Firkin pub before we'd sold the Fleece. I didn't let him know the problem was even worse than he feared as we'd spent several thousand pounds more than we'd anticipated on the crumbling fabric of the Ferret building. We were able to survive thanks to our 'white knight', Antony Fletcher, who agreed to lend us £40,000 over three years with the proviso that he had the opportunity to become financially involved with the development of the Phoenix. Antony had become imbued with the spirit of the Firkin vernacular and would say 'Every Ferret ale has a happy or hoppy ending' and another of my tortuous inventions that, as ever, crucified the English language but appealed to him: 'You can tell it's Ferret Ale because it's wease-ly recognisable and stoat-ily different.' Could they get any worse?

Chris Fawcett and Antony Fletcher, with his lawyers, started to put together a government-approved investment plan called the Business Expansion Scheme (BES). BES was attractive to high-risk entrepreneurial investors who wanted to take a punt on smaller but expanding businesses. Investors could claim back up to 40 per cent of their investment capital against income tax immediately and, provided they stayed in the scheme for a minimum of five years, any capital gains would be tax free. This was a bold piece of legislation that appealed to Antony and several of his similarly well-heeled friends.

While Chris was spending time with Antony on the BES scheme for the Phoenix, I was continuing to try to find a suitable bank or venture capitalist I could sell some group equity to. It was during one of these meetings at the Ferret that County Bank, the investment division of NatWest Bank, introduced me to the unforgettable abbreviation CCRPPO, about which I had to declare total ignorance. I was told it stood for cumulative convertible redeemable participating preferred ordinary shares. One of the men in suits, now on his third pint, said, 'Well, basically, it means that if you do well the bank does well and if you do badly the bank still does well.' County Bank joined the ever-increasing list of rejected financial leads.

The Fleece & Firkin even features in the graffiti on the Berlin Wall

The Firkin Saga

On 31 August, the Fleece & Firkin was finally sold to Halls of Oxford for £260,000. This was only a little more than we'd invested but at least we were free of the albatross that had been round our necks since its opening. In addition, I would also receive an annual £10,000 consultancy fee for three years to assist when necessary with technical advice on the brewing operation. At last, the place that had almost brought my fast-expanding London ventures to a grinding halt had been disposed of at a reasonable price and its long-term future was assured under the direction of one of the big brewers. I was able jubilantly to report to Lloyds that we were now well in order and I was able to let Mike Middlemas at Touche Ross know that all his recommendations had been implemented within six months of his report being produced.

Andy McDonald realised, several weeks following the opening of the Ferret, that while he'd been appointed managing director of the group, being a resident pub manager wasn't as much fun as he'd anticipated. We had a long and frank discussion about his future and it was agreed amicably that it would be better if he moved on, as the company was becoming more structured following the Touche Ross report. It was a tough decision, as Andy and I went back a long way to the days at the Artesian in Notting Hill when we'd first joined forces at LSD Entertainment. The only problem we experienced following the decision that Andy would leave was how to value the 10 per cent of the equity in the group that Louise and I had given him as recognition of all his hard work and enthusiasm in the early days of the Firkin pubs. As the company was in such a state of transition, it was almost impossible to value professionally the various shareholdings of the now eight companies. Even Andy warned us of the difficulties of attempting to value a private company's equity. The issue was further compounded by what Andy referred to as the BUF or 'bugger-up factor'. What this meant was that if we couldn't agree a price that was acceptable to Andy, he'd remain a 10 per cent shareholder for the future. None of us wanted that but it made us focus on agreeing a value that was acceptable to all parties, and Andy duly resigned as MD.

It was part of the Firkin ethos to let our hair down from time to time and where possible to raise money for charity. We took part in the 1983 *Sunday Times* Fun Run in Hyde Park and organised an all-day barbecue. As the number of our staff grew and customers multiplied, so our entrants in the race increased. That year we entered close to 100 runners in various teams. Each runner received a T-shirt with the Ken Pyne cartoon of the fat jogger on the front holding a pint of beer and on the back the words 'I'm Firkin Knackered'. I'm sure most of the so-called runners agreed to join us only because they would get one of the much-coveted T-shirts. To help the party go with a swing, we organised a team of runners, working in relays, to push the pub piano, with a series of pianists playing it, from the Frog & Firkin in Notting Hill all the way down Ladbroke Grove, over the Bayswater Road, across Kensington Gardens and into Hyde Park, then all the way down to the Serpentine, where the Firkin Flyers had roped off an enormous compound for the revelries.

Back to brewing, Stephanie and I joined Hans Hopf, our Bruwel agent, at Brau '83, the International Brewing Exhibition in Nuremberg. It marked the first occasion in the history of brewing for a trade stand at an international brewing event to feature a full working brewery, producing beer on the stand. We'd managed to overcome all the problems associated with milling grain, boiling liquids, extracting heat and steam from the area, not to mention the special drainage needed to cope with the huge amounts of water involved in brewing and in cleaning the equipment after each brew. The stand, masterminded by Hans Hopf, caused a sensation over the four-day event and it became the talking point of the entire exhibition.

It was good to meet Crown Prince Luitpold of Bavaria, who was starting to sell his Kaltenberg beer, brewed in his own Kaltenberg Castle, in Britain. By the end of the show we'd secured four firm orders and received several further enquiries for our German agents to follow up.

Back home, I was keen to secure another property ripe for development as a Firkin. It seemed the Phoenix & Firkin wouldn't be open for at least another six months or more and just before Christmas

1983, I viewed the closed and boarded-up Highbury Brewery Tap on Holloway Road. This site was on the market through Fleurets for £78,000. Ind Coope no longer wished to own the freehold of the tied house and were happy to sell on the open market as a freehold free house but would prefer to sell it to a company prepared to continue selling some of their beers. This could fit the Firkin formula and I was keen to get a good look around the premises to see what promise it might hold for us. There had been a dispute with Fleurets over the wording in their sale document about an enclosed yard they claimed could be for trade use such as storing dustbins. I interpreted this as more of a covered yard that I could convert into a trading area for customers rather than a repository for waste.

Early one December morning, armed with the sale details, I banged on the front door of the premises. Eventually the door was opened by a bleary-eyed, scruffy, hippy-looking type who asked me what I wanted at this early hour. I told him I wanted to look around and waved the Fleurets' details at him. He was joined by two or three others, who said they were officially squatting in the pub and no one would be allowed to inspect the premises as they'd be trespassing on squatters' rights.

I argued with them for several minutes and eventually persuaded the hostile group to let me have a quick walk round the place. I had to rely on torchlight as usual, as all the downstairs windows were boarded up and the electricity had been switched off by Ind Coope when the tenant had left the pub. The squatters had broken in through a rear skylight and they followed me closely as I made my tour. I was concerned to see a pile of tapes containing a selection of songs in support of the Irish Republican Army. This tied in with the local gossip that the pub had been a meeting place for the local IRA. I didn't dally long. The place sent a shiver down my spine as I flashed my torch around the darkened scene. While the pub was long and narrow, I felt that if we could properly cover the yard at the back by creating a new roof, it would almost double the trading area of the existing bar, and the cellar was certainly big enough to incorporate a brewery as it extended under the yard at the back of the premises.

The day after my encounter with the Highbury squatters saw me wrapped up warmly against a biting north-easterly gale some 100 feet above the railway lines at Denmark Hill station. The topping-out ceremony was taking place to mark the completion of the restoration of the external structure of the station by Bovis on behalf of British Rail. Neither Jeremy Bennett nor I relished climbing up the outside of the recently restored structure, traversing the roof and up to the highest chimney on which the final brick was about to be laid to mark the completion of stage one of the project. We completed our aerial adventure but climbing a series of ladders was an unpleasant experience as my Bovis hard hat, several sizes too big, kept falling over my face. I was glad I didn't suffer from vertigo like Louise.

Lessons and learnings

🍺 **Lesson 3: Be brave, ambitious and determined to overcome all obstacles**

When bureaucrats try to stifle your ambitions, fight bureaucracy and red tape and never let a bigger rival get the better of you. Whenever I tried to obtain a new licence for a pub, most of the big brewers objected to my application on the sole grounds that they didn't want any more competition on their patch. Fighting for and protecting your business can be very time consuming and sometimes expensive, but it's essential in order to achieve what you want.

🍺 **Lesson 6: Control the cash**

If any part of your new business doesn't work out, then close it down or sell it before it loses too much cash, as I experienced at the Fleece & Firkin.

Skirmishes with squatters, losing directors and becoming a dad

1984

As New Year's Day 1984 beckoned, I looked back on the previous year as near make or break. The Touche Ross report probably saved our bacon as it made me realise it was time to get some proper management controls in place and reduce our borrowings. The loss of Dick Putland at Lloyds Bank was a blow, as his successor showed none of Dick's willingness to help. The support Antony Fletcher had given us to save the Ferret development and help with the Phoenix lifted a worrying burden while the sale of the Fleece in Bristol removed a financial millstone and injected much-needed cash back into the business. We'd gained a finance director but lost an old friend in Andy McDonald. I continued to be disappointed by the merchant banks and the failure of other commercial lenders to appreciate the Firkin phenomenon and its investment potential.

The year got off to a flying start when Fleurets called me to say that Ind Coope had accepted my offer of £105,000 for the freehold of the Highbury Brewery Tap. This was a real fillip as for once not only could we just about afford it but also more importantly it would represent my second freehold, which would boost the strength of the balance sheet. This would allow us to borrow more money against it for future expansion of the group while being ever mindful of the dangers of a domino effect occurring. We managed to scrape together enough money for the 10 per cent deposit, which enabled us to exchange contracts on the Highbury premises, although several months would pass before we could complete the deal due to the squatters' determination to carry on living in what was now our property. This was probably a blessing in disguise, as the relationship with our manager at Lloyds was deteriorating fast. It was imperative for me to start afresh with a new clearing bank and leave behind the hairy memories of general impecuniousness and the recent disagreements with Lloyds.

Rumours were reaching me that Richard Branson was thinking of expanding his Virgin empire by moving into pubs. It occurred to me there might be some synergies between Virgin and Firkin, and if there weren't, I didn't relish the prospect of becoming a rival of his in the London pub market. While he'd never been involved in pubs, he seemed to make a success of anything he turned his hand to. I managed to obtain the phone number of his houseboat on the Regent's Canal in Little Venice and arranged to meet him one afternoon. When I arrived on board, he beckoned me into his office, where he was on a transatlantic call to Hollywood. I sat and waited… and waited… and waited, until eventually the call came to an end. I'd just introduced myself when the phone rang again and another lengthy call ensued, at the end of which I started to outline my proposal, but I'd hardly started when the phone rang once more and another long transatlantic call interrupted us.

After a couple of hours of continual interruptions by the phone, I'd hardly had a chance to scratch the surface. Branson was perfectly friendly and charming and interested to hear what little information I'd been able to give him between the telephone calls, all of which seemed to be about much more exciting and glamorous matters than developing pubs in London. I attempted to follow up our meeting on a number of occasions but it was clearly not meant to happen. A few months later, Branson did invest in pubs for the first time by opening the Vulture's Perch in Shepherd's Bush, but within months he'd abandoned his new pub venture, mainly due to a murder taking place within weeks of its opening. As I'd discovered in Newcastle some years before, a murder can, not surprisingly, ruin a fledgling business.

Building work was continuing at the Phoenix & Firkin but, with no windows or doors, the weekly site meetings in February were freezing occasions that could drag on for a couple of hours, although there was now a roof to keep out the snow and rain. During one of these meetings, it occurred to me that none of us was wearing a hard hat. By amazing coincidence, no sooner had I asked David du Boulay for a hat than a brick fell from the new mezzanine level some 30 ft above us, landing on the exact spot where I'd just raised my foot while attempting to keep warm. If I'd been standing still or leaning my head forward to check my notes, I'd have either received a badly broken foot or the Firkin story would have come to a sudden end. The shock of how close I'd been to calamity only dawned on me later and from then on, regardless of health and safety regulations, we all vowed that hard hats would be worn at all times.

As the building took shape, it became clear that trying to cover the vast amount of wall space with suitable bric-a-brac and posters would pose a major problem. Sally had heard that British Rail stored a collection of railway memorabilia in an old warehouse behind Euston Station. She paid a visit and announced that she'd not only bought a load of signals, posters and other material, but she'd also seen a small card advertising a railway clock for sale for only £50. When she asked why it was so cheap, she was told that it measured some 5 ft in diameter and it would need a warehouse-sized building to hang it in.

It sounded ideal, but Sally was warned it needed dismantling and removing from its location in a small and unpronounceable railway station in north Wales. Sally was a keen hill walker and was duly dispatched with her husband Rob the following weekend for an all-expenses trip with the proviso that they returned with photos of the enormous hanging clock from all angles. When we saw the fruits of her expedition, two of du Boulay's subcontractors were sent the following week with an enormous toolkit and firm instructions not only to dismantle the clock but also to remember how to reassemble it once it was in its new home in the Phoenix. The magnificent timepiece became a central feature of the pub and it scarcely lost a second from the day it was installed.

The Phoenix & Firkin with its amazing station clock

I wanted more memorabilia, so I took a day trip to York, where I spent a fascinating day wandering around the National Railway Museum. Disappointingly, I returned with only a small selection of reproduction railway posters to adorn the walls of the pub. As a result, I phoned my friend Liz Farrow at Dodo, where we'd bought all our beery posters over the years, and explained I was on the hunt for railway-themed posters to fill the vast amount of wall space at the Phoenix. She rang back a couple of weeks later and said, rather gloomily, that she had nothing much in the way of railways or trains but had located a source of large travel posters that she hadn't yet inspected, though she was confident they were sufficiently large and colourful for my purposes. We went to inspect them and couldn't contain our delight when every one of the original posters, going back to the 1930s, turned out to be an advertisement for seaside resorts from Northumberland to Cornwall, each one proclaiming the merits of travelling by train. They were perfect, so I bought the lot and spent a small fortune having them framed, but they were worth every penny and helped transform the rebuilt shell of the railway station.

As my Firkin empire continued to grow apace, office politics and intrigue were bound to rear their ugly heads at some point, as in any business with an ever-increasing number of employees. There was one notable occasion when two of my directors objected to a decision I'd made to sack a pub manager due to her continuing poor profitability. For some reason, they felt so strongly that they both threatened to resign from my board if I didn't agree to reverse my decision. I refused to comply with their demands and suggested they reconsider for the next hour, but I warned them if they didn't change their minds at the end of that hour I'd expect their resignations along with their car keys. I surprised myself at the strength of my resolve. I left them both in the boardroom and walked home, where I briefed Louise on the extraordinary turn of events. She endorsed my view that no one should have a pistol held to their head by two new directors. We realised that if our bluff were called we'd lose half of the new board we'd formed as a result of following the recommendations of the Touche Ross report only a year earlier.

One hour later, I returned to the office where I found them sitting defiantly in the boardroom with two sets of car keys on the table in front of them. They said they wouldn't withdraw their threat and wished to resign immediately. Much to their surprise, I accepted without further ado. I made three phone calls, the first to let Louise know the outcome and then to explain what had happened to our manager at Lloyds Bank and Mike Middlemas at Touche Ross, who could hardly believe his ears. Both completely understood my decision to accept their resignations and Mike offered to send temporary help. With their departure, we needed someone to do the weekly wages, pay the bills and generally keep on top of all financial matters. Mike seconded one of his young assistants, Robert Aitkin, to assess the financial situation and keep the monetary side of the business flowing while I drafted an advertisement in *Accountancy Age* for a new finance director.

Later that day, Sally called an impromptu meeting of all managers and brewers where I told them what had happened earlier that day. The only surprise expressed by the staff was that it had taken me so long to take such a firm but necessary stand. The poor atmosphere improved immediately and life started to return to normal – but not quite for me, as soon after, Rebecca Emily Bruce was born at St Thomas's Hospital on 1 March 1984. This was a wonderful moment for both of us as Louise and I had been married for 11 years, so no one could accuse us of being hasty in starting a family.

Sally helped keep the TWs (time-wasters), as she referred to them, at bay as I juggled fatherhood with the development work at the Phoenix & Firkin. Half of my board resigning did little to relieve the pressure and there was also the Highbury Brewery Tap to consider. We were hampered by the squatters, who continued to squat in spite of several visits by court bailiffs. I became quite an expert on squatters' rights and each time a bailiff was appointed to remove them, the bailiff had to name each squatter before it became a legal requirement for them to leave the premises. The squatters also became experts on the legal niceties by replacing previously named squatters with new ones unknown to the bailiff, and they continued to squat until he interrogated them prior to his next visit. They'd be removed, only to be replaced by yet another new group. It took five months of this merry-go-round to finally remove them legally with the aid of some very large bailiffs. The squatters moved on, and I was finally able to invite the licensing justices to inspect the premises.

In their usual unhelpful fashion, I duly received notification from the clerk to the licensing justices at Highbury and Islington Magistrates Court that the premises would be inspected between 8.30 am and 4.30 pm on a given day. I was fastidious about timekeeping and arrived at the pub at 8.30 am precisely. There was no electricity, the windows were still boarded up and the squatters had wrecked the place. There was nowhere to sit and the place stank. After two hours of shivering in the dark or waiting by the half-open door trying to read a newspaper, I walked to the nearest phone box and rang the court to be told the magistrates were on their tour but I couldn't be told when they'd visit me. By lunchtime there was still no sign of them and by then I was becoming increasingly cold, despondent and hungry. I phoned the court again to be told the magistrates had returned to the court for their lunch hour. I was also told their visit to the Highbury Brewery Tap, as it was the closest pub to the court, had been made at 8.15 am, 15 minutes before they were due to start their tour. As they were unable to gain access, they'd crossed it off their list for the next hearing and I'd have to wait a further six weeks before they were prepared to visit again. Some days, life just didn't seem fair.

As May 1984 approached, the three-year anniversary of Antony Fletcher's investment in the Frog & Firkin in Notting Hill would be due. It had been agreed that I'd buy him out at the end of three years according to a formula based on average annual sales. I was just about able to pay back Antony's investment, enabling him to double his money over the period, while I secured for Bruce's Brewery its first 100 per cent-owned freehold free house, complete with its own brewery in west London. None of this would've been possible without the vision and support of my old running pal, to whom I am eternally grateful.

Lessons and learnings

🍺 **Lesson 2: Build a trusted support network**
As the founder and leader of the team you've developed, always be the assertive boss. I really had to be the unwavering leader one day when 50 per cent of my board threatened to resign over one of my decisions, so I called their bluff and they subsequently had to leave within the hour.

12

Avoiding trains and finding a helpful bank

1984

Converting a derelict, burned-out railway station into a new pub with its own brewery was proving to be a major challenge. There were two sets of builders on site: Bovis rebuilt the shell for British Rail while du Boulay Construction was responsible for all interior work. One of the most demanding tasks was excavating hundreds of tons of earth from the railway embankment under the old stationmaster's flat to enable us to install the brewery in the cellar. This entailed many hours of laborious shovelling by hand as there was no room to use a mechanical digger. It was only after the excavation work was completed that I realised just how close the new brewery would be to the railway lines, which were a few feet away.

Every few minutes, the ground vibrated when a train thundered through the station. This was a cause for concern as the last thing a brewer wants when settling beer in storage tanks or casks prior to serving it is for any vibration that would disturb the sediment at the bottom of vessels, resulting in cloudy beer. We agreed to carry on fitting out the brewery but with the firm understanding that if the vibration did upset the clarity of the beer, there would have to be remedial work, such as suspending floors and inserting rubber cushioning. We wouldn't know if there would be any problems until beer had been brewed and the pub opened.

Owing to the large number of organisations engaged on the project, our weekly site meetings involved as many as a dozen people. The British Rail team, despite being more than an hour late for one meeting due to train delays, for which they were mercilessly ribbed, were incredibly helpful. There were architects, surveyors and engineers, all of whom were responsible for making sure the conversion of a station spanning four railway tracks into a new pub and brewery didn't collapse onto a passing train.

During one of the site meetings, the engineer responded to a technical question with an enormous suck on his teeth and the announcement that 'Well, that all depends on whether or not we can get PICOPs on that day.' The assembled company looked quizzically at him as we didn't have a clue what he was talking about. As the proposed work required structural improvements to the underside of the building, all four tracks would have to be shut, probably on a Sunday, to minimise inconvenience to one of the busiest commuter routes in the world. However, essential trains, such as those carrying nuclear waste from Dungeness to Sellafield, which usually passed through the station in the dead of night, would have to be allowed through.

It was agreed by the Engineers' Department that British Rail would have to find a PICOPS prepared to work for double time over a weekend. It was eventually explained that a PICOP was a Person In Charge Of Possessions: each track needed two PICOPs, one with a red flag and one with a green flag. There were four tracks, so eight people were needed to work double time at the weekend to provide extra safety precautions over and above what could be obtained using modern electric signalling equipment. I felt I was part of a secret war cabinet where serious people talked in strange acronyms. I had no idea when I embarked on the Firkin journey that I'd be privy to the curious inner workings of British Rail.

With less than a month to go before the scheduled opening day, David du Boulay phoned me late one afternoon to say that one of his electricians had found extensive dry rot in the one portion of the roof that hadn't been destroyed in the fire. Further investigations had shown that the rot was seriously widespread and he'd declared the structure unsafe, so all work had stopped while we took stock. My first call the next morning was to the director of the environment at British Rail headquarters, who'd been immensely supportive of all our efforts so far. I explained the last-minute setback and that I didn't have the £30,000 du Boulay had estimated it would cost to remove the rot and rebuild, all within a tight deadline.

The director immediately grasped the severity of the situation and recognised the project couldn't be completed unless British Rail contributed a further £30,000 to solving the problem. Disaster was averted by bending the rules yet again, particularly as the British Rail contribution to the project had already overrun the budget considerably as a result of the specialist work required in restoring the shell of the building.

Finally, on 5 June 1984, I attended Camberwell Green Magistrates Court for the granting of the final order of the licence application for the Phoenix. It was granted by the magistrates at 11 am on the informal understanding that I'd reserve a table for the whole licensing bench to have lunch at the pub that day, followed by a brewery tour.

The first day of trading was phenomenal. The pub was mobbed by literally thousands of people and the takings for the first day amounted to half of what I'd budgeted for a full week, which was £6,000. The success of the first day continued for the next 12 weeks, with sales running at £18,000 a week, roughly three times our forecast. The biggest problem was keeping up with the demand for our beer, Rail Ale in particular, which built up a strong following. It was the weakest of the range but it was most suitable for drinking during a warm and sunny June.

Within days of opening, we received complaints from the police that the road outside the pub was blocked by customers standing outside to drink. Traffic was unable to pass in either direction and we were forced to try to keep people back on the steps or the pavement and not allow them to spill into the road. On opening night, I was busy until 1 am sweeping up broken glass that was a danger to passing cars and could have punctured their tyres.

One Friday lunchtime, there was an enormous crash and the model electric train I'd bought at Hamleys toy shop to run along the top of the back-fitting behind the bar was derailed for some reason and the engine and four carriages crashed down, breaking bottles on the way and landing on the shoulder of a barmaid. She was sufficiently hurt to be rushed to A&E at King's College Hospital where the reason for her admittance caused some consternation as it read 'Train crash victim at Denmark Hill railway station'. No one mentioned it was only a toy train.

There were regular showings on close circuit television of wonderful archive footage collated by John Shearman, who'd organised the Rudyard Kipling Nights at the Fox & Firkin. John had been the official photographer and archivist for British Rail and had edited some unique footage of steam trains around the UK going back to the 1920s. The films were an enormous source of interest to the many train enthusiasts who came to the pub and swelled the ranks of our real-ale buffs. One of the rail enthusiasts berated me one day for hanging the arm of a signal the wrong way up. To me, it was just one piece of bric-a-brac we'd bought as part of the railway memorabilia but to the steam buff it was a piece of living history that needed to be properly displayed, with the little red arrows facing the right way – up and not down. We took steps to rectify this unforgivable act of railway barbarism.

Once the excitement of the Phoenix opening was behind me, I set about recruiting a new finance director. The advertisement in *Accountancy Age* had produced a wide choice of candidates, and we squeezed in interviews at all hours of the day for those we shortlisted. At 10 am on the first Sunday morning following the opening of the Phoenix, we met Paul Adams. He possessed all the necessary qualifications and experience for the Firkin Group as he'd worked as finance director for Ladbroke Casinos' London outlets. Instinctively, we knew he'd be a great guy to work with, and his experience and expertise would benefit the business. To back his appointment, we promoted Rory Garden to production director.

Avoiding trains and finding a helpful bank

'No you can't speak to David Bruce - he's in a communications meeting'

In July, some seven months after exchanging contracts on the Highbury Brewery Tap, we were finally able to complete the purchase of the freehold as the last of the squatters was evicted. The delay was probably a blessing in disguise in view of the complexities of opening the Phoenix & Firkin, compounded by half my board resigning. As always, we were short of liquid funds. This was mainly due to the Phoenix development eating spare cash, and while the pub was booming, it hadn't yet started to generate funds. I found myself in a corner with not enough cash to complete the Highbury property. At the risk of spoiling a beautiful friendship, I gritted my teeth and rang Antony Fletcher at home one Sunday morning and explained my predicament. To my astonishment and relief, he said he'd be happy to lend Bruce's Brewery (Highbury) Ltd £85,000 for six months at 2 per cent over base rate, secured against the freehold of the property.

We were saved once again but this time I decided I really had to renew my efforts to find an alternative bank to Lloyds. It was only thanks to Antony's assistance that I'd managed to acquire more Firkin opportunities, not with the help of any bank. I decided to write a cold letter to the chairs of six banks, ranging from the Allied Arab Bank to Williams & Glyn's, taking in the National Giro Bank and Allied Irish Bank. I was covering a complete range of clearing banks and thought I might have more success by writing to the people at the top rather than being brushed off by their minions at branch level. This unusual and, even for me, unprecedented approach bore fruit. The chair of Williams & Glyn's replied by return and suggested I should meet one of his top managers, Alan Twort, at their Croydon branch.

As a result, Paul Adams and I went to Croydon to introduce ourselves. After around 20 minutes, he suggested it was time we went to his favourite restaurant for lunch. We didn't leave the restaurant until 5.30 pm, a measure of how well we got on. It didn't take any time for Paul and I to agree we'd found a bank and a manager who understood the booze business and wanted to back our plans for the future.

The Phoenix & Firkin continued to trade at levels between two and three times our best forecasts and the pub was selling enormous amounts of not only our own-brewed beer but also lagers, stouts and bottled beers from Watney's. At the start of the project, we'd secured a £30,000 free trade loan from Watney's at 5 per cent interest. As we were selling three times as much beer bought from the brewery than we'd predicted, we asked if they'd like to increase their free trade loan to £100,000 to match the volume of barrelage. They said no so we decided to switch our business to Courage in return for a free trade loan of £100,000 at 5 per cent. This switch of trade supplier enabled us to repay the investors in Antony Fletcher's business expansion scheme. They not only doubled their money in six months but were also compensated for any loss of tax relief to which they would've been entitled if the scheme had run for its full five years. I was keen that we should own 100 per cent of such a prime asset at the earliest opportunity, and with such a huge amount of money available from Courage at 5 per cent, it was an ideal opportunity to pay back the minority shareholders.

There was much amusement in the office with all the talk of high finance flying around, including changing banks, paying back BES investors and refinancing brewery loans. On top of these, I announced

I was going to attend a special seminar at the Institute of Directors entitled 'How to be chairman of a PLC company'. I thought this would be a useful exercise in improving my knowledge of corporate governance, as I'd started to harbour ambitions of floating the Firkin Group on the Unlisted Securities Market (USM) of the London Stock Exchange.

The pubs continued to be very busy as Christmas approached. We had a further boost to trade at the Goose & Firkin when London Weekend Television ran a five-minute feature after the peak-time evening news, which would've been worth hundreds of thousands of pounds if we'd purchased the airtime as advertising. Business soared even higher and the Goose, which had less than 1,000 square feet of trading area, took more than £10,000 for the first time in one of the weeks before Christmas. Beer had to be shipped in from other Firkin breweries as we couldn't cope with the demand created by the unexpected TV exposure. The power of public relations, when used to good effect, is immeasurable, yet we never employed either a PR company or an advertising agency.

Antony Fletcher, my old pal and knight in shining armour, having had his investment in the Phoenix & Firkin BES scheme repaid after six months rather than five years, was keen to provide us with further finance. One day, he brought into the office details of the Liberty Cinema near Clapham South Underground station, which had recently come on the market. This enormous empty cinema would've been a fantastic opportunity but the sheer scale of it frightened even me. After the hairy three years or more I'd spent on resurrecting Denmark Hill station, even my own naked ambition was diminished by the thought of taking on such a challenge. However, we all agreed that if we'd gone ahead and turned it into a Firkin pub, it would definitely have had to be called A Firkin Liberty.

Lessons and learnings

🍺 **Lesson 3: Be brave, ambitious and determined to overcome all obstacles**

Building a subterranean brewery adjacent to four of the busiest railway lines in Britain was one of my most ambitious projects. Let no challenge prove to be insurmountable, as there's always a solution, usually achieved by patience and hard work.

🍺 **Lesson 8: Encourage and nurture free PR, even if it entails fancy dress**

Nothing can beat good PR, so spread the word widely about your success. One of my most effective features was on London Weekend Television, when there was a five-minute slot on the Goose & Firkin directly after the evening news and the pub was mobbed for weeks afterwards.

13

Fishy work in Highbury and finding out the Queen is my Hackney landlord

1985

Du Boulay Construction started in January 1985 on the £100,000 project to convert the Highbury Brewery Tap from an Ind Coope tied house, run by a tenant, to the Flounder & Firkin, another freehold free house with its own brewery. Little thanks to the squatters, it was only one year after our offer of £105,000 had been accepted that we could start the restoration and conversion programme.

My plan had been to more than double the existing trading area by covering over the enclosed yard at the back. I'd had lengthy discussions with Fleurets about whether it was an enclosed yard or a covered yard. I'd always maintained that 'enclosed' implied 'covered' but apparently I was wrong and extensive work entailed fixing the new roof to the three party walls of the adjacent properties. This was an expensive and time-consuming legal process that required a separate party wall agreement with each of the three property owners for permission to tie our new roof into their premises.

Once the roof had been fitted over the enclosed yard, it became clear that, with no windows at the back of the premises, it would be claustrophobic and gloomy at the far end of the new trading area. In order to create light as well as a visual attraction, David du Boulay and I hatched a plot to build an enormous aquarium that would fill the whole of the end wall of the new structure. Nobody had any experience of keeping fish, so Sally was given the task of becoming an expert in both tropical fish and the design and maintenance of the tank. As she became increasingly knowledgeable in her new subject, we discovered that a tank large enough to fill the wall would have to hold five tons of water. David and I had visions of disaster striking one Saturday afternoon when a marauding mob of away supporters turned up for a match against Arsenal, whose ground was just around the corner at Highbury. When Arsenal were playing at home, Holloway Road was closed between the Tube station at Highbury Corner and the football ground while mounted police with riot shields tried to control the supporters of home and away teams. Bitter experience told us that there was always a group of supporters with more than drinking on their minds who managed to get into pubs on match days. Publicans dreaded the prospect of a major punch-up breaking out between rival supporters. The Flounder was perfectly located for such an event. You didn't need too much imagination to see the chaos that would ensue if flying tables and chairs were thrown around the pub with five tons of water flowing through the building, accompanied by flapping and dying fish. We decided the only way we could protect the fish and the pub's internal fittings was to line the front of the fish tank with reinforced, bullet-proof glass. As we'd sought advice from Pilkington Glass over how thick the glass panel should be above the cellar of the Frog & Firkin, we now spoke to them about the right specification to make the fish tank football hooligan proof.

While the team at Bruwel were manufacturing the equipment for the new brewery at the Flounder, they were also building the kit for our fourth order from Allied Breweries, this time for a Tetley pub by the water at Hull docks. It was gratifying that one of Britain's biggest brewing groups should be placing repeat orders with our specialist brewery design and fabrication company. A further accolade was received when Colin Summers won the top postgraduate award for brewing studies from Heriot-Watt University. I'm certain our beers received such widespread accolades due to the two Heriot-Watt graduates, Rory Garden and Colin Summers, who worked as our production director and production manager respectively.

Weighing the hops at the Flounder & Firkin

Since the birth of our daughter Rebecca the previous year, Louise and I had been considering moving out of London to bring up our first child in a more rural environment, even if it meant I'd have to commute to the capital. Our determination to leave had been strengthened by being burgled no less than three times at our house in Clapham. After much searching, we bought a beautiful, Grade II-listed Georgian townhouse on Hungerford High Street, about one hour west of London.

At the beginning of March, the first mash was brewed at the Flounder & Firkin and in view of its fishy theme we'd put several portholes in the floor to enable customers to watch the brewing process from the bar. The Flounder opened on 19 March 1985, and the enormous fish tank was an instant success. A trend quickly set in for people to rush to the back of the pub and take up all the nearest seating so they could have a close-up view of the dozens of brightly coloured tropical fish swimming around. People found them incredibly relaxing but I hoped it wouldn't put them off consuming our beer, as it might remind them of waiting in a dentist's surgery.

The invitation and logo for this latest Firkin were predictably based on a suitably fishy theme and punned to within an inch of sanity with the slogan 'I've Flounder a great plaice worth whiting home about'. Closer examination of the fat flounder with the beer gut revealed that Jamie Nimmo, the graphic designer, had managed to include his signature in his typical but quirky form. This time it was expressed in Morse code, which he'd used to spell his name down the flounder's beer gut. The mark of Jamie's ownership was apparent to only a few special confidantes.

One morning, details of a pub in Hackney landed on my desk. The Queen's Hotel was a Truman's lease and was being offered by the freeholders, the Crown Commissioners, who'd appointed their agents, Drivers Jonas, to find a new lessee, as Truman's didn't want to renew their lease. This new opportunity had the benefit that the pub was still trading, although not with the sort of customers we'd normally try to attract to a Firkin. This was a problem as I didn't wish to alienate the existing customers too much with my proposals to transform their local from a grotty Truman's pub into an exciting Firkin free house and brewery. The full Firkin team of Paul, Rory, Sally, Louise and me met with Nick Shepherd of Drivers Jonas to inspect the premises. We were astounded by the size of what was on offer. It had an enormous bar with an unused function room above it that would take up to

100 people. There was a car park and a beautiful garden looking on to Victoria Park, which is the East End's equivalent of Hyde Park. Next to the pub was a large, empty building that had been used as a warehouse by Brown & Pank, a wine merchant owned by Grand Metropolitan, who also owned Truman's. We weren't enamoured to be told by Nick Shepherd that he was only looking for offers on the understanding that the lessee would also take on the ramshackle warehouse, which would be superfluous to our normal Firkin needs. None of us could think what to do with the warehouse, but we were keen on the size and location of the pub and decided to make an offer for the entire site and worry about the warehouse later. We put in an offer of £29,500 a year rent for a 20-year lease with five-year rent reviews. As it was a Crown Commission property, I was intrigued that the draft lease showed the premises were being granted to Bruce's Brewery (Hackney) Ltd by Her Majesty the Queen. This was a first for me in having the Queen as my ultimate landlord, and I thought I'd better pay the rent or I'd be sent to the Tower of London!

Once word had got round that there was a chance the pub would be converted into a Firkin free house with its own brewery, a group of customers, who were pretty hard-bitten East Enders, drew up a petition pleading with me not to spoil their local. This wasn't surprising as the pub had, unknown to me, acquired a reputation that had been instrumental in Truman's surrendering the lease. It was during one of the meetings with local residents, when I was explaining how a Firkin pub and brewery would enhance their drinking experience and would be a more fun place to visit, that I was struck by the number of young children running about the place. While the parents drank at the bar, kids from age two upwards were playing undaunted, sometimes up to the 11 pm closing time. It suddenly dawned on me that rather than putting the brewery in the cellar, we could locate it in the empty warehouse and make a visually accessible glass panel in the wall between the pub and the warehouse. This would not only give us a bigger and better-looking brewery but we could also build an indoor playroom for children, instead of them running riot in the pub. And if we were to spend money converting the warehouse into the brewery and playroom, we might as well incorporate some smart new loos as well. Suddenly, we had a brilliant use for the empty warehouse that we were paying rent on.

Sally had become an instant expert on fish from the design and installation of the aquarium at the Flounder & Firkin and she was now charged with becoming an expert on indoor playroom facilities for children. There was nothing similar on offer in any London pub, so Sally and I headed north on a trip that took us to Sunderland and across to Manchester, where there were some feeble but pioneering attempts at the sort of thing we envisaged. The visits helped us learn what not to do rather than cribbing the ideas, but it did help us to formulate our own plans. The Crown Commissioners agreed to our terms for the lease of the Hackney pub, which would become known as the Falcon & Firkin. The logo, which Jamie Nimmo decided should depict a falcon and the ubiquitous firkin, showed the falcon wearing a crown on its head with the top of the crown sprouting a beer engine handle.

With the deal for the Falcon under way, in May 1985 I flew to Denver, Colorado, to once again be the keynote speaker at the American Craft Brewers' Conference. My friend Charlie Papazian had invited me to talk further about the development of what he referred to as the 'Holy Firkin Empire'. Charlie made a ridiculously grand entrance into the auditorium of the Colorado State Conference Center in Denver on an enormous elephant. This extraordinary start to the conference brought the house down with rapturous applause for his mad originality. I received an equally large round of applause when, at the end of the conference party, I'd decided to wear the spurs I'd been awarded as a thank you for my speech. I was being whizzed around the floor by a large blonde Coloradan lady when the back of the spurs became interlocked and I fell to the dance floor like a sack of potatoes, much to the amusement of the assembled company.

The company seemed to be settling down into some form of efficient routine with the new board of Paul and Rory working well with me, supported by Sally.

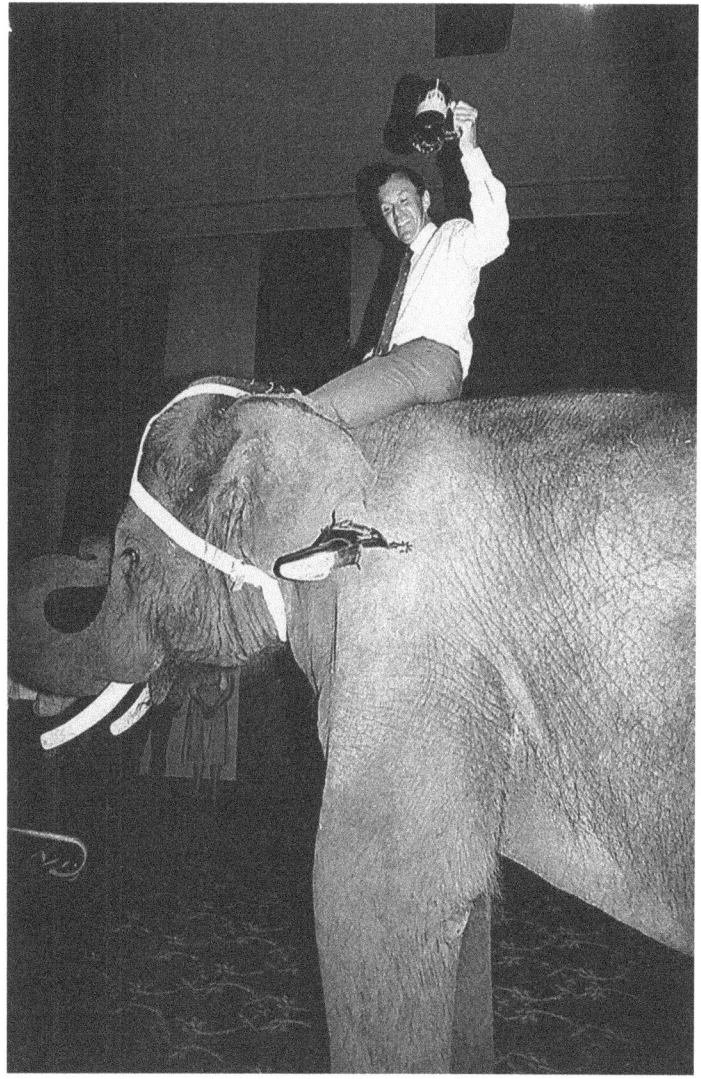

Riding high in Colorado wearing my new spurs!

The stability of the company was clearly understood in the City, as that autumn I received a number of lunch invitations from stockbrokers. This change from pariah to being sought after was both novel and flattering. A number of prestigious stockbrokers were now all enthusiastic at the prospect of launching Bruce's Brewery and the Firkin pubs on the London Stock Exchange's Unlisted Securities Market.

Lunching with the City boys was keeping me busy, while du Boulay Construction had started work on the Falcon & Firkin. As a result of the additional work needed to refurbish the warehouse as a brewery and playroom, complete with the new toilet block, the original budget would be exceeded by at least £50,000. A visit to the managing director of Courage was arranged and we managed to secure a further free trade loan of £75,000 at 5 per cent, provided we sold their bottled beers and lagers in the new Firkin pub.

The layout of the children's indoor playroom was kept between the Firkin and du Boulay Construction teams and it was great fun designing a jungle theme from which the name Bo Junglies sprang. This was decided as the most politically correct name and owed its origins to the old Cat Stevens number 'Mr Bojangles'. The rough idea of the playroom was that children should climb up into a tree house, along a precarious swaying net, and then slide down into a snake-like swamp, which in reality was an enormous pit full of brightly coloured plastic balls. While we were building the new toilets, we also incorporated two separate children's loos with access from the playroom and, most innovatively for the time, we were able to provide nappy changing facilities in both the ladies' and gents' loos.

David in the ball pond at Bo Junglies at the Falcon & Firkin

Lessons and learnings

🍺 **Lesson 2: Build a trusted support network**

My small team developed as the company grew, and eventually we had a close-knit group focusing on finance and production with my executive PA and I handling new site development, marketing and PR. We all worked closely together, held regular meetings, there were no office politics, and the greatest thing is that we're still friends more than 35 years later. The days of lone (and lonely!) entrepreneurs are over, and most successful entrepreneurs recognise the importance not only of surrounding themselves with kindred spirits but also incentivising them not to want to leave the business.

🍺 **Lesson 3: Be brave, ambitious and determined to overcome all obstacles**

Always try to find the positives in any situation. When I was told I could only take on the lease of what became the Falcon & Firkin if I also leased an adjacent large, empty warehouse, I nearly lost interest. However, it did provide the opportunity for me to build my largest brewery ever and London's first indoor children's soft play area.

🍺 **Lesson 7: Inspire and educate others and put something back into your community**

Keep helping others to start their own new ventures. As my reputation spread, I was invited to speak at more conferences around the world and also to MBA students who were studying entrepreneurship as part of their course.

14

A Falcon, a Phantom, a Fuzzock and a Flamingo all join the Firkin menagerie

1986–1987

The Falcon & Firkin opened to great acclaim on 28 January 1986. Its ten-barrel brewery was twice as big as the other Firkin breweries and also featured London's first pub with a separate indoor children's play area. Hackney had never seen anything like it, and we were mobbed from day one. Our slogan, 'Falcon well buy me a Firkin pint' was well received by the regulars, who loved how we'd transformed their local.

I'd now opened nine Firkin pubs in seven years, with each one in London a huge success. I resolved to step up the roll-out but that would entail bolstering our finances as well as intensifying the search for new sites. To raise more money, I had to spend even more time wearing a suit and tie and then showing the City suits (or shitty suits, as I called them) around the Firkin pubs in the evening.

My search for new sites resulted in identifying two exciting freeholds and one leasehold site, to be rented from Watney Combe Reid, as was the Ferret & Firkin. The two freeholds were in an area as equally tasty as Hackney, namely Plaistow, in the East End, and Kentish Town, in north-west London, neither for the faint-hearted. I had to turn down a brilliant opportunity to develop an old army drill hall in Turnham Green, near Chiswick. Once the neighbours in the adjoining flats heard it could become 'one of those noisy Firkin pubs' they petitioned the landlord not to lease it to us. It was a great shame as it was a cracking site and I'd already thought of a brilliant slogan: Bruce's Beers Turnham Green.

In April 1986, the head office team had outgrown our original office in Clapham that was only 100 yards from our old home and to which I often used to commute in my slippers, much to the amusement of the neighbours. Sally found an ideal office building over four floors adjacent to Ladbroke Grove Underground station, which meant I was only three stops from Paddington for my commute home to Hungerford. That month, I became a Tutti-man during Hungerford's ancient Hocktide Festival, which dates back to John of Gaunt in the 14th century. Tutti-men could be recruited only from the residents of Hungerford High Street, all of whom enjoyed commoners' rights, namely to graze cattle on the common, fish in the River Kennet or shoot duck on Freeman's marsh – three privileges I never took up. Each year, two Tutti-men had to wear top hat and tails and visit each of the houses on the High Street and accept a drink, usually alcoholic. One year, one of the Tutti-men had so much to drink he had to be delivered home at the end of the day in a wheelbarrow – and no, it wasn't me. What made the day even more demanding was that if a 'fair maiden' was seen hanging out of an upstairs window, which there usually was, the Tutti-man would have to climb up a ladder and give her a kiss in exchange for an orange from the Orangeman and his Tutti wenches. It wasn't an easy task for me as I'm a bit wobbly on ladders at the best of times, as had been proven on the roof of the Phoenix & Firkin, and certainly not while wearing a top hat and flapping tails after a few drinks.

Word was clearly getting around that I was looking for new sites and out of the blue, one day I was approached by New Zealand Breweries to help them find a freehold site in London's West End where they could showcase their main brand, Steinlager. In view of the distance between Auckland and London, they'd want me to operate the pub for them and even install a brewery. I had a discussion with the chair over whether I could create a new brand called Firkin Steinlager or even a Firkinstein Lager. While I was scouring the West End for New Zealand Breweries, details dropped onto my desk of a new-build pub in Brentford. This was exciting, as it would be a purpose-built pub and brewery on the water's edge of the dilapidated but soon-to-be-restored Brentford Dock on the Thames at the mouth of the Grand Union Canal. It was good that developers and architects were now approaching me to create a Firkin as part of their developments. The Brentford opportunity was soon followed by an invitation from the London Docklands Development Board to open a Firkin as part of their rejuvenation of London's derelict docklands that would eventually become Canary Wharf, a massive rival office development to those in the City of London.

While I was busy site hunting, I was delighted to be honoured for my involvement in restoring the fire-ravaged Denmark Hill station that had risen from the ashes following an arson attack. The Duke of Gloucester presented me with a coveted Civic Trust Award for the 'outstanding contribution to the quality and appearance of the environment and benefit to its local community'.

David's most beautiful development ever

One wet October night, I ventured down to Plaistow to look at a really rough pub full of West Ham United football fans behaving badly. Next morning, my offer for the freehold was accepted by Allied Breweries and planning to develop the Phantom & Firkin began. Early on the Sunday morning following completion, I drove through London's deserted East End streets to Plaistow in order to have a quiet look around my latest freehold acquisition to work out how best to develop it. I parked my Range Rover a discreet distance from the pub and approached the front door holding a fistful of keys. To my horror, I noticed there were three bullet holes in the door and two in the front window. On the doormat inside was a card saying 'Congratulations! You have been visited by the Inter City Firm and we will be back to get you'. It wasn't the sort of welcome I wanted from the toughest and most vicious supporters of West Ham United football club, who clearly didn't want one of their locals to become a Firkin.

I'd never been so busy finding sites and fundraising, but I managed to fit in a trip with Louise and Rebecca, aged two, to Auckland for Christmas, all expenses paid by New Zealand Breweries, including the use of one of their private jets while we were there. Who could refuse such an offer?

Suitably refreshed from our month's holiday, I was raring to go, developing the three new sites I'd identified while still attempting to find the money to pay for them. In spite of the bullet holes left by the Inter City Firm, the Phantom & Firkin opened on 17 February 1987 with its slogan 'I spectre Firkin ghoul pint when I ghost to the Phantom & Firkin', which proved my puns were not improving as the Firkin chain expanded. My abiding memory of the opening night was that, as it was mobbed as usual, the queue for the small ladies' loo was so long that a new line formed outside the pub in order that women could climb through the loo window to queue-jump the more orderly line of cross-legged women inside.

As the company grew, inevitably so did the corporate responsibilities, and it was not long before the National Association of Licensed House Managers started to persuade my managers to join its trade union. I found this disappointing, as I'd personally recruited and developed a really special team of managers whose welfare and remuneration were paramount to the success of my Firkin pubs.

The weekend following the opening of the Phantom & Firkin, I was honoured to be the guest speaker at the Heriot-Watt Brewing Postgraduate Dinner, which was always held after the Scotland versus Ireland rugby match in Edinburgh. I phoned Louise after the match from a call box outside Murrayfield Stadium. When she asked what all the shouting and screaming and sound of breaking glass was about, I told her Scotland had lost and the Irish weren't very popular.

There were few entrepreneurs in the pub industry at the time and many of my fellow pioneering independent brewing entrepreneurs had gone bust. As a result, it was fun every now and then to chew the fat, literally, over a curry with my fellow pub entrepreneur Tim Martin, founder and chair of J D Wetherspoon. Tim had started his first pub about the same time as I'd started mine, his in north London and mine at the Goose in south London. Neither of us could ever imagine in those early days that his company would eventually own more than 800 pubs while I sold up with only 12 Firkins under my belt. Tim's focus and fortitude are to be admired.

Our next freehold acquisition was adjacent to railway arches at the end of a cul-de-sac in the roughest part of Kentish Town. Du Boulay Construction yet again transformed the really run-down wreck of a pub, this time into the Fuzzock & Firkin, which opened on 16 June 1987. The more Firkin pubs I opened, the more desperate I became for creatures spelt with an 'f' or a 'ph' to alliterate with Firkin. I mentioned this to my Uncle Dick, and he suggested, being a Yorkshireman born and bred, that the Yorkshire colloquialism for a donkey is a fuzzock, and that choice of name really foxed all the unsuspecting Londoners when I unveiled my latest offering. In keeping with my dubious puns, the slogan was 'Donkey me waiting for a Firkin pint Eeyore I might get Fuzzock Ale'.

I'd successfully opened two Firkin freeholds within four months but my usually supportive Allied Irish Bank manager, Alan Twort, was becoming nervous about expanding too quickly and consuming too much cash before my latest sites could be profitable. His concerns were correct and understandable. As a result, I stepped up my efforts not only to raise new equity capital but also to find a stockbroker who could help me float the company on the Stock Exchange's Unlisted Securities Market, and sooner rather than later. So, it was back into my suit and tie, which I tried not to wear in Hackney, Plaistow or Lewisham for fear of being beaten up as a 'toff'. Over the next few months I spent hours extending my list of merchant banks and brokers to visit. Among them was the brewing analyst who had scrawled on my business plan eight years earlier, 'This project has absolutely no chance of succeeding, I suggest you abandon it immediately', and now his firm was pitching for my business…

Word had got out that my entrepreneurial helter-skelter, roller-coaster ride so far would make a good case study for MBA students at both the London Business School and Cranfield School of Management. It was more a case of the students learning how not to start and develop a new venture. Through my various lectures, I met Paul Burns, professor of small business development at Cranfield. Paul loved my story and introduced me to Tony Kippenberger. They were writing a book together called *Entrepreneur – Eight British Success Stories of the 1980s* (1988). I was flattered to be invited to feature in the book and spent a lot of time with the authors, sharing my trials and tribulations of building the Firkin empire. I was delighted, when the book was published, that the prime minister, Margaret Thatcher, wrote the foreword, in which she said: 'I congratulate all those featured in this book for their drive and determination to succeed, despite the many difficulties they faced.' It was good to know that I wasn't alone in tackling so many different challenges while growing my business.

One evening, I was invited by London's Capital Radio to appear on their equivalent of *Desert Island Discs*. I chose an eclectic selection of favourite pieces, ranging from Johnny & The Hurricanes' 'Rocking Goose' to the 'Sanctus' from Fauré's *Requiem*. I almost missed the programme as the London traffic that evening was even worse than usual. It was gridlocked from Ladbroke Grove to the studios near Euston. It took me nearly two hours to crawl there. I had allowed an hour, just in case, for the normally 20-minute journey. Further stress was added while I was listening to Capital Radio en route, with the DJ repeatedly saying, 'And we have with us tonight in the studio, David Bruce of London's Firkin pubs, who we're all looking forward to hearing from.' That trailer must have been played at least a dozen times while I was stuck in traffic. I was still breathless when I went on air. I'd eventually abandoned my car in sheer desperation on a double yellow line and run the rest of the way to the studio.

In June, I was delighted to be asked, as an independent London brewer, to make a submission to an investigation by the Monopolies and Mergers Commission into the power of Britain's big brewers. The investigation was an initiative by the Conservative government into the constraints against free enterprise in the licensed trade. Incidentally, I've always wondered why there's is only one Monopolies Commission…

For decades, the national brewers – Allied, Bass, Courage, Grand Metropolitan (Watney and Truman), Scottish & Newcastle and Whitbread – had built up huge, tied estates of pubs, several thousand in some cases, and each pub was tied to the owning brewer and could sell only its beers. Under both monopoly and fair competition laws, this was now deemed unfair for the consumer, who could drink only that brewer's products in a tied house. On top of this, the tenant, tied to his landlord's products, had to pay more than a free house would pay to the same brewer for the same products, which included wines, spirits and soft drinks as well as beer.

It was one of the major campaigns that SIBA had waged. I was pleased to give my evidence to the commission about how unfair it was that small brewers were unable to sell their products in most of the country's 75,000 tied houses as they were all owned by big brewers. Within a few months, the commission made its ruling, saying the brewers had to turn most of their pubs into free houses. This judgement had a crucial impact on how I viewed the future of my Firkin free houses.

On Wednesday 19 August 1987, a date I'll never forget, my weekly production meeting was interrupted by a phone call from Louise, who sounded distressed. This was really worrying, as we'd just heard the good news she was ten weeks' pregnant and had been ordered to take life easy. Louise said there were sounds of machine-gun fire all round Hungerford and she was frightened for her and Rebecca's safety. They'd taken cover under the dining room table at the back of our house on the High Street. It was a normal sunny market day until the peace had been shattered by gunfire from one of its residents, Michael Ryan, who was running amok, armed with three guns. I suggested to Louise that she and Rebecca might be safer upstairs but Louise didn't want to go to the front of the house, where the staircase was, in case the gunman fired through the front door or windows. It was a good decision on her part as it turned out that some of those shot had been killed in their own halls or front rooms.

I went off to a meeting near Oxford Circus, never thinking as I passed Paddington to jump on a train home. In fact, as it turned out, that was a good decision, as I could've been confronted by the gunman between the station and my home. He was on the rampage all afternoon until he was eventually cornered by the police in the John O'Gaunt School, where he shot himself.

Imagine my horror, when I came out of my meeting, to see on an *Evening Standard* billboard, '12 slain in High Street massacre'. I tried ringing home, at 104 High Street, but all the lines were engaged, so I caught the next train, which was almost empty, as all sensible and caring people would've hurried home on hearing the terrible news.

As I got off the train, there was an eerie silence, broken only by the sirens of ambulances and the whirring of circling helicopters. I had no idea as I walked up the High Street whether the gunman was still at large, but I had to risk it to reach my home. As I walked past bodies with blankets over them and blood running down the road, I feared the worst for Louise and Rebecca. Imagine my relief when I reached the front door and found it was still in one piece. Louise and Rebecca were still cowering under the dining table but now with the TV on, they could see live transmission of what was going on all around them. By the end of the day, Michael Ryan had killed 16 people, including his own mother, seriously injured a further 15, burned down his home and three adjoining properties and even shot his own dog. The supreme irony of this tragic day is that we moved to the sleepy market town of Hungerford only because we wanted to bring up our family away from the high crime rates of south London.

As if a massacre in my own home town wasn't enough to slow me down, I was back in London the next day for a meeting with Mike O'Dwyer of Watney Combe Reid. He was so impressed with the success of the Ferret & Firkin, which I leased from him, that he offered me the leasehold of a large, closed pub in Kingston upon Thames to turn into a Firkin. Cash was still very tight and Alan Twort, our bank manager, was becoming increasingly nervous. Nevertheless, I let du Boulay Construction loose on it and on 8 September 1987, the Flamingo & Firkin opened with the slogan 'Flamingo buy me a Firkin pint'. Jamie Nimmo this time cleverly made the flamingo's beak match the curve of the tap of a firkin.

I'd opened a third Firkin during 1987 and my company's finances were becoming ever more stretched. As a result, I spent even more time with professional advisors, especially David Wadsworth, a corporate finance partner at Touche Ross. It was beginning to look as if a 'trade sale' to a larger company might be the best solution, rather than hanging on for a Stock Exchange listing on the USM and dealing with all the additional work and cost that would entail. On top of this, the National Association of Licensed House Managers was pushing my managers more and more to join the union, which I felt was unnecessary and would spoil the ethos and culture I'd created.

It was also a frustrating time, as some terrific sites were being offered to me, such as Kew Gardens railway station and the Fountain, an enormous pub by Tooting Underground station in south London. Sadly, I had to turn them both down as I'd run out of cash by expanding too quickly that year. On a lighter note I was asked by BBC TV if I could brew a red-coloured beer for them to have in the studio when they launched Red Nose Day to raise money for Comic Relief. I'd never had such a weird request before. I chatted it through with my team and we decided to brew a very pale beer and add cochineal to colour it red. Someone from the Brewing Research Foundation warned us that cochineal would stain everything, especially lips and tongue, and we'd be better off using beetroot juice, which we duly added. This unique brew was exactly what the BBC wanted but what none of us knew is that if you had more than a pint it would turn your pee bright red. That night, 1,500 pints were consumed in London and a lot of worried people went to see their doctors the next morning, fearing they had blood in their urine, particularly as the more they had drunk, the darker the red…

Lessons and learnings

🍺 **Lesson 3: Be brave, ambitious and determined to overcome all obstacles**

I always exhort entrepreneurs to be brave and strong to tackle the many challenges they'll inevitably encounter. However, the 'welcome' I received at the future Phantom & Firkin was more sinister than my usual challenges. Fortunately, my worst fears never materialised. Let nothing deter you from achieving your ambitions.

🍺 **Lesson 7: Inspire and educate others and put something back into your community**

Share your experiences in the hope that it will encourage others to abandon being employees and to take the big leap of faith into starting their own business. I was delighted to have a chapter devoted to my entrepreneurial journey in a book for which the then prime minster, Mrs Thatcher, wrote the foreword to encourage future entrepreneurs to follow our example and take the plunge.

🍺 **Lesson 9: Look after yourself and your family**

Creating and developing your first business can be incredibly stressful, so try to balance some time with friends and family to help prevent burnout or pure exhaustion. The great joy for me was that, as soon as I'd built the nucleus of a loyal team, I took my family to New Zealand for a month. This was a great opportunity to reflect on what I'd achieved so far and to recharge my batteries for tackling the next phase of challenges.

15

A Firkin farewell

1987–1988

During Christmas 1987, I had time to reflect on the future of the Firkins and considered whether to 'flog 'em or float 'em', weighing up the consequences of each choice. One cold, misty Monday morning in January, I was driving along the M4 into London for yet another week of interminable meetings with accountants, lawyers, bank managers, trade union officials, merchant bankers and stockbrokers. Suddenly the traffic ground to a halt. This wasn't an unusual event on that motorway when there'd been a bad accident. I was stationary for two hours, so I used my new car phone to ring Barry Gillham, my pal who was chair of Fleurets, for a chat. Barry asked me where I was and I told him, 'Stuck on the M4 and really pissed off at the thought of yet another week of wearing a suit and tie while trailing round professional advisors in the City.'

Barry responded, 'Sounds like you want to get off the merry-go-round, so why don't you call it a day now and let me sell your Firkin pubs for you?' I told him the sales figures for the previous week and the year-to-date figures and he said, 'Great! Sounds like a £5 million deal to me but come in and we'll have a chat.' The die was cast. It was another epiphany, like all those years ago when I knew I had to start my own brewery in a pub cellar. It dawned on me that the Firkin pubs should all be sold and I wouldn't be floating them on the USM after all.

I felt a massive relief that I had at last made a decision. I rang

Louise from the car, still stationary on the M4, and said, 'We're selling up and Barry reckons he can get us £5 million plus. We'll celebrate finally making a decision, and it's definitely the right one!' However, it was such a big decision to make that we agreed we must first compile a list of pros and cons, both commercial and personal, just as Winston Churchill used to do at critical times in his life, especially while prime minister during the Second World War. You can see the full lists on pages 267 and 268.

I'd made the big decision and, supported by our list of pros and cons, where the pros of selling up far outweighed the cons, I had to let people know before rumours started spreading. The first to know had to be my co-directors Paul Adams, the finance director, and Rory Garden, the production director, and, most importantly, my long-suffering PA Sally Smith.

Barry Gillham was instructed to sell the assets and trademarks of the Firkin empire. John Power and David Wadsworth of Touche Ross would handle all tax and corporate finance matters and Richard Williams of Bishop & Sewell all legal aspects of the sale. I then had to break the news to my various stockbrokers and merchant bankers, who'd thought they might earn massive fees floating the company. The biggest shock was for my pub managers and head office team. Many of them had been with me from the beginning, so I called them all together for a routine managers' meeting in the function room at the Falcon & Firkin. Top of the agenda was 'Joining the National Association of Licensed House Managers'. I bounced into the room, where some 30 of my senior staff were waiting, and announced: 'Before we start on item one on the agenda, I just want to share some important news with you.' There was much huffing, puffing and wriggling around while I played dramatically for time before blurting out: 'We won't need any agenda today because I've made the decision to sell up, lock, stock and barrel, so there won't be any need for you to join a trade union after all.'

Jaws dropped and you could've heard a pin drop. After the stunned silence, all hell broke loose with many questions, mainly to do with job security, which was guaranteed whoever the buyer turned out to be. The final two people to learn of my decision were Alan Twort, our bank manager, who showed visible signs of relief that all our many bank loans would soon be repaid, and Graeme White of 3i (Investors in Industry), which had ended up owning 10 per cent of one of the companies. My meeting with 3i didn't go well, as I'd deliberately left it until the evening before the announcement of the sale was due to appear in the *Financial Times*. Graeme was furious that I'd left it so late to inform him and said I couldn't sell the company without his consent, even though 3i owned only 10 per cent. I said it was too late, I'd quadrupled the value of their investment in only two years and he should take the money and run. A blazing row followed, during which Graeme threatened to stop the advertisement appearing in the next morning's *Financial Times* by slapping an injunction on me. He phoned his legal department but they'd all gone home, so he rang the *FT*, who told him the advertisement was already printed and they couldn't withdraw it. Graeme had to admit defeat and I was delighted to have outwitted him.

Meanwhile, Fleurets were busy contacting every potential buyer across the UK, both brewers and pub companies, and dozens of 'men in suits' were soon spotted trailing round all the Firkin pubs trying to look not too conspicuous among the locals, all of whom by then knew what was going on. After a few weeks, Barry Gillham confided he was concerned that no one had made an offer, especially as we'd both thought this 'unique opportunity' would be quickly snapped up. Then, one Monday morning, Barry rang me to say the board of a company called Midsummer Leisure, which I'd never heard of, had visited all the Firkin pubs the previous Saturday evening, when fortunately they would've been packed with happy punters. Midsummer was prepared to make an offer and I authorised Barry to negotiate the best price in millions, preferably with a six at the start. An hour later, Barry rang back to say he'd secured £6.6 million in cash, provided we took the company off the market immediately, with a quick exchange of contracts, which we duly did on 16 March.

That was fraught with problems, as by then Louise was wired and tubed in the Wellington Hospital awaiting the arrival of our second child. There were masses of legal documents for her to sign as company secretary. Our lawyer waited patiently outside her room before going back to his office to formally exchange contracts with Midsummer Leisure. Three days later, on 18 March, our second daughter Hannah was born, so there was much to celebrate. Louise wasn't drinking as she'd had a Caesarean but that didn't stop me having a few beers.

The one and only offer for the Firkins had been a good one and I was invited to meet the board of Midsummer Leisure at their head office in Leicestershire, Swithland Hall, known in the trade as Swizzleland Hall. Adam Page, the chair, had made a fortune running nightclubs and had recently bought the pubs owned by CAMRA Real Ale Investments, a spin-off from the main campaign, which had changed its name to Midsummer Inns. Adam Page felt the Firkin pubs would be complementary to that deal and changed the name of his company to Midsummer Leisure. I was delighted to receive such a high price for the Firkin pubs and was further pleased to accept a new consultancy role with Midsummer Leisure, with a fee of £1,000 a day, to help them open new Firkin pubs. My first task was to convert an old cinema in Derby into a Firkin pub complete with its own brewery, which was a novel idea for beer drinkers in that city.

Just before completion of the deal, I asked the Midsummer board if I could have 50 per cent of the agreed £6.6 million in Midsummer shares, as they were doing so well on the stock market. Adam Page said a firm no, as he didn't want to dilute his equity holding, and confirmed I must take all the sale proceeds in cash, as had been agreed. It was just as well, because soon after the sale Midsummer sold the Firkin chain on to Stakis Leisure in Glasgow, so my suggested £3.3 million in shares might never have been converted into cash.

While contracts had been exchanged on the sale of Bruce's Brewery and the Firkin pubs, there were still many appointments in my diary that I wanted to keep for the sake of good manners. One was to show a group of MBA students from Cranfield around the brewery at the Falcon & Firkin and bring them up to date on my entrepreneurial journey. Several of them were using my hard-won experiences as a case study for their MBA.

No sooner had the press coverage of the sale of the Firkins died down than Humphrey Smith, the chair of Samuel Smith's brewery in Tadcaster, phoned to ask if I'd like to move to the Lake District, where he'd just bought Jennings Brewery in Cockermouth and was looking for someone to run it. Intrigued by the idea, Louise and I headed off on the long drive north for our discreet inspection, as Humphrey had requested. We'd completely forgotten that our Range Rover was still emblazoned with car stickers proclaiming 'Firkin Boozers do it falling over!' and 'Follow me to the nearest Firkin pub' and we were both wearing Fox & Firkin sweatshirts with 'For Fox Sake Buy Me a Firkin Pint!' on the back. With our car and clothing covered in Firkin slogans etc we suddenly realised we were hardly discreet when we pulled up in the visitors' car park and didn't dare to get out of the car after our six-hour drive, let alone look around. The next day we went to see Humphrey Smith in Tadcaster and said we'd enjoyed our visit but had decided we didn't want to move back north, however much I'd enjoyed brewing at his rival Yorkshire brewery, Theakston's of Masham.

Another diary date I didn't want to miss was the week I'd booked, well before deciding to sell up, to walk the 100-mile West Highland Way with Jonathan Swales from my brewing days in Masham, when he was Lord Masham's estate manager. Most people, suddenly finding themselves a cash multi-millionaire before their 40th birthday, would've headed off to the Caribbean for some serious sun and relaxation. Instead, Jonathan and I set off from Glasgow to walk 100 miles along old military tracks all the way to Fort William, carrying our rucksacks across the most spectacular Highland scenery.

My blisters were still healing when the following week, Louise and I took all 50 of our pub managers, brewers and head office staff to Paris for a two-day celebration of selling the Firkin pubs. Everyone behaved pretty well, considering the amount of booze that was consumed from the moment we arrived at Heathrow. The one exception was me. After a late dinner at the Folies Bergère Cabaret Club, everyone went back to the hotel bar for the proverbial nightcap, apart from me and our travel courier, who persuaded me, without much effort on her part, to visit a little bar she knew round the corner in Montmartre.

A serious problem arose at 3 am when we both fell out of the bar after yet more drinks, as neither of us could remember the name or address of our hotel, which proved she wasn't a very good courier. Dawn was rising over Paris when we eventually and literally stumbled upon our hotel, and I sheepishly went up to my room, where Louise was sitting up in bed absolutely furious at my behaviour, having feared – or perhaps hoped – I'd drowned in the River Seine.

The day of completion – 23 May – was very exciting. We received the rest of the £6.6 million in cash and were able to pay off all our bank loans and overdrafts and get rid of 3i's 10 per cent stake in the company. Louise and I heaved a huge sigh of relief that the whole sale process had gone so smoothly but we also never forgot that we'd only received one offer for what we'd spent nine years working so hard to achieve.

Every day from May onwards, there was much celebrating to be done and the summer of 1988 was like no other, before or since. There were innumerable lunches and dinners in all our favourite London restaurants and, during too many weekends, Raymond Blanc's Oxfordshire restaurant Le Manoir aux Quat'Saisons. I was running even more than usual to stop putting on too much weight with all the food and booze I was consuming. As the company had given notice on its lease for the head office in Ladbroke Grove, I soon realised I'd need a new office of my own, and I had yet another moment of divine inspiration. What about a mobile office that I could drive and park anywhere? Considerable research into this novel idea resulted in the purchase of a luxury six-berth, air-conditioned motorhome, complete with shower, WC, kitchen and dining area that would become my new 'workstation'. However, for this 20 ft-long purchase to qualify as a legitimate company asset, our professional advisors insisted we also buy a mobile phone, which in those days was the size of two bricks with a large, fixed aerial. It had to be kept permanently on the dashboard. Only then could we justify our investment in a new mobile office that would allow me to work from anywhere. Once the word spread that I'd sold up so profitably, people approached me out of the blue with all manner of ideas about what I should do with my new-found wealth. Estate agents pestered me to arrange viewings of farms for sale but

A Firkin farewell

I never wanted to farm, however tax efficient investing in farmland might be. It was even suggested that I now had enough cash to be put forward as 'a name' in a syndicate at Lloyds Insurance Market in the City of London. Apart from being deemed socially acceptable and good for future networking, neither of which appealed to me, the idea of risking my hard-earned cash helping to insure risks from around the world didn't enthuse me at all. This turned out to be a good decision because, for the next few years, hundreds of Lloyds' names lost enormous amounts of money from insurance claims as a result of both natural and human-made disasters around the world.

After many years of trying to service innumerable loans and bank overdrafts, I was enjoying having cash on deposit, especially as the bank rate had returned to 16 per cent and my cash was generating £1,000 in interest every day. While we enjoyed living on Hungerford High Street, double yellow lines and parking meters had recently been installed, which often meant we could no longer park outside our own home, which Louise found increasingly difficult with a newborn baby and a four-year-old.

One Thursday in June, I was browsing through houses for sale in the *Newbury Weekly News* when the photo of a Georgian farmhouse between Hungerford and Kintbury caught my eye. Inglewood Farmhouse was situated at the end of a long avenue of lime trees and was surrounded by 18 acres of paddocks and featured a tennis court and stables. What more could a young family want at that stage of their lives?

Two days later, on a hot Saturday afternoon, I went to have a snoop around and found the owners playing in the garden with their children. I apologised for not making an appointment to view and explained it was exactly what I could ever dream of owning and was dismayed to be told there were already dozens of viewings due to start on the Monday. The owners confirmed they were looking for offers in excess of £400,000, so I said if I offered £600,000 in cash, with no chain involved and agreed to exchange contracts within 48 hours, would they cancel all the viewings and take it off the market there and then? To my great surprise, they agreed on a handshake, so I went back home and told Louise I'd found our dream house and had just done a deal to buy it, without her having the chance to look around her future home.

My 40th birthday on 5 July doubled as a 'retirement party' where we enjoyed celebrating both milestones with a dinner and disco for 100 of our nearest and dearest in a marquee in our back garden, which I don't think pleased all the neighbours. Before I made my inevitable speech, I crept out undetected from the dinner to change into my dirty old man 'retirement' costume – a grotesque latex mask depicting a wrinkly, old, toothless, bald man with wispy white hair, a dirty brown raincoat with baler twine as a belt and scruffy old walking boots with string for laces. I then returned to the party as a shuffling old man, bent double while pushing a Zimmer frame from which hung an incontinence bottle filled with Lucozade. My appearance was met with a stunned silence by my guests, who were embarrassed and mystified by this horrible apparition who had somehow managed to gatecrash this special occasion. It was only after I'd shuffled up, stood on my chair and removed the mask that the guests realised, with much booing and laughter, that my dressing-up had completely fooled them.

In spite of all the partying and celebrations that memorable summer, one of the Firkin pubs, the Flamingo in Kingston upon Thames, was causing a problem with Watney Combe Reid, the lessors (which they also were at the Ferret & Firkin). They were furious, as my clever lawyers had found a way round the clause in the Ferret lease that if the lease was sold then first refusal would have to be given to them as my landlord. Our ingenious way round this assignment clause was not to sell the lease to Midsummer Leisure but to sell my company, Bruce's Brewery (World's End) Ltd, which owned the lease, for £1 with a separate premium of around £400,000. Unfortunately, the later lease on the Flamingo had tightened up this loophole and when I tried to sell the lease to Midsummer Leisure my landlord, purely out of spite, refused to let me assign the lease or sell the company and demanded to take back the property. They promptly de-branded it as a Firkin, resulting in it immediately returning to being an empty pub, as it had been until I Firkinised it. Talk about a Pyrrhic victory for Watney Combe Reid.

Ironically, the first new development by Midsummer was to create the Flamingo & Firkin in Derby, to which I sent all the bric-a-brac, pictures etc from the original Flamingo.

All my lovely Kingston locals and Firkin supporters were so incensed by this attitude from one of the big brewers that they organised a grand closing-down party and wake at the dead Flamingo. The highlight of this sad occasion was when the beautiful pink stuffed flamingo behind the bar was carefully removed from its position next to the firkin and was lowered into a specially made black coffin. Six pallbearers, including me, then carried the open coffin out of the pub with the flamingo's long neck and head hanging over the side. The only good thing that came from the closing down of Kingston's Firkin was that my first consultancy for Midsummer Leisure resulted in converting the cinema in Derby into the Flamingo & Firkin, using all the Flamingo's bric-a-brac.

A few days after handing back the original Flamingo, we were cheered by a fun event. Louise and I were conscious of how lucky we'd been in selling the Firkins that we wanted to thank all our professional advisors who had guided us through the complex sale process. Our thank you involved hiring a private Lear jet to fly to the military airfield at Rheims for a few days in the Champagne region. Our guests were Barry Gillham at Fleurets, John Power and David Wadsworth of Touche Ross, and Alan Twort from Royal Bank of Scotland, all with their wives. We stayed at the three Michelin-starred Hotel Domaine les Crayères and the highlight of the trip, which included visits to several Champagne houses, was lunch at the House of Krug, arranged for us by our pal Nick Davies, the owner of the Hungerford Wine Company.

This was hosted by Henri Krug himself, who showed us around his vineyard and amazing cellars before we sat down to a ten-course lunch with a vintage Krug for each course. We were astounded by Henri Krug's generosity but all became apparent at the end of the lunch when I presented the legendary Champagne producer with a can of my Dogbolter home brew kit with Bruce's Brewery on the label. Henri thanked me, studied the label, and said, 'But I thought you were all from the famous Bass Brewery in England. I've never heard of the Bruce Brewery but I'm very pleased to have met you all today.' How very gracious of him.

It was soon after this extravagant trip to Champagne that I bought my first Rolls-Royce. It wasn't mine for long. Our lawyers Bishop & Sewell had run up a considerable bill handling all aspects of the Firkin sale but they asked me not to pay any of their fees. As the three partners were all keen Rolls-Royce enthusiasts, they'd chosen a beautiful classic model from Frank Dale & Stepsons in Hammersmith, which they could share between them. The cost was the same as their fees, so all four of us went to collect the car from the dealer. I handed over the cheque, received the keys, passed them on to Jill Sewell, the senior partner, and my 20 seconds of owning a Rolls-Royce were over.

At the beginning of August we completed the purchase of Inglewood farmhouse, an acquisition that would last longer than the Rolls-Royce. The great joy of being able to pay cash and not be stuck in a chain resulted in my owning two Georgian houses in West Berkshire. This was a long way removed from our first home in North Yorkshire, a two-up, two-down terrace house that cost £3,500 – and we had to borrow £500 from my mother for the deposit.

Day by day, my diary was beginning to ease. The final pub-related event was on 1 September, when Paul Adams and Rory Garden, my former finance and production directors, opened The Flower at Kew Gardens railway station. This was the result of my 'severance pay' deal for them when I announced I was selling and their Firkin careers were about to come to an abrupt end, especially as neither of them would want to work for Midsummer Leisure.

As a result of my success in restoring Denmark Hill railway station and creating the Phoenix & Firkin, the British Rail Property Board offered me the lease on Kew Gardens station, which was in a sad, dilapidated state. I was excited at the prospect and even thought of an appropriate name, the Fuchsia & Firkin, with the slogan 'The Firkin pub with a rosy Fuchsia'. But negotiations dragged on for so long that I'd decided to sell up before the lease was signed, so I was then able to offer the site to Paul and Rory, together with £50,000 each towards its development costs.

The Flower took off immediately and became a great success, as it would've been as a Firkin. But I had to remind myself that reflecting on what might've been another Firkin success was purely academic and only then did I appreciate that my Firkin days were now well and truly over. Two dates in October 1988 underscored the fact. On 11 October, I changed the name of my company from Bruce's Brewery plc to Dunbrewin plc, which really said it all. Little did I realise then that it wouldn't be too long before I missed the wonderful world of brewing and had to start all over again.

I'd Dunbrewin and resolved to concentrate on pursuing my new philanthropic ambitions, especially as I now had the time and the cash to enable me to do so. It was also exciting to embark on a completely new project, nine years after becoming a pioneer in the brewing industry. It was great to know that out of brewing my Firkin beer came the opportunity to put some of my hard-won gains to good use for many years to come.

Lessons and learnings

🍺 **Lesson 1: Follow your instincts and demonstrate your motivation to succeed**

It's always hard to recognise the best time to sell your business as there are so many factors to take into account. The only way I could follow my instincts that it might be time to sell up was to follow the example of that great decision-maker, Winston Churchill, and list all the pros and cons, both commercial and personal. In that way I proved that my instincts were correct and it was the best time to put the business up for sale. Whenever a major decision has to be made, it's often best to have a brainstorming session with your closest confidants at work and socially.

🍺 **Lesson 10: Savour the special moments**

Starting and developing your own successful business is an amazing achievement, so when you come to sell it, feel free to indulge yourself and revel in your hard-won success. Don't feel guilty about enjoying the fruits of all your labours, whatever form they take. It's a wonderful feeling to have cleared your debts, proved the doomsters wrong, make a few bob along the way and to have secured your future.

Being a lover of excruciating, appalling puns, I enjoyed creating the invitations to the openings of the Firkin pubs, a sample of which can be seen below:

PHOENIX & FIRKIN at Denmark Hill Railway Station

Providing you're not **on the wagon**, never again need you get all **steamed** up or nearly go **off the rails** in your search for some decent **points** of beer or even a glass of **Brunel**. At this **junction** in your life you can now refresh those **tender** parts that the big brewers' beers simply cannot reach.

Only those on the wrong **tracks**, such as dreamy **sleepers**, **old buffers** with **tunnel** vision or those **in loco parentis**, will miss the obvious **connection** that they must revise their **timetables** from 5th June.

If you are a cut above your **station** and want to make a **whistle stop** tour of the brewery to see how we brew **porter**, then do drop us a **line**. It would be just the **ticket** to hear from you but, please, don't wear your **platform** heels otherwise we might just have to give you a **Rocket**.

When, after a couple of drinks, you can't tell **a signal** from a double, let alone say **Chattanooga choo choo**, then you're probably fairly well **stoked up** or even a little bit **piston** Bruce's.

However, rather than risk **a shunt** on the way home, be on your **guard** and happy to say "**ASLEF** my **wheels** behind" remembering that – this is the Age of the Train!

FALCON & FIRKIN

We're so **chough**-ed with our new pub we're almost **puffin** out our chests with pride! Hopefully, you **toucan** find it a **pheasant** experience but don't **crow** on about it too much to your friends. If they all **diver** down at once for a quick **gander** someone could get hurt in the **thrush** to leave when the landlord calls **ptarmigan**.

When we're busy you may have to be a good **egg** and

wader minute or two **teal** you're served. Please don't **snipe** at the barmaid or try to **harrier** up as she may throw a **warbler** and we don't want you to end up hitting **heron** the head.

You may just want to **swallow** a **swift** half, a glass of **brown owl** or a **nightjar** before going to bed. Sadly, we **egret** that we don't **avocet** menu but real **gannets** may want to **shoveler** down **eider** some **pigeon** casserole or our special **magpie** and two veg.

If you consider, purely on an ad **hawk** basis, how much some of the big brewers charge, it's hard not to think they are **robin** you blind or at least trying to **rook** you in order to **feather** their own **nests**. You have to be a **raven** lunatic not to feel our beer is relatively '**cheep cheep**'.

You'd certainly have to be slightly **cuckoo** not to agree that our beer **goose** down well. In fact other beers can taste like **shearwater** in comparison, but don't drink too much of ours in case you feel **ruff** next morning.

Dodo remember the **pecking** order when its your **tern** to buy a round, otherwise you could be **ostrich**-ised by your friends who'd say, 'Look, **cock**, **flamingo** buy us a drink' and that really could throw a **sparrow** in the works.

FLOUNDER & FIRKIN

A free house with its own small **scale** brewery, it really is a **plaice** worth **whiting** home about. Although our menu is extensive we were **caught** out recently by a **spawn**-again Christian asking if we served **monkfish**, but unfortunately we had to apologise and say we had Nun.

If you feel as if you've **haddock** 'nough to drink then don't **dace** with death by trying to **weever** in and out of the traffic – leave the car. It's only two **minnows** walk to the Underground or you could always hitch-**hake** home…

Part 2

Foreword

By Charlie Papazian

My worldly view of beer was non-existent until I met David Bruce. It was an eye-popping introduction to the beer world outside America.

In 1980, beer enthusiast Paul Freedman, a *Washington Post* editor, contacted me and proposed the idea of two stories for our *Zymurgy* magazine about the UK's CAMRA and an account of his recent visit to a little-known quirky brewpub called the Goose & Firkin.

The story's accompanying sidebar began, 'To visit Bruce's brewhouse you enter the door to the ladies' room and make a sharp right...' Thus began my journey with David Bruce. I was intrigued. Who was this guy David?

In the late summer of 1981, I travelled for three weeks in the United Kingdom. It was my first time across the Atlantic, specifically to the UK and Ireland.

In the first part of this book, David recalls my initial visit, and that I 'was keen to see how commercial brewing could be carried out in a small space within a pub'. Hmmmm. Maybe in fact it was the free beer. I do recall that I became quite ill with stomach distress immediately after my transatlantic flight across 'the Pond'. I was feeling very queasy when we met up at the Frog & Firkin. David insisted he had a cure for whatever was 'ale-ing' me at the time. That was the first of many David Bruce puns I endured. That prescribed pint at the Frog seemed to have disinfected me – miraculously my stomach settled, and I was good to go through the remainder of my Firkin visits to the Goose & Firkin and Fox & Firkin.

My life forever changed, while David continued non-stop with his endeavours. *The Firkin Saga* is David's gift to us, sharing his experiences, business lessons and above all his never-ending sense of humour. With a constant bombardment of one-liners accompanying every step of life, you don't need to read between the lines.

David's experiences are more outrageous than a Monty Python movie because his accounts are all true. He is a world-class contrarian. His mantra 'Never listen to the experts' resonates with any entrepreneur who has defied all odds and succeeded. His never-ending battle with bureaucracy is absurd, macabre, consistently encountering the unpredictable and the retroactive. He reminds us of the battles that all entrepreneurs have experienced, 'constantly being observed by an army of civil servants and local authority bureaucrats, many of whom seemed hell-bent on pointing out innumerable violations of obscure rules and regulations in an effort to impede my progress.'

He has a story for every move and every name. He admits and invokes and celebrates 'a professional standard of amateurism'.

You can spend your life doing nothing. You can spend your life doing something. David Bruce seems to have spent his life doing everything! We are the benefactors of his shared experiences, so many of which are portrayed in these wondrous chapters.

In this second part of the book he shares the diversity of his post-Firkin era activities that have included beer, brewing, pubs, food, farm shops, vineyards and perhaps above all charitable and philanthropic endeavours. Cheers!

Charlie Papazian lives and still brews for family and friends in Boulder County, Colorado. He is the author of The Complete Joy of Homebrewing, *a founder of the American Homebrewers Association, the American Brewers Association, the Great American Beer Festival and the World Beer Cup.*

16

From Firkins to philanthropy

1988–2016

The dramatic year of 1988, during which our second daughter, Hannah, was born and we sold the Firkin pubs for millions, ended with me receiving a personal letter on 28 December from none other than the prime minister, Margaret Thatcher. She had kindly remembered that I featured in the book *Entrepreneur*, for which she had written the foreword, and I was delighted to read her opening paragraph: 'I am most encouraged by your new project to help the disabled and underprivileged. If you make it anywhere near as successful as your brewing business you will have contributed a great deal to helping the less fortunate. I wish you every success in your new venture.'

I was also honoured to have been invited by her in October to address the Cabinet Office and share my entrepreneurial adventures developing Bruce's Brewery and the Firkin pubs – many of which were well known to several members of her cabinet!

It had been several years since I'd first encountered a charity that provided holidays for people with special needs on accessible boats. The London Narrow Boat Project, a Lewisham charity, held their monthly meetings in the Fox & Firkin. The chair, Richard Brierley, asked if I'd like to join their committee. The project provided holidays for disadvantaged young people from south-east London, mainly from New Cross, Peckham and Lewisham, on a narrow boat on the

Grand Union Canal at Braunston, Northamptonshire. Thanks to the Lewisham Narrow Boat Project, I enjoyed my first experience of canal cruising and was pleased to contribute to the highly motivated team that had set up the project. Little did I realise at the time that it was this experience that helped give me the inspiration some years later to start my own charitable work involving canal boats.

As soon as we'd sold the business, I instructed our lawyers, Bishop & Sewell, to set up the Bruce Charitable Trust so that we could transfer some of our Firkin sale proceeds into our own charity and start thinking about developing our ideas for a boat for disabled people on the Kennet & Avon Canal. A few weeks later, we were told that the Charity Commissioners didn't believe our purely charitable intentions and assumed, wrongly, that it must be a clever tax dodge to enable us to buy and moor a gin palace on the Thames near Windsor, exclusively for our own selfish use. Déjà vu, all over again! Nine years earlier everyone thought our idea of brewing in a pub was doomed to fail. Now we wanted to gift £80,000 of our own cash into our own charity but the commissioners didn't trust our honourable intentions. Yet another battle was about to begin as we pioneered our way into the whole new world of philanthropy and charities.

We were dismayed to learn that creating your own charity was almost as difficult as starting your own business. However, this time my entrepreneurial and pioneering spirit would be focused on creating a new boat that would enable disabled people to enjoy canal holidays.

On 20 October, after several months of wrangling with the Charity Commissioners, the Bruce Charitable Trust (registered charity number 800402) was finally created. This was only possible after Louise and I had each signed an affidavit before a judge in his Lincoln's Inn Chambers that our new trust would provide only 'holidays for disabled, disadvantaged or elderly people'. Only then did we convince the sceptical commissioners that our proposed boat on the Kennet & Avon Canal would not be built for our personal use as a 'gin palace'. We opened a bank account for the trust and transferred £80,000 of our Firkin sale proceeds ready to cover the cost of its new, specially designed, purpose-built, wide-beam boat, the *Rebecca*, named after our eldest daughter.

One of the last appointments I'd agreed to keep even after selling the business was to show a group of Cranfield MBA students around the brewery at the Falcon & Firkin in Hackney. One of the students asked me what I was going to do following the sale. I said I'd like to set up a charity that would provide holidays for disabled people on a boat on the Kennet & Avon Canal. When asked what I knew about canals, boats or special facilities for disabled people, I said, 'Absolutely nothing but, as always, I'm prepared to learn, as all pioneers have to and as I had, the hard way, in the early days of the Firkins.' The student replied, 'I can help you. I live on the Grand Union Canal in Hertfordshire and I'm always seeing boats full of children in wheelchairs or with learning disabilities cruising past my flat with a name and phone number in large letters on the side of the boat.' He said the next time he saw such a boat, he'd phone me with the details. Two weeks later, he rang with the details of Reach Out for Kids, sponsored by the Diocese of St Albans and run by the Reverend Mike Shaw, the diocesan youth officer. Serendipity had struck again.

Mike had launched Reach Out for Kids (ROK) some 15 years earlier to provide holidays on the Grand Union Canal for disabled and underprivileged children. We arranged to meet at the ROK base at Nash Mills on the Grand Union Canal, where I was able to inspect his specially designed, purpose-built boats. I was able to explain more about my hopes and aspirations, bearing in mind I'd never stepped aboard a canal boat, let alone provided holidays for disabled people.

Mike and I hit it off from the moment we met and, before I left, he'd reassured me he'd be more than happy to share his 15 years' experience to help me achieve my charitable objectives.

I was hugely encouraged by my first meeting with Mike and felt sufficiently confident to outline my plans to British Waterways, who owned all 2,000 miles of canals in the UK. My first meeting was with their regional director at Gloucester Docks, who seemed a little alarmed by my complete ignorance of canal boats and lock operation. Nevertheless, he kindly introduced me to the manager of the Kennet & Avon Canal, Terry Kemp, whom I met at Kintbury Lock. In common with Mike Shaw, we got on like a house on fire.

Terry introduced me to Commander Nick Wright, who was the

general secretary of the Kennet & Avon Canal Trust, which had been restoring the canal since the mid-1950s. Back then, the government had planned to close the entire canal by pouring concrete into the locks at Reading, Newbury and Bath on the grounds that the canal was no longer economically viable.

I'd now shared my vision with the key people involved in the canal and I arranged to have regular, almost weekly, meetings with Mike Shaw, usually on a Friday over lunch at our favourite steak house. Mike arranged for me to meet all the key volunteers involved in ROK, in particular Charles Cocksedge, a civil engineer who offered to design a boat, plus David Paull, John Grimshaw and Roger Merivale. They were, respectively, a marine engineer, heating engineer and electrician.

The ROK team introduced me to their boatbuilder, Mike Gration, of Steelcraft near Daventry. Mike worked closely with Charles on the design for our 12-berth boat, complete with ramps, hydraulic lifts and special toilets. Mike wanted to know, once he'd constructed the steel shell, who I'd employ to provide the flooring, insulation, bunks and galley. I mentioned this to Peter Hannam, a friend of Richard Barker-Harland, who was doing some building work at our new home. Peter suggested we could use a lot of mahogany and iroko wood, which was lying around in Richard's workshop in Somerset, where he used to fabricate all the bars and back-fittings for the Firkin pubs. Problem solved and material costs virtually nil!

While this work and planning was going on, Nick Wright asked me if I'd take on the challenge of raising the final £10,000 needed to finally reopen the Kennet & Avon Canal following 27 years of voluntary fundraising. I liaised with Bill Scrope, the local land agent, and formed a committee to start work on the Last Lock Appeal. It occurred to me one day that, as work on the boat was progressing well, it would soon need an accessible base where it could be moored and operate from. Terry Kemp suggested I should meet Bob and Gloria Lucas, whose company, Southern Boat Services, leased Great Bedwyn Wharf from British Waterways. In common with everyone I'd shared my vision with, they were enormously enthusiastic, and Bob was duly appointed to be the boat's marine surveyor as well as my trust's landlord.

In October 1989, Mike Gration laid the boat's 60 ft-long steel baseplate and work started on constructing her hull, decks and cabin. During one of my regular meetings with Mike Shaw, he suggested that, as I knew absolutely nothing about operating a boat or canal cruising, it might be wise if I attended a weekend training course run by the ROK team. I mentioned it to my new secretary, Danese, who'd played an integral role in helping me to develop my plans and researching innumerable canal and charitable contacts. She agreed to join me on our residential weekend training course and off we headed, complete with sleeping bags.

As neither Danese nor I had any previous boating experience, we resolved from that weekend to start devising the ultimate training programme for future hirers of the boat. The content was designed to be absolutely Bruce-proof, ie idiot-proof for those who were as ignorant as I'd been.

On 21 December, the new boat was delivered to Great Bedwyn Wharf on a low loader owned by a haulage company called Knights of Old, Old being a village near Northampton. Fitting could then begin with all hands on deck, literally! Recruiting voluntary helpers began, the boat was painted and then sign-written on both sides with her name. On 13 April 1990, the *Rebecca* embarked on her maiden voyage to Hungerford Wharf with a full complement of everyone who'd helped to bring her to fruition.

The *Rebecca* cruising past Hungerford Church

On 5 May 1990, a group of severely disabled people, including some with learning difficulties, from the Home Farm Trust at Lympne in Kent, arrived as our first hirers and the Bruce Charitable Trust became fully operational and was fully booked for its first season.

When the *Rebecca*'s first season ended in October 1990, she'd provided holidays on the Kennet & Avon Canal for 243 disabled people along with their carers. It was especially encouraging that more than half of the hirers booked again for the following year, so we had the evidence that a second boat should be built to satisfy the demand.

We'd paid for the first boat using some of the proceeds from the sale of the Firkins. This time, we decided to launch a fundraising campaign to raise £100,000 to cover the costs of the trust's second 12-berth boat, the *Hannah*, named after our second daughter. Word of the trust spread rapidly and the fundraising went well. As a result, on 13 January 1992, the *Hannah* arrived by road from Mike Gration's boatyard and she was craned into the canal at Great Bedwyn. During the summer of 1992, I was delighted to launch the *Hannah*, which made its maiden voyage on 9 May, having been blessed, like the *Rebecca*, by the Rev Mike Shaw.

The *Hannah* and a steam train pass near Crofton

From Firkins to philanthropy

Christmas card by Ken Pyne 1991

By June 1994, my trust had purchased its third boat, which was named in honour of my mother, Rachel. The six-berth boat had been spotted by Louise and me on BBC TV's *Songs of Praise*, and we learned it had been purpose built to provide holidays for disabled people on the River Thames. It had been mentioned on the programme that the owner was selling it, so we made enquiries and, hey presto, it was soon added to our ever-expanding small fleet.

As if developing my own trust wasn't keeping me busy enough, in 1996 I was amazed and delighted to be appointed a governor of Queen Anne's School in Caversham near Reading. So much for me being too thick to be accepted by any university! Subsequently, as chair of the governors of Queen Anne's School, I was pleased to be appointed a governor of the Grey Coat Hospital School in Westminster, a large, inner-city comprehensive school, and also a trustee of the Grey Coat Hospital Foundation, a charitable trust established in 1698 for the provision of education. As chair, I was also privileged to read the lesson at Westminster Abbey during the Queen Anne's School biennial service.

In January 1997, my trust launched an appeal for £120,000 to raise sufficient funds to build our fourth boat, which would accommodate ten people. I'd named the first three boats after my two daughters and my mother, but Louise didn't want a boat named after her. I thought that if I named the new boat after Diana, the Princess of Wales, who'd died tragically in a car crash in Paris in August 1997, I might be able to raise some money from the memorial fund that had been set up in her memory.

I wrote to the fund and received a very curt reply, saying absolutely no way, not ever, especially as Diana had shown no interest in boats. Nevertheless, I named the boat *Diana* and, in March 1998, after a huge £120,000 fundraising campaign, it was launched, the third brand-new boat designed by the Bruce Trust.

Fast forward to October 2006, and I was asked to open the new £3 million Science Centre at Queen Anne's School. I was surprised when I was inspecting the building to see that one of the laboratories had been named the Bruce Physics Laboratory, after the chair of governors. This was a great honour but I didn't dare tell anyone that I'd done so badly in my mock O-levels that I wasn't allowed to sit any of the physics, chemistry or biology exams as my teachers knew I'd fail them all.

While I was busy fundraising commercially, the spring of 2008 marked the launch of the appeal for my trust's new six-berth boat, budgeted to cost £150,000, also to be named the *Rachel*, in honour of my mother. Unlike her predecessors, the *Rebecca* and the *Hannah*, both 12-berth, the first *Rachel* had brilliantly proved there was a strong demand for a six-berth boat from families with members with special needs.

In June 2011, I was delighted to be appointed president of the Kennet & Avon Canal Trust, around the time the government was ending its taxpayer-funded responsibility (through British Waterways) for Britain's 2,000 miles of inland waterways and creating a new charity, the Canal & River Trust, to take on that responsibility. By this time, I knew enough about canals to know that the government proposal would be difficult to make work and spent an inordinate amount of time lobbying Parliament and the media. I also shared my views with the trust's branch members along the Kennet & Avon Canal from Reading to Bristol via Newbury, Hungerford, Devizes and Bradford-on-Avon.

David donating his trust's four boats to Rob Dean, president of the KACT

I made such a fuss that on 14 October 2011, the *Times* ran a feature reporting that I 'delighted in getting up the noses of the establishment' and my 'latest target is British Waterways'. I accused its board of incompetence while having their "snouts in the trough".

In 2012, I started to explore an exciting commercial opportunity on a stretch of the waterway. There was a ten-acre freehold site with planning permission for a 100-berth marina and a hotel near Hungerford. I knew that the Kennet & Avon Canal was becoming more popular with boaters since it had been reopened by the Queen in 1990 and became excited at the prospect of owning and developing a new marina roughly halfway between the two existing ones at Newbury and Devizes.

The site was owned by a property developer, St Modwen, and after much haggling I managed to agree a sale price of £250,000, which I considered cheap considering local property values. I knew the biggest challenge and cost when digging an enormous basin on which 100 boats could eventually be moored was what to do with the thousands of tons of excavated earth. The problem could be solved immediately, as I knew that there were several acres of freehold land available over the road that could easily absorb the soil.

Commercial property lawyers at Henderson Boyd Jackson were instructed and it was agreed we'd exchange contracts and complete on the same day. But it wasn't to be. The Canal & River Trust's lawyers had refused to be legally bound to provide water access from their canal into my new marina, with the result that there was a small 'ransom strip' of land the Canal & River Trust simply wouldn't agree to sell to me.

On the morning of completion, my lawyer, Kirsty Nicholson, told me the Canal & River Trust were absolutely intransigent about their decision. As a result, Kirsty wouldn't allow me to exchange contracts on the deal with St Modwen as she feared I'd be the proud owner of a new 100-berth marina with no water in it or access to or from the canal for the boats. What a waste of a huge amount of my time and effort, as well as writing off several thousand pounds in legal fees. The marina still hasn't been created, presumably because the Canal & River Trust simply won't grant access to their canal.

After 23 years of providing canal cruising holidays for thousands of people with special needs, it dawned on me one day that there might be a strong demand for land-based holidays for people with similar special needs. The Great Bedwyn Wharf, where the Bruce Trust boats were based, was an ideal site to build four purpose-built lodges, each one featuring special facilities for disabled people. Detailed plans were drawn up and planning permission applied for that resulted in a mass of objections from far and wide, in particular the residents of Great Bedwyn.

I'm not normally someone who shies away from a challenge, but the last straw that persuaded me to abandon my latest philanthropic initiative was a gloomy report from the Environment Agency on its flood risk assessment of my proposed site for the lodges. Would you believe it, the bureaucrats, without a site inspection, had decided from the comfort of their offices that the canal would flow *uphill* in a flood on to the higher wharf rather than *downhill* into the river just below and parallel to it. Unusually, I gave up the unequal struggle and pulled the plug on the entire project. It was more valuable time and professional fees down the drain – or rather *up* the drain if you believed the Environment Agency's version of the laws of gravity.

I'd been thwarted once again but had a sudden brainwave. If I couldn't develop a marina or build canal-side lodges, then I could provide something new for disabled people that wouldn't need planning permission or any kind of permission – a *motorhome!* Twenty-three years earlier, I'd never built a boat suitable for disabled people and now I vowed to build a motorhome, using all the experience I'd gained developing my small fleet of specially designed, purpose-built boats.

As with many of my start-up projects, going right back to each of my Firkin pubs being in a separate company in case one of them failed and brought down the rest, I didn't want to put my trust at risk if this latest pioneering initiative didn't work out. Louise and I decided to create the Bruce Charitable Foundation, which would design, develop and operate one of the world's first few motorhomes specifically planned to accommodate disabled people and probably the only one available for private hire.

As I knew little or nothing about building motorhomes let alone ones accessible for disabled people, I embarked on a huge amount of research, just as I had when I was researching canal boats for people with special needs.

In April 2012, my daughter Rebecca, who had succeeded Danese after her 22 years as trust administrator, and I met up with Neil Pallett, whose company, Event Homes in Scunthorpe, had designed and built several bespoke wheelchair-accessible motorhomes for private ownership by disabled people, but he'd never been asked to build one for hire. Neil introduced us to two of his customers, Roy Townsend, whose wife Sally suffered with MS; and John Clayton, a brilliant mouth-and-foot painter. Neil agreed to build the six-berth motorhome on a Mercedes commercial chassis and its dimensions would be 32 ft long, 8 ft wide and 11 ft high. The special features included a wheelchair lift up to the wide-access double doorway, a scissor-action hospital bed and a ceiling hoist for transfer from the hospital bed to the wet room. Such a high-specification vehicle wouldn't be cheap, so the Bruce Foundation launched an appeal to raise £120,000 to cover the motorhome's costs.

There was great excitement on the Kennet & Avon Canal in June when the Duke of Gloucester came to inspect Crofton Pumping Station near Marlborough. As the president of the Canal Trust, it was my privilege to show him around the two Boulton & Watt beam engines, dating back to 1812. These historic machines are the only beam engines in the world that can still serve their original purpose of pumping one ton of water at each stroke 40 ft up from the nearby Wilton reservoir to the summit of the canal in order to maintain its water levels flowing both east and west.

During tea after the tour, I asked the Duke if he recalled me giving him a watercolour of the Phoenix & Firkin back in 1984, when he officially opened the pub as a result of his special interest in architecture and the restoration of historic buildings. To my delight, the Duke said not only did he remember meeting me on that auspicious occasion, but also that the painting I gave him had hung ever since in the downstairs loo at his home in Kensington Palace. I felt flushed with success on learning this fact!

Before the 2012 Paralympic Games, my trust prepared one of its boats, the *Diana*, for the 82-mile journey to the Olympic Stadium in east London. The plan was for the *Diana* to moor in Victoria Park, in Tower Hamlets, to provide accommodation for disabled visitors to the Paralympics, which were only a short wheelchair ride from the Olympic Stadium.

On 18 August, the *Diana* left Great Bedwyn Wharf with a large sign on the roof stating, 'Paralympics here we come!' The sign featured in the many photos taken as the boat passed the Houses of Parliament and Big Ben, then was dwarfed under Tower Bridge before leaving the Thames at Limehouse Basin to join the Regent's Canal. On the outward and return stretches of the Kennet & Avon Canal from Great Bedwyn to Reading, the *Diana* was crewed by members of the Rotary Clubs of Hungerford, Newbury and Thatcham. Each stop provided day trips for groups of people with special needs. Once we were on the tidal Thames at Teddington Lock, some of my experienced trust volunteers came on board to assist the professional pilot, who was required to skipper the boat for the rest of its journey.

During the Games, dozens of disabled people and their carers enjoyed sleeping on the *Diana*. They included members of the armed forces who'd been injured in the wars in Iraq and Afghanistan and were being rehabilitated at Headley Court. When the Games were over, I received two letters. One was from the Duke and Duchess of Cambridge, which said that they 'hope that those staying aboard Diana had a wonderful and memorable experience'. The second was from Lord Sebastian Coe, chair of the Olympic Organising Committee, stating, 'The Games would not have been possible without the help and support of so many organisations and individuals like you and for this we will be eternally grateful.'

The *Diana* heading to the Paralympics

No sooner had we recovered from the five-week return trip to the Paralympics than it was time to collect from Scunthorpe the Bruce Foundation's brand-new, purpose-built motorhome for wheelchair users. The vehicle was even better than I could ever have imagined, and Neil had done a superb job in building it to perfection. The only snag was that it was so long and high that I didn't want to drive it. Luckily, many of my volunteers were happy to do so, claiming it was much smaller than a double-decker bus or a combine harvester. The vehicle's first public appearance was at the Motorhome and Camping Show at the Birmingham NEC. Enormous interest was shown in its unique layout and facilities, and bookings to hire it came flooding in for the start of the 2013 season.

I decided that Neil Pallett had done such a fine job building the Bruce Foundation's new accessible motorhome that he should be let loose on refurbishing the Bruce Trust's first boat, the *Rebecca*, 24 years after she was launched. She was craned from the water at Great Bedwyn and taken on an enormous lorry, with lots of flashing lights, for the long journey to Scunthorpe. Not only did she have a complete refurbishment but also a full-sized, scissor-action hospital bed fitted for use by quadriplegics or stroke victims with locked-in syndrome, which means they often can't move or speak at all. Neil, with brilliant skill, cut a 6 ft x 4 ft hole in the side of the boat so that occupants of the hospital bed could lie flat or sit up and still see the countryside slowly passing by through the panoramic bed-height window.

Lessons and learnings

🍺 **Lesson 1: Follow your instincts and demonstrate your motivation to succeed**

Even after successfully selling your business, you can still have instincts! My instincts came to the fore fairly quickly after selling up as I became increasingly bored just resting on my laurels and not really using my brain. I needed a new challenge where I could use all the skills and experience I'd gained commercially but this time to apply them to creating and developing my own charity. It can take a while to get used to applying your experience to new areas, but your skills in business will be incredibly useful to many other organisations such as charities, school governing, etc.

🍺 **Lesson 3: Be brave, ambitious and determined to overcome all obstacles**

However noble your intentions, you're still going to experience obstructive and negative attitudes. My early attempts to create my own charity were greeted with the same degree of scepticism as I'd experienced when starting my own business. If you're working in new areas you may encounter new obstacles, so you need to learn new ways to overcome these.

🍺 **Lesson 5: Delegate as soon and as often as possible**

Even with a new philanthropic venture, you should always delegate responsibilities as soon as possible. With my charitable trust, I was lucky that my PA was sufficiently interested in what I was trying to achieve that she became the trust administrator in charge of virtually everything from bookings to training and organising the volunteers, leaving me to raise funds to build more boats.

🍺 **Lesson 7: Inspire and educate others and put something back into your community**

Local charities are vital to your local community, so actively support them in any way you can, either financially or with your time. My first experience of doing so was at the Fox & Firkin in Lewisham, where the trustees of the London Narrow Boat Project used to meet monthly and I provided them with supper and beer as my small contribution. They reciprocated by inviting me to help on their canal boats with groups of disadvantaged children, which was my introduction to boating for people with special needs.

🍺 **Lesson 10: Savour the special moments**

Every now and again, it does you no harm to pat yourself on the back. I remember the joy and pride I felt when my trust's first canal boat was finally launched after months of research and sheer hard work.

17

Back to brewing and pubs

1990–1998

After selling the Firkin pubs, for 18 months I'd focused exclusively on my trust and developing the boat for people with special needs, so I rarely had time to think of anything else. However, soon after the *Rebecca* became fully operational, I started to realise I was missing the buzz of entrepreneurial business start-ups. I tried to suppress such thoughts as it was less than two years since I'd sold Bruce's Brewery and the Firkin pubs, but as the weeks went by, I couldn't resist trying to see if I could do it all over again. However, my first attempt at starting another new business failed dismally!

I'd already taken cash off deposit after Peter Hannam, who was building an indoor swimming pool and conservatory at our home, persuaded me to set up a new joint venture building company with him. I invested £80,000 for 80 per cent of Brock Court Developments and Peter invested £20,000 for 20 per cent. Our £100,000 investment bought a collection of ancient tithe barns near the railway station at Castle Cary in Somerset, complete with innumerable badger setts.

Using Peter's formidable skills as a builder, the plan was to dismantle the barns stone by stone, number each one and then rebuild the shell on new foundations, stone by numbered stone, in order to develop five four- to five-bedroom homes. What could possibly go wrong? In order to finance this new entrepreneurial journey, it wasn't necessary this time to approach banks or outside investors to support my latest initiative. I'd paid off all my Firkin debts plus £1.3 million of capital gains tax to HM Revenue & Customs, and I still had around £2 million on deposit earning £1,000 in interest every day.

I'd been at the sharp end of developing a business for the past decade or more and didn't want to be in the front line of management again. As a result, I asked Paul Adams, the former finance director of Bruce's Brewery plc, to become managing director of all my new and future ventures, starting with Brock Court Developments. While Paul was settling into his new role, I accepted an invitation to be a guest speaker at the American Microbrewers' Conference in San Francisco in August 1989. As I'd sold my brewery and pubs the previous year, the title of my talk was, 'Done Brewing, the Future Now' and I was introduced as the chair of the UK's Dunbrewin plc.

Once safely back in the UK and even with the words of our best man Bob Loosley ringing in my ears, 'Pay the tax and relax', I resolved to abandon my Dunbrewin strategy and invest £500,000 in developing two new breweries. But this time I had to invent an alter ego as I'd sold as intellectual property the brand name of Bruce as in Bruce's Brewery, along with Dogbolter, my legendary strong ale, and Firkin as in Firkin pubs. As part of the sale, I'd agreed not to trade in London for five years, and as a result I decided to focus on the south coast. I agreed to lease two pubs from Inntrepreneur Ltd, one in Southampton and one in Hove, near Brighton.

In March 1990, I started to plan my latest venture, which would be called 'Bertie Belcher's Brighton Brewery Company at the Hedgehog & Hogshead – it's really in Hove, actually'! The rather cumbersome name was subsequently ratified in the *Guinness Book of Records* 1992 as the longest pub name in the world, although the pub traded simply as the Hedgehog & Hogshead. This time the slogan was in Greek rather than Latin, thanks again to Michael Kaye, but it still meant 'Drink until you die!' – although some people wrongly translated it as 'Drink yourself to death', which it was certainly not meant to mean.

My alter ego soon became established as 'Bertie Belcher – brewer of the beer you'll want to repeat', and his range of beers included Brighton Breezy Bitter, Hogbolter and Prickletickler. Bertie Belcher also claimed that 'Hogswill do anything for a pint of Belcher's – there's snout better!'

Back to brewing and pubs

The Belcher's Brewery Christmas card, 1990

Bertie Belcher savouring his latest brew

On 24 July 1990, I opened my new brewing venture, followed on 9 October with the second Hedgehog & Hogshead pub in Southampton, which also brewed on the premises. As if opening two new breweries wasn't keeping me busy enough, I also bought a freehold pub near Newbury which I reopened as The Water Rat at Marsh Benham, selling Bertie Belcher's beers, of course. Jamie Nimmo, who'd designed all the logos for the Firkins, produced a beautiful, acid-etched mirror to hang by the entrance that everyone could see as they arrived. The mirror showed a water rat rowing a boat among the reeds. The boat was named *Wachts Yoars*, which confused everyone, who then asked what it meant. Question: Wachts yoars? Answer: Mine's a pint!

David checking hops and a sack of roasted barley, 1990

I'd purchased the freehold and opened the Water Rat and it became increasingly clear my Firkin funds were being fast depleted. This was the result of the latest recession and the crash in house prices, and no one was interested in buying any of the superb, award-winning homes Brock Court Developments had developed from the derelict barns in Castle Cary.

I mentioned this parlous state of affairs to a friend, Simon Bowes, who offered to introduce me to his neighbour, Tim Thwaites. Tim was a legend in the brewing industry. When he was a director of Whitbread's, he brought from the United States the concept of 'Thank God it's Friday', better known as TGI Friday, which the brewing group rolled out across the UK. Tim invited me for coffee and I outlined what I'd been doing since selling the Firkins four years earlier. I also told Tim that I was fast running out of cash to develop Bertie Belcher's true potential. I asked if he had any ideas and he said he was chair of Grosvenor Inns plc, which had just gone public on the Unlisted Securities Market of the London Stock Exchange in order to raise the capital to buy the Slug & Lettuce chain of pubs.

Tim arranged for me to meet the vice chair of Grosvenor Inns, Roger Looker, who was also a director of Rea Brothers, the City merchant bank. I met Roger at his office in the City on 24 April and told him about my hopes and aspirations to develop Belcher's Brewery further, but it would require considerable new capital. Roger and I hit it off and he liked my plans and ideas to the extent that he wanted to visit all three of the Belcher's Brewery pubs and introduce me to the rest of the Grosvenor Inns board.

I met Tim Thwaites at his home just before Christmas 1992, and he asked me if I'd like to join the Grosvenor Inns board, not only to build a chain of Belcher's pubs and breweries but also to develop the Slug & Lettuce brand they'd bought but weren't quite sure what to do with.

As if I wasn't busy enough with my new responsibilities at Grosvenor Inns and keen to prove my worth, I took a phone call in March 1993 from two MBA students at the INSEAD Business School near Paris. Paul Chantler and Thor Gudmundsson said they were fed up with drinking only Kronenbourg lager and wanted to start their own brewery in Paris, but admitted they knew absolutely nothing about brewing or running pubs. Fearing they were TWs (time-wasters, of whom there always seem to be many in my life), I tested their resolve by inviting them to travel from Paris to Marsh Benham and meet over lunch at the Water Rat.

On 29 March 1993, they outlined their plans to launch the Paris Real Ale Brewery. Paul and Thor were delightful people and I agreed not only to be a director and investor in their new venture but also teach them to brew and develop a Firkin-style pub. In June, I went with David du Boulay by Eurostar to Paris to inspect the proposed site for the brewery that would be in the large cellar of a building that closely resembled the size and layout of any of my Firkin pubs. Paul and Thor announced that the pub would be called the Frog & Rosbif. They felt this would amuse, if not irritate, both our target markets: the French, who don't like being called frogs; and ex-pat Brits living in Paris, who don't like being called '*les rosbifs*' by the French.

While I was busy at Grosvenor Inns looking for new sites for Slug & Lettuce, and freehold pubs to buy and develop as Belcher's pubs, I was approached by the executive team at Joe Allen's restaurant in London's Covent Garden, who wanted to leave and launch their own business called Bar Central. The Grosvenor Inns board embraced their idea and we set up a new joint venture company with the four from Joe Allen. We'd just bought the freehold of a pub next to the Old Vic in Waterloo and David du Boulay was tasked with creating our first Bar Central restaurant, which opened on 26 April 1994.

Back in France, the Paris Real Ale Brewery produced its first beers and the pub opened with two bitters, Inseine (after the river) and Parislytic (after the city), along with a dark mild called Dark de Triomphe.

I'd worked well with the Grosvenor Inns' board, who'd given me free rein to develop all my ideas since I joined them. In October 1993, I was delighted to be asked by Roger Looker if I might be prepared to sell my two Bertie Belcher's Hedgehog & Hogshead pubs and the Water Rat in exchange for equity in Grosvenor Inns. As trading in the early 1990s had proved to be really tough, especially outside London and during a long, deep recession, I took little persuading and found myself the largest private shareholder in Grosvenor Inns along with a new title of development and marketing director and a decent PLC salary to match. My feet scarcely touched the ground. I was busy buying freehold outlets for Belcher's pubs, opening new Slug & Lettuce sites and developing Grosvenor Inns' first Belcher's Brewery in the basement of Daly's Wine Bar in the Strand in central London. In March 1995, I was delighted to receive the highest personal accolade at the Publican Awards for 'Outstanding Services to the Industry'.

I was continuing to develop Grosvenor Inns' new restaurant concept of Bar Central and our latest site opening next to the Angel Underground station in Islington. While I was in London for the opening, I was delighted to attend the 1996 Publican Awards, where Grosvenor Inns won the Best Independent Pub Operator category, which was great recognition for my small team's efforts to build Slug & Lettuce, Belcher's Breweries in the Hedgehog & Hogshead pubs, and Belcher's pubs.

In April 1998, I was back in London for some serious business as a director of Grosvenor Inns. It had been agreed with the board of Regent Inns that most of the non-branded pubs owned by each company would be sold to a new company to be called the Ambishus Pub Company. As a result, 31 pubs from Grosvenor Inns and Regent Inns were bought for cash and new equity by the Ambishus Pub Company for £16 million. The equity was split with Grosvenor holding 17.5 per cent and Regent 8.5 per cent.

On 5 May 1998, the *Times* referred to the share register of the new company that was about to be launched on the Alternative Investment Market of the London Stock Exchange as 'a *Who's Who* of the pub and restaurant industry and includes David Bruce of the Firkin pub chain, Luke Johnson and Hugh Osmond of Pizza Express and Michael Cannon of Devenish Brewery and the Magic Pub Company'.

Lessons and learnings

🍺 **Lesson 1: Follow your instincts and demonstrate your motivation to succeed**
Keep following your instincts wherever they may lead you. As soon as my trust had launched its first boat, I realised that I missed the cut and thrust of business and my instincts were soon telling me to start all over again.

🍺 **Lesson 2: Build a trusted support network**
Working as a team is by far the best way to succeed in business. As soon as I'd decided to start in business again, I appointed my former finance director to be both the managing director and the finance director and my former head brewer to be the production director. This left me free to look for and develop new sites from day one. For new enterprises, you may be able to ask members of your existing team to be involved, or you may need to develop a new network.

🍺 **Lesson 4: Seize opportunities as they arise**
Explore new markets and be prepared to take your experience and knowledge to other countries. Having established a reputation as a brewing entrepreneur, I was delighted to be invited to help start and also invest in new breweries in France and North America.

18

Off to the Big Apple in the Land of the Free

1994–2013

Ever since Charlie Papazian, president of the American Brewers' Association, had first invited me to dress up as a frog to be the keynote speaker at a conference in Colorado in 1982, I'd enjoyed speaking at several beery events across America. On one of these occasions, Louise accompanied me, as we'd always wanted to visit Yosemite National Park in the Sierra Nevada mountains, so we hired a flashy convertible car from Avis, whose slogan was 'We try harder'.

On the second day of touring the park, we noticed smoke coming out of the bonnet and I stopped the car. Before we could lift the bonnet to investigate the smoke, flames started flickering upwards and we realised our hire car was on fire. We grabbed our suitcases out of the boot and the briefcase holding my speech for the conference and ran as fast as we could from the car as it became engulfed in flames. We were horrified as the flames started to shoot 20 ft into the air, but fortunately we'd stopped in a clearing in the forest. As we looked on helplessly, we were conscious that Yellowstone National Park had suffered a massive forest fire only the year before and we could be held responsible for starting an equally devastating fire in Yosemite.

By the time the car was completely burned out and all the tyres had exploded with the heat, a truck pulled up as we stood in the middle of nowhere with our bags beside us. The driver was very helpful and let us use his phone to tell Avis what had happened to their car. When I told the Avis receptionist their car had caught fire, she couldn't understand my English accent and kept asking, 'What, yer've gotta flat tyre?' to which I kept responding, 'No, your car's caught fire.' From then on we changed the Avis slogan from 'We try harder' to 'We fry harder'. It took several hours for a tow truck to collect the remains of the car and deliver us to the nearest Avis depot in Monterey. It was closed by the time we arrived and we left the charred shell of the car outside their entrance.

We needed a room for the night as it was too late to continue our journey to San Francisco, where I was due to make my speech the following morning. The only room we could find was in a temperance hotel, of all places, when all we wanted was several large drinks to drown out the memories of our unforgettable visit to Yosemite. Next morning, we were up early to hire a Hertz car (not an Avis!) and we only just made it by the skin of our teeth for my keynote opening speech.

In spite of that fiery experience, I'd grown to love my visits to America, so was delighted when Roger Looker suggested that we should visit New York City for a long weekend, staying in the Ritz Carlton on Central Park, all expenses paid. This was hugely exciting for me as I'd never been to NYC before, although Roger knew it well. He'd worked there previously as vice-president of County Bank.

With Roger as our leader, we spent our time in Manhattan 'researching' bars, clubs and restaurants, and I fell in love with the 24/7 buzz of the city. We even discovered the English-style beers of the Manhattan Brewing Company in SoHo, which had been launched in 1984 by an Englishman, Richard Wrigley. His beers were delivered in Manhattan by a horse-drawn dray that had belonged to Whitbread's Brewery in London. The two shire horses that pulled the dray were English Clydesdales, also provided by Whitbread. The brewery had one major snag: the hygiene-conscious residents and workers of Manhattan didn't like having to negotiate piles of horse manure whenever they wanted to cross the road.

Off to the Big Apple in the Land of the Free

There wasn't time during my inaugural visit to Manhattan to discover more about its eponymous brewery, but I assured Roger that I'd find out more. I discovered when I returned home that, since 1990, its brewmaster had been Garrett Oliver, who had been taught to brew by Mark Witty, the head brewer at Samuel Smith's Brewery in Tadcaster, Yorkshire. In June 1994, Roger Looker and I returned to meet Garrett at the Manhattan Brewery. We hit it off immediately and learned a lot from him about the brewery. The company wasn't in good shape financially and Garrett was worried about his future there, although all his beers were superb.

It turned out that the brewery could be bought for the grand sum of one dollar but there was more than $2 million of debt that any new owner would also have to take on. Once Garrett realised we weren't interested in buying the brewery, he told us he was thinking of resigning before it went Chapter 11, ie bankrupt. He said he was considering joining a new brewery that was starting up in Brooklyn, whose co-founders were Steve Hindy and Tom Potter, a journalist and banker respectively, and neither of them a brewer.

Garrett asked if we might like to meet them, as he knew they were looking for money to finance their new venture. We agreed to meet them for breakfast the next morning at Garrett's favourite diner opposite Radio City in the Rockefeller Plaza. As is so often the way in the burgeoning entrepreneurial world of small breweries, we had a great time listening to Steve and Tom outlining their plans to start the Brooklyn Brewery in an old warehouse near the Williamsburg Bridge. Since 1988, they'd been selling Brooklyn Lager in Manhattan but it had been brewed under licence at the F X Matt Brewery in Utica, upstate New York. The beer was based on an authentic pre-Prohibition recipe and it was important to Steve and Tom that they should prove the flavour and consumer market were right for their beer before they invested in building a brewery from scratch and buying new trucks to distribute their products around New York City.

Following our first meeting, Roger and I could hardly curb our enthusiasm to join Garrett in teaming up with Steve and Tom as co-founding investors. By November 1994, we'd received from Steve the Brooklyn Brewery offer document to raise $1.2 million of new equity for a New York limited partnership in $20,000 units. Roger and I immediately agreed to invest in five units each for $100,000, and we committed Roger's friend Colin Herridge to invest $100,000 on Roger's assurance that Colin would love the business once we'd told him all about it.

In May that year, Charlie Papazian again invited me to be a guest speaker at the American Craft Brewers' Conference in Denver, Colorado. A fellow speaker was John Hickenlooper, who had founded the Wynkoop Brewery in Downtown Denver in 1988. We got on like a house on fire and inevitably chatted about breweries over dinner one night. Wynkoop owned 50 per cent of the Phantom Canyon Brewing Company in Colorado Springs and 50 per cent of the Broadway Brewing Company in Denver. John was proud that Wynkoop had been awarded the title of the Biggest Brewpub in the World, brewing 5,008 barrels that year. John had heard on the pioneering new breweries' grapevine that I'd invested in Brooklyn Brewery and asked if I'd take a look at his business plan for Wynkoop. There were exciting plans to develop new breweries, with three sites already identified: Upstream Brewing in Omaha, Nebraska; Titletown Brewing in Green Bay, Wisconsin; and Racoon River in Des Moines, Iowa. I was on board from that day on, and assured John I'd invest personally and would attempt to persuade Roger Looker and fellow Brits to invest as well, as we'd already done with Brooklyn.

While I was in Denver, Charlie Papazian mentioned that he'd been invited to speak at a brewers' conference in Germany and would like to visit the Paris Real Ale Brewery en route. Better still, we thought it would be a great opportunity for the founder of the American Brewers' Association to brew with me while he was in Paris. Charlie suggested we should brew a unique beer: we weren't sure what that could be until our nostrils started to twitch as we walked past a stall in a street market that was selling exotic spices from around the world. Charlie spotted a huge pile of fresh coriander that we bought to add to the malt in the mash tun and the aromas we produced were exquisite – and the beer tasted wonderful a couple of weeks later.

I'd set the ball rolling with John Hickenlooper in Denver, so I headed back to New York to pick up with Steve Hindy and Tom Potter. They'd been granted planning permission to start building their new brewery and we revelled in two brilliant articles in the *New York Times* about their ambitious plans.

Shortly after building work began, Steve and Tom were alarmed early one morning when a big black stretch Lincoln limo pulled up outside and six large men wearing long, dark overcoats stepped out. The unsmiling men demanded to know why the building site wasn't using their union labour. Steve and Tom assured them that in future they'd always comply or face the consequences. The New York mafia had wasted no time in introducing themselves.

Steve let me know he still needed to raise $600,000 to meet his budget of $1.2 million. Roger and I decided to spread the word among our friends and soon several Brits had taken up the slack, enabling Brooklyn Brewery to progress from a limited partnership to a full-blown New York corporation. The initial investments of $100,000 each from Roger, Colin and me made by secured promissory notes could then be converted into 1,979.2 Class A shares each. We were soon joined as founding shareholders by Antony Fletcher, my loyal friend from the Firkin days, Tim Thwaites and Gary Pettit, chair and managing director respectively of Grosvenor Inns, and Tony Vickers, my brother-in-law, who was married to my sister Pippa.

Now fully funded thanks to my fellow Brits, building work continued apace and before long Garrett Oliver, as the inaugural brewmaster, was able to fire up his mash tun and copper. On 28 May 1996, Brooklyn Brewery was officially opened by Rudy Giuliani, the mayor of New York City.

Little did I know that when Steve Hindy published his book *The Craft Beer Revolution* in 2014 that he'd refer to me as 'The Monty Python of the British micro-brewing movement'. The foreword was written by John Hickenlooper and Steve made further reference to the three of us: 'At one point in the late 1990s both of us were courting the investor David Bruce, the legendary British pub chain developer. We shared lunches with Bruce and his entourage in both Brooklyn and Denver.'

Soon after the grand opening of Brooklyn, Roger and I decided to pop over one weekend to see how well our money had been spent. We were queuing at the business class check-in desk at Heathrow with only overnight bags when we were approached by a smart, uniformed woman who invited us to follow her. She told us she had spotted us, two blazer-wearing businessmen, and thought we might like to be upgraded to Concorde, where she had two spare seats. So, instead of arriving in New York for lunch, we landed in time for breakfast after only a three-hour flight.

In the fall, as the Americans call autumn, I was back in Denver as an international judge at the Great American Beer Festival. Between sessions judging some incredibly high-quality and imaginative beers, I was approached by a burly, bohemian-looking chap who introduced himself as Dave Buhler. He wasted no time in telling me he wanted to open a brewery in Seattle with two colleagues, Dick Cantwell and Joe Bisacca. There was a slight snag, as usual – they were short of funds and he wondered if I might be interested in backing them. Here we go again, I thought.

John Hickenlooper had sidled over and, overhearing our conversation, butted in with, 'Yer know, personally I wouldn't touch it with a bargepole, especially as Wynkoop is still looking for more funds.' Undeterred, Dave Buhler gave me his business plan to launch the Elysian Brewery in Seattle. Impressed with his proposal, I mentioned it to three directors of du Boulay Construction, David Budd, David du Boulay and Michael Reed. The four of us decided to invest in this new venture at $75 a share. My brewery investment company, Brew Securities Ltd, bought 600 shares for $45,000, giving it 6 per cent of the Elysian Brewery. The three du Boulay directors bought 400 shares for $30,000, giving them 4 per cent of the brewery. From day one, the Brits owned 10 per cent of the brewery. There was a total of 26 founding investors who raised $250,000, plus a bank loan of $500,000, so Dave Buhler had achieved his aim of securing the $750,000 he needed to start his new brewery. We didn't appreciate at the time that 20 years later, investing in that start-up business would turn out to be one of the best investment decisions any of us ever made.

I'd invested in three American breweries and it was a huge privilege to have met so many lovely people who shared my passion for starting and developing our own breweries. As a result, it was great fun to welcome my new Brewing Buddies to my new home to inspect my exciting new plans for Grosvenor Inns. Around Christmas 1995, Louise and I hosted visits from Charlie Papazian, John Hickenlooper and Dave Buhler with Hans and Wilma Hopf from Bavaria, and we grew a very special international bond with our new brewing fraternity and we've kept in touch with all of them ever since.

Once the directors of Rea Bros could see I'd invested my own money in new breweries in New York City, Denver, Seattle and Boston, Roger Looker suggested we should create a new investment fund, to be listed on the London Stock Exchange, for Brits to invest in North America's burgeoning craft beer movement. This exciting new initiative, amusingly called NABIT (North American Brewery Investment Trust), was launched in March 1996 and Roger was joined in the project by Jo Welman and Tim Andrews of Rea Bros while I had the role of investment manager.

Back in Denver, Wynkoop was fast expanding with three new sites identified: Half Moon Brewing in Jersey City, overlooking the Hudson River towards the Twin Towers of waterfront Manhattan; Nail City Brewing in Wheeling, West Virginia; and Old Market Brewing in Evansville, Indiana. It was the usual entrepreneurial story and Wynkoop needed a new equity fundraising to finance its expansion. John Hickenlooper produced a proposal for a private placing of new shares in minimum tranches of $400,000 at $206.93 per share. I'd just invested in both Brooklyn and Elysian breweries and was strapped for cash but I managed to scrape together $200,000 via Brew Securities.

Roger and his colleagues at Rea Bros were now thinking beyond their NABIT initiative and Roger wrote to John Hickenlooper offering to launch Wynkoop on the London Stock Exchange to raise

$10 million to finance his expansion plans. Amid all this corporate finance excitement, Hickenlooper launched a further private placing in November 1996 to raise $2 million at $300 per share, which gave existing shareholders a notional paper profit of around $100 per share in less than a year. Eleven Brits, together with Rea Bros putting in $500,000, invested $1.7 million, with Louise and I following our money by investing a further $250,000, bringing our total investment in Wynkoop to $450,000 – a commitment not to be sneezed at.

Outside a potential Wynkoop Brewery, New Jersey

On one trip to New York I was introduced to Elliott Feiner, who had started a brewpub in Boston in 1994 called Brew Moon, with 'a vision for food and a passion for beer'. By the time I met Elliott, he had opened three Brew Moons in Boston, Saugus and opposite Harvard University in Cambridge, each with annual sales of around $4 million. Elliott and I got on well and we both attended the New York Craft Brewers' Conference organised by stockbrokers Dean Witter Reynolds whose offices I'd previously been to on the 35th floor of 2 World Trade Center, one of the Twin Towers. Needless to say, Elliott was looking for new equity capital of $3–$5 million to expand the Brew Moon concept. It wasn't long before Roger Looker and Tim Andrews from Rea Bros joined me for a tour of the three Brew Moons in which Elliott had already invested $8 million.

We returned to the UK with Roger and Tim as excited as I was. My next visit to Boston was with Jo Welman from Rea Bros, who was in charge of our NABIT initiative. Jo was particularly impressed when Brew Moon's lawyer wrote: 'Brew Moon are as enthused about David Bruce's vast amount of knowledge as they are about his dollars.'

The summer of 1996 was a whirlwind of travelling around all my brewing investments from Paris to Seattle via New York and Denver, with stops in Chicago, Omaha, Des Moines, Princeton and Vail, Colorado, where I was a judge at the World Beer Cup competition.

On another trip flying around North America looking at potential new sites for Wynkoop, Charlie Papazian invited John Hickenlooper and me for an evening of relaxation at his riverside ranch on the edge of the Rockies just outside Denver. We discovered that not only was Charlie an expert brewer but he was also a keen maker of mead, using local honey from the flower-filled meadows around his ranch. He hosted us in his genuine Cherokee tepee or wigwam, where the only drink he produced for us was his lethally strong mead. As the night wore on, our conversation became more and more intense until John and I persuaded Charlie to phone a girl he'd met recently on a beach in Brazil and ask her to marry him. Soon after that night in the tipi, Charlie did marry Sandra, and I'm proud to be godfather to their daughter, Carla.

As the tepee was pitched on the other side of a raging torrent carrying snowmelt down from the Rockies, the only way to reach it was to cross the river holding on to four fixed ropes rather than risk being swept away. Whenever I needed a pee that night, which was more often than usual with the sound of rushing water and the amount of mead we were knocking back, Charlie warned me to 'beware of the rattlers'. Charlie and John knew all about the danger of treading on a sleeping rattlesnake in the dark but the one Brit present did not. When the snake is fast asleep it doesn't rattle its tail to warn people of its presence, so the first thing you know if you tread on it is its venomous and often lethal bite.

Our memorable, drunken, soul-searching evening came to an abrupt end at first light when a taxi collected me for the hour's drive to Denver International Airport. When we arrived, the driver struggled to wake me from my mead-induced stupor and I was grateful for the airport baggage trolley as I weaved and stumbled my way to the check-in desk for my flight to Boston.

I was joined by Jo Welman and Tim Andrews from Rea Bros in Boston, where Elliott Feiner outlined his ambition to launch Brew Moon on the NASDAQ market of the New York Stock Exchange in 2000 with an IPO (initial public offering) to raise $20 million at a projected $600 per share. However, in the short term, Elliott asked the Brits to help him raise $2 million to open more sites by mid-1999. So off we went once more, with the Brits, led by me, following their money. In August 1997, Brew Moon announced, 'The Rea Bros Investment Club is to invest $2 million in Brew Moon in preferred stock at $100 per share, alongside David Bruce, the father of the British brewpub industry who is also credited with providing the model for the US brewpub movement.'

In April 1998, I was invited to be a guest speaker at the American Craft Brewers' Conference in Atlanta, Georgia. Charlie Papazian asked if I'd mind dressing up as a frog again and I asked my PA, Danese, to hire a Kermit the Frog outfit for me to wear during my presentation on sales and marketing.

I didn't arrive at my hotel until the morning of the speech as my scheduled flight from Washington, DC had been cancelled due to thunderstorms. I was assured by the concierge that my costume was in my room. I rushed upstairs to find that on a coat hanger was not a frog costume but a long green *frock* – a further example of what Winston Churchill called 'two countries divided by a common language'. The concierge phoned several costume hire shops and just half an hour before I was due to hop onto the stage of the Georgia State Convention Center, my Kermit costume was delivered to my room. I hadn't had time to try it on at the hotel and didn't realise the frog's head was so large that my mouth was nowhere near the frog's mouth. I was only a few seconds into my speech when members of the audience started shouting, 'Take yer effing head off, you stupid frog, we can't hear a word you're saying.' The sound engineers couldn't help by adjusting their microphones, so I had to do as politely requested and remove my enormous frog's head. I placed it in front of me on the lectern among all the multi-language mics, feeling rather like a ghost with his head under his arm.

Soon after, I flew to Singapore to meet James Weschler, an American I'd first encountered in New York during one of my speaking engagements. James wanted to start a Firkin-style brewery in a beautiful, mid-19th-century building with wood terraces and verandas on Penang Road, almost opposite the legendary Raffles Hotel. It was a great location and I joined James on the board of the newly formed Firkin Pub Company Asia Pacific Pte Ltd.

As negotiations got under way to take a lease on the building from its landlord, Wing Tai Investments, it became clear that Wing Tai didn't want a brewery on their premises. They also felt that 'Singapore is far too sophisticated for the rural look of a Firkin pub' and were further concerned about the use of the word Firkin. That was one new and exciting venture that never took off but at least I hadn't invested in it.

As it was only a short hop from Singapore to Bangkok, I enjoyed visiting my old friend Hans Hopf's new brewpub, the Hopf Lodge and Brew House in Pattaya, Thailand. This was proving a huge success, especially as it was located in the heart of Pattaya's notorious red-light district. Hans had teamed up with a well-known Thai businessman, Virabhongse Bodhipakti, who was a director of the newly formed (another one!) company, Micro-Brew Asia Co Ltd, which operated the venue, as Virabhongse's local knowledge was vital in achieving its success. Virabhongse, Hans and I had many happy meetings, both in London and Pattaya, and Virabhongse and his wife hosted an amazing visit to Bangkok for Louise and me. They took us on a cruise in his private launch along the mighty Chao Phraya River for dinner in one of his restaurants.

I'd been endlessly flying around the world from Europe to North America to Asia and began to realise there was more to life than being a buccaneering international entrepreneur. I spent more time in airport departure lounges and hotels than with my young family back home. I'd enjoyed a unique time for several years investing in new brewery start-ups from Paris to Seattle via New York and Denver and resolved it was high time to stop my globetrotting life and focus again on opportunities in the UK, particularly as I could then spend more time at home.

However, I still had to tie up a lot of loose ends on the other side of the pond. Brew Moon continued to expand rapidly and had won two gold medals for its beers at the 1998 World Beer Cup in Atlanta. In September that year, Elliott Feiner launched Brew Moon's final fundraising prior to its proposed IPO on New York's NASDAQ. Brew Securities bought an additional 233 shares at $100 a share under a rights issue. After Elliott pleaded with me, 'Your name and prestige carry a great deal of weight in this industry', I put in a further $50,000.

While this fundraising frenzy was going on in Boston, in Brooklyn the brewery was doing well on every front – so well that it had set up the Craft Brewers' Guild to help rival small brewers distribute their beers in the hugely competitive New York market. Sadly, in the Midwest, Wynkoop wasn't enjoying such good fortune and was haemorrhaging cash on a daily basis.

In response to a heartfelt letter, signed by John Hickenlooper as 'Your pal in the Rockies', I agreed to cease being paid as a director but remained as a non-executive director on Wynkoop's advisory board. In October 1998, both Jim Caruso, chief executive, and Barbara Burrell, chief finance officer, resigned and Roger Looker arranged for Tom Gill of Regent Inns and Philip Snook of Ambishus Pub Company to take on the finance and operations functions. John Hickenlooper agreed he 'would discontinue direct involvement in the company'. It was one of John's favourite expressions more than a decade earlier that 'it's always the pioneers who get the arrows – it's the settlers who get the land'. Sadly, a poignant truth had been proved.

In January 1999, it seemed a solution may have been found to end Wynkoop's woes when an unsolicited offer was received from Big River Breweries of Chattanooga, Tennessee, to buy the company. The deal eventually fell through but it galvanised the Wynkoop board to take steps to placate the increasingly concerned British investors, led by me, that we might lose some if not all of our not inconsiderable investments. In May 1999, Wynkoop offered to buy out all the foreign investors – ie the Brits – at $217.15 per share. This gave me back $391,187 for my total of 1,801 shares. I later received a further $39,108 that, with the $65,000 director's fees, resulted in a break-even result for my investment. It wasn't exactly making millions by floating the company on NASDAQ, which had always been John Hickenlooper's and my hope and aspiration. However, I'd enjoyed some of the most exciting and fun experiences working alongside John and his enthusiastic team, so it had all been worth every dollar. Poignantly, once the deal was done, the *Denver Post* reported, 'Multimillionaire Bruce says, "As usual all my best ideas are mistakes."'

As the year 2000 approached, my American adventures were starting to crystallise. Brooklyn Brewery and Wynkoop Brewing Company had each returned at least my investments in them. However, Brew Moon and Elysian Brewery had yet to reveal their returns on my investments.

The new millennium started without any of the fears being fulfilled that all computers around the world would crash after 11.59 pm on 31 December 1999. We all woke on New Year's Day relieved that we could start afresh with not only a new millennium but also a new century. However, there were soon rumblings that the new IT and biotechnology industries were being overpriced on the world's stock exchanges as investors piled into this exciting new financial sector. In spite of dire warnings, investors continued their support for the new companies, so conventional businesses such as Brew Moon in Boston could no longer attract capital to finance their expansion. In June, Elliott Feiner sent an email to all investors in Brew Moon stating, 'NASDAQ's IPO market does not favour restaurants and breweries anymore as they are only interested in the IT and biotechnology sectors of the market.' This proved to be the death knell for us shareholders. We'd invested our money on the understanding we'd get it all back and a lot more when Brew Moon launched on the New York Stock Exchange later that year. One of my fellow investors, Ron Pearson, later wrote to all Brew Moon shareholders, 'Brew Moon will "crash and burn" without new equity.' How right he turned out to be.

Soon after, economies around the world crashed due to what became known as the dot.com bubble bursting. The overhyped new IT sector imploded as nervous investors started selling their shares. It was all horribly reminiscent of the collapse of the New York Stock Exchange in 1929 that heralded the Great Depression. Elliott had to abandon all hope of his IPO for Brew Moon and on 31 October 2000, the company's assets were sold to Rock Bottom Restaurants of Denver, Colorado. It was a cruel irony, as Rock Bottom was Wynkoop's greatest rival.

On 11 November, Brew Moon filed for Chapter 11 insolvency. Every investor, including me and my pals in Rea Bros's North America Brewery Investment Trust, lost all their money, totalling more than $2 million. I'd still say today that if it weren't for circumstances beyond our control – the bursting of the global dot.com bubble – Brew Moon would've deserved a successful IPO, delivering excellent returns for its investors. It was the sad end of a great business, through no fault of its own.

With all the excitement of our latest venture, I'd almost forgotten I was still a founding shareholder in the Brooklyn Brewery in New York City. In March 2004, Tom Potter, the original founder with Steve Hindy, resigned and sold his shares to the Ottaway family, of publishing fame. By September, the Ottaways mounted a full takeover of the company and I was delighted to receive $70 for each of my 1,978 shares, totalling $138,460.

This tremendous result from investing in the Brooklyn Brewery underscored a quote from a profile of me in the *Daily Mail* in August 2004: 'The more fun I have, the more money I make!' Brooklyn had always been a lot of fun with lovely people – and it made us all a few bucks along the way.

I wondered one day what might be happening to my investment in the Elysian Brewery. It was 18 years since my three pals at du Boulay Contracts and I had bought 10 per cent of the start-up venture but, apart from receiving the occasional newsletter and the annual accounts, we had no idea when we might ever get our money out. I asked Charlie Papazian who he'd recommend to establish the value of our investment. Charlie suggested Andy Christon of corporate valuers Ippolito Christon in Florida. They agreed to provide a valuation report for a fee of $40,000 that we could use in our negotiations with Elysian to see if they were prepared to buy out our investment.

Elysian had grown to become a well-established brewery selling its beers in 11 states with annual sales of $15 million and profits of $1.5 million. It brewed 29,500 barrels of beer a year in its 35,000 square foot brewery, with three brewpubs in Seattle. By December 2013, Ippolito Christon had put an enterprise value of $22 million on Elysian. This was good news and it enabled me to warn the board of the brewery that the four Brits were about to start seeking a buyer for their 10 per cent of the equity, and would they like first refusal?

I was delighted to be distracted one day by a phone call from Joe Bisacca, the CEO of the Elysian Brewery in Seattle. Joe swore me to absolute secrecy but he could hardly wait to tell me that 'a major global brewer was sniffing around' and reckoned Elysian could be worth $35 million, $13 million more than Ippolito Christon had valued it at the previous year. If the global brewer's valuation ever came to fruition, the $45,000 founding investment I'd made via Brew Securities would be worth $2.1 million – not to be sneezed at.

It was hard for me to keep such amazing news quiet and not shout it from the rooftops. But I kept schtum and by December the $35 million offer from Anheuser Busch (AB InBev), the world's biggest brewer, was formally accepted by the board and shareholders of the Elysian Brewery. To my delight, the original cost of a $75 share had risen to a value per share of $3,500, a compound interest rate over 19 years of 22.4 per cent – one of my best deals ever.

Lessons and learnings

- **Lesson 6: Control the cash**
  Beware of the dangers of running out of cash, especially if you're expanding your new business too quickly. Two of my investments in America were expanding so fast and were on such a roll that they nearly went bust as they couldn't raise new finance or make a profit fast enough.

- **Lesson 7: Inspire and educate others and put something back into your community**
  Keep helping others to start their own new ventures. As my reputation spread, I was invited to speak at more conferences around the world and also to MBA students who were studying entrepreneurship as part of their course.

🍺 19 🍺

Honeypot buzzes along to a sticky end

1998–2000

There had been many opportunities during long, transatlantic flights to ponder what best to do to re-establish my business life back in England. I remembered how well Mike Foster and I used to get on when he was managing director of Courage Brewery. He'd recently left that job to become chair of Brakspear's Brewery in Henley-on-Thames. In October 1998, I met Mike for lunch and we agreed to create a new 50:50 joint venture company between Brakspear's and Brew Securities. As the logo of Brakspear's Brewery was a honey bee, we decided to call our new venture Honeypot Inns, with me the head beekeeper rather than chief executive.

The summer of 1999 was spent negotiating with W H Brakspear & Sons to create Honeypot Inns. There was much legal work to be done as neither of the companies had ever started a joint venture company before and there were no precedents to crib from. When I wasn't bogged down in interminably long meetings with corporate lawyers and Brakspear's directors, I was busy developing the business plan and looking for potential acquisitions for my latest UK-based venture. The key points of the business plan for what was first called Brewspear Ltd were that each company would invest £250k, Brakspear would grant Honeypot Inns 21-year leases on each of its existing seven managed houses and Honeypot would acquire, develop and operate up to six freehold or leasehold managed houses a year. As a gesture of goodwill, Brew Securities bought 27,000 shares in Brakspear at £2.25 a share for £60,750.

Bee Day was 6 September 1999, when Honeypot Inns was launched with a considerable fanfare in the national press thanks to both Mike Foster's and my excellent PR contacts. A large photo of me dressed as a honey bee, flanked by Mike and Jim in their sombre grey suits, featured on the front page of the business section of the *Sunday Telegraph* with the headline 'Firkin founder's new Honeypot'.

On 11 November, the *Financial Times* reported under the headline 'Stumbling from one idea to another' that 'There is no method behind the innovation strategies devised by David Bruce, the serial entrepreneur. He says he just stumbles on ideas and "creating the right ambience is an innate skill, not something I can explain". He says: "Beehive Yourself will be our motto and our pubs with accommodation will offer Bee and Bee."'

Flushed with the success of yet another new start-up venture, I was delighted in November to be appointed a liveryman of the Worshipful Company of World Traders. One of the reasons why Nigel Pullman, the clerk (CEO) to the Company of World Traders, had nominated me was because many of the members worked in 'invisible exports', such as insurance, banking and information technology (IT). Few of them traded around the world in anything tangible such as malt, hops and brewing equipment. I'd certainly worked as a world trader and got my hands dirty. I was also granted the Freedom of the City of London, which was a great honour. As a freeman, under ancient custom, I'd be permitted to shepherd a flock of sheep over London Bridge once a year, but felt that would probably never happen in my case.

The first month of the new millennium was a busy one on the pub front. I added three leasehold properties to the Honeypot estate of seven Brakspear managed houses. New 30-year leases from the Unique Pub Company were bought for the Rising Sun in Harrow and the Good Companion in Warlingham, Surrey, with £500,000 allocated for their much-needed refurbishment.

A new, 25-year, free-of-tie lease was acquired for the uniquely named Pewter Platter Tavern in the heart of Spitalfields, bringing Brakspear's beers to the City of London for the first time. Sadly, these three exciting acquisitions and development opportunities completely spooked Brakspear's board and by February I realised that we'd never get on as a team.

It soon became clear that more working capital would be needed to help the company to continue its expansion. We were discussing cash flow one day and I was told 'each shareholder will just have to dig deeper into their pockets and the one with the deepest pockets will win'. Who will win what? A new joint venture company isn't meant to be a hard battle but it had turned into one with a 200-year-old, family-owned brewery valued on the London OFEX market at £42 million.

In July 2000, Brew Securities invested a further £100,000 as a short-term loan to Honeypot Inns, on top of its original £250,000 shareholding. The loan of £100,000 was matched, grudgingly, by Brakspear. In the same month, Honeypot obtained the lease of the Chequers in Marlow, a prestigious pub with accommodation, so it was indeed a Bee & Bee! By August, the company was running 14 pubs, all selling Brakspear beers from Henley across London to Hackney and Tottenham. It wasn't a bad achievement for a new pub company less than a year since it started trading.

One day, out of the blue, Mike Foster, the chair of Brakspear, announced in his statement with the interim results to 30 June 2000 that, 'To date the performance of our joint venture company, Honeypot Inns, has been disappointing and before the year end we will be undertaking a strategic review of this investment.' Brakspear immediately made sure that all my Honeypot managers received a copy of the interim report, which was a massive blow to the morale of all fellow worker bees. In effect, Mike's comments in his chair's statement heralded the beginning of the end for my new venture.

The trade press reported 'Brakspear finds Honeypot not so attractive' and 'Brewer to review Honeypot venture'. The *Times* headline on 22 August announced 'Brewer in joint venture considers future'. Talk about the death knell for Honeypot Inns! The negative publicity reached the ears of Roger Looker, who kindly offered to help me try to find a solution now the world at large knew that Brakspear was disenchanted, to say the least, with Honeypot. Roger agreed, for a fee, of course, to try to sell six of the pubs using his extensive contacts in the licensed trade and the City, which would help restructure the company and strengthen its finances.

In October, Brakspear wrote to me, saying, 'The ship is sinking fast' and 'Honeypot Inns is in a parlous state and will likely perish at the month-end.' No wonder we'd never got on – the eternal pessimist versus the eternal optimist.

At a Honeypot board meeting on 6 November, it was agreed that each shareholder in the joint venture could agree to buy out the other as long as they undertook to invest a further £500,000 to restructure the company. Brakspear easily had £500,000 to inject new equity into the company but Brew Securities did not, having already invested £350,000.

On 10 November, I met Clive Watson, who'd recently left Regent Inns and started his own company, Bar & Kitchen Ltd, which he was keen to develop from its first bar in Waterloo. I shared with Clive all the information I had on Honeypot Inns and, unlike Roger, who was keen to sell some of the assets to generate cash, Clive considered whether to invest in Honeypot and continue to operate all the pubs.

Neither Roger nor Clive could provide a definitive solution before the next Honeypot board meeting on 15 November, held at the offices in Portman Square of the British Licensed Retailers' Association, of which Mike Foster was chair. It was a miserable meeting as I fretted over losing my £350,000 investment in the company. There was also the not-insignificant fact to consider that in August both Brakspear and I had each guaranteed £250,000 to the company's bank, the Royal Bank of Scotland, to help secure Honeypot's overdraft of £1.5 million.

As neither shareholder wanted to buy out the other for a reasonable sum, there was complete deadlock. As a result, we agreed to consider putting the company into some form of administration

Honeypot buzzes along to a sticky end

or receivership. Frantic phone calls ensued, day, night and weekend, between me, Roger, Clive, Mike, lawyers and the bank manager while we tried to find a solution to avoid the company failing completely, which would have been disastrous for the reputations of both Mike and me. It soon became clear that it would be preferable for me to write off my £250,000 equity investment, try to retrieve as much as I could of my £100,000 loan and, most important of all, to persuade Brakspear to take on, as part of a settlement agreement, my personal guarantee to the bank of £250,000. If the bank ever called that in, as part of an administration process, then I'd probably have to sell our home to find the money. Louise would not be best pleased.

During the weekend following the board meeting, Mike and I agreed by phone that Brakspear would purchase Brew Securities' 50 per cent share of the joint venture for just £1, resulting in a loss to my company of £249,999; Brakspear would pay back only 50 per cent of Brew Securities' £100,000 loan to Honeypot Inns, incurring a further loss of £50,000; and Brakspear would indemnify me personally to ensure the bank wouldn't be able to call in my personal guarantee for £250,000. It was this last point that persuaded me to write off £299,999 of my first venture back in the UK. It wasn't a good start, but the company hadn't fallen into administration and my reputation remained intact, which was important for my next entrepreneurial adventure.

Honeypot Inns had been going for just 14 months when it was taken in-house by Brakspear on 22 November 2000. Jim Burrows said in a press release that Brakspear had 'acquired David's interest in the business for an undisclosed sum'. If people only knew how much I had lost…

The moral of this sorry saga was to make sure you can work with your fellow directors before embarking on any new venture. The joint venture had failed dismally and I vowed never to become involved in any such joint venture ever again.

Ironically, just two years later, on 25 July 2002, Brakspear announced that following 230 years it was 'going to quit brewing'. Soon after, all the Brakspear pubs, including those that Honeypot

Inns had owned, were sold to London pub operator J T Davies. The entire brewery site in Henley, overlooking the River Thames, was sold for £10 million and is now – rather oddly, given its brewing history – called Hotel du Vin. Brakspear reported that brewing operations alone had been losing £500,000 a year, in spite of annual sales of £6 million.

The final comments about the end of Brakspear's brewery in the *Morning Advertiser* trade paper were most apt, quoting Oscar Wilde: 'Cynics are those who know the price of everything but the value of nothing.' The paper added, 'Something precious has been lost.' Tell me about it!

Lessons and learnings

🍺 **Lesson 6: Control the cash**
Try to keep control of your company and avoid joint ventures. I learned the very hard way that it's better to have 100 per cent of something small than 50 per cent of something you can't completely control.

20

Brewing up some capital ideas

2000–2011

While Honeypot Inns was going down the pan, I spent a lot of time with Clive Watson. We both wondered whether his new company, Bar & Kitchen, might have been interested in investing in Honeypot. It was a good opportunity to get to know Clive and to attempt to work out what might be best – to try to save Honeypot or to team up together in a new venture.

It was a breath of fresh air getting to know Clive after the ghastly Brakspear experiences and we had a lot of fun putting together ideas for the future and developing our respective plans. I was still reeling from the imminent downfall of Honeypot and was keen to start looking at new opportunities. Clive had left Regent Inns and was equally hungry to develop something new. The most important thing to me was that Clive and I should get on well, which we most certainly did.

Clive had been in fundraising talks with Noble & Company, an Edinburgh-based merchant bank with an office in the City of London. On 12 September 2000, Clive and I had our first meeting with them, where we tentatively outlined our rough ideas for a new pub company. Noble was represented by Patrick Booth-Clibborn, Shane Elliot and Henry Chaplin, and Clive and I enjoyed great rapport with them. Every meeting was a positive and stimulating occasion and more often than not we'd end up in the pub around the corner from their office near Bank Underground station.

The Noble team introduced us to Andy Ley, their corporate lawyer at Henderson Boyd Jackson in Edinburgh, and also Lenny Norstrand and Matt Brown at RAM Capital, who were experts in fundraising for new ventures. Everyone we met through Noble was a pleasure to deal with and by Christmas 2000 Clive and I had put together a business plan that was greeted with enthusiasm and approval by all our new professional advisors.

Noble insisted that the corporate governance for Clive and my new venture should be exemplary, especially as it was to be launched as a full-blooded PLC. On 8 February 2001, The Capital Pub Company plc was launched, with an offer for subscriptions document that we hoped would raise £10 million of new equity under the Enterprise Investment Scheme. The EIS is a government initiative to help new start-up companies raise capital to develop their business from scratch. The main benefits for an EIS investor are: income tax relief of 20 per cent refunded by HMRC, based on each personal investment made; exemption from capital gains tax, which meant no tax would be paid on any gain in the value of the EIS shares; and loss relief – should the company fail, then any losses could be set against other capital gains or taxable income.

I didn't know then that this first experience of raising new equity capital under the EIS would eventually result in me raising more than £120 million for future ventures. What a great way to attract new investors to a potentially risky business using a government-approved, tax-efficient method of securing OPM – other people's money! While Clive and I considered ourselves to be equal business partners, Noble insisted we should have formal titles, so I was appointed chief executive and Clive, being a chartered accountant, became finance and commercial director. The prime objectives of our new venture were: to acquire, develop and manage a group of pubs in and around Greater London; the pubs would be non-branded, un-themed and cater for their local markets; the pubs would be liquor led, free-of-tie and not dependent on primary locations; the pubs would be well refurbished, operated on an individual basis (ie no chain) and serve food cooked to order, using fresh ingredients.

As soon as the company had been launched, our time was spent visiting banks and independent financial advisors and on the road searching for our first acquisition. We hoped to buy 12 pubs in our first year, assuming we raised the entire £10 million. In the spring of 2001, we attracted amazing public relations with articles in the *Times*, *Guardian*, *Independent* and *Daily Telegraph*, many with photos of Clive and me in fancy dress in order to grab national press coverage. The first of these stunts involved the pair of us dressed respectively as a Grenadier Guard and a Beefeater. We took a boat to the Tower of London, where we were photographed under Tower Bridge. The photo featured in colour on the front page of the *Sunday Telegraph* on 4 February 2001 and it got tongues wagging around the City about our venture.

David and Clive under Tower Bridge fundraising for Capital Pubs

Patrick Booth-Clibborn should've been in the photo, dressed as a London bobby. However, when the three of us gathered for a team photo in the Mall, with Buckingham Palace in the background, a real policeman warned Patrick that it was illegal to impersonate a police officer and he suggested Patrick should change out of his costume to avoid imminent arrest.

Funds started to trickle in, which was very exciting, in spite of one notable occasion when Clive and I took a City financial advisor around some East End pubs one evening. He was clearly underwhelmed by our plans and said at the end of the tour, 'Well, I've listened to you both all evening and I don't think you'll raise any money at all and, even if you do, there aren't any decent freehold pubs in London for you to buy.' Yet another prophet of doom!

Capital Pubs held its first formal board meeting at Noble's offices in the City on 11 September 2001. When the meeting ended, we all went to the pub around the corner for some lunch and a couple of well-earned pints. While we were standing at the bar waiting for our food to arrive, someone switched on the television in time to see a plane fly into one of the Twin Towers in New York. The whole pub gasped in horror, followed by an incredulous silence, and then everyone started speculating on what could've happened, assuming it was a small plane flying off course. We were all glued to the TV and forgot about our food as any feelings of hunger had left us. When a second plane hit the other Twin Tower, the pub erupted in shrieks and howls of horror.

We were deeply shocked by the loss of more than 3,000 American lives on their home turf, with the threat that the US might start a new war in Afghanistan. However, Clive and I resolved to buckle down to raise more money and find new sites to buy and develop. But it was immediately clear after 9/11 that potential investors were spooked. For a while they sat on their cash and didn't invest in any new ventures, and as a result it became hard for a while to raise new equity despite the tax advantages of the EIS scheme.

On 10 October 2001, our new company started trading with the purchase of the free-of-tie lease on Smithy's Wine Bar that was renowned as 'the best kept secret in King's Cross'. It was called Smithy's as the beautiful, mid-19th-century building had once been the blacksmith's shop when London Transport's horse-drawn buses needed to have their horses' hooves reshod.

Our company suddenly started to grow. Smithy's was followed a few weeks later by the purchase of a 30-year, free-of-tie lease on the Lord Nelson on Old Street on the northern outskirts of the City. In November, the freehold of the White Hart in Whitechapel was bought, as were Clive's two free-of-tie leaseholds, the Square Pig in Holborn and the Prodigal's Return near Battersea Bridge. By the end of November, our new company was running five pubs as a result of raising £7.8 million from 312 investors since we'd launched in February.

In February 2002, Noble & Company organised a second fundraising for the company, this time selling shares at £1.10 each. Once again it extolled the benefits of the EIS, with a target of £8.8 million on top of the original £7.8 million. To publicise the new offer, Clive and I dressed up once more, this time as Lord Nelson and Dick Whittington. The colour photo, with St Paul's Cathedral in the background, featured on the front pages of the *Sunday Telegraph* on 10 February and the *Independent* on 6 March – amazing national press coverage.

Dick Whittington and Lord Nelson, aka Bruce and Watson, outside St Paul's Cathedral, fundraising again!

Funds soon started to flow into our coffers and in June 2002 we were able to honour our pledge to all our professional advisors that we would take them on a celebratory trip to Paris for a couple of nights once we'd raised our first £10 million.

Acquisitions continued apace. They included an Italian restaurant in Teddington that became the Teddington Arms; an enormous freehold pub, the Alexandra, overlooking Clapham Common; the freehold of the Ladbroke Arms in Notting Hill; and in August 2002 one of London's most iconic and much-loved free houses, the Anglesea Arms in South Kensington.

I'd been told that the freehold of the Anglesea Arms was available for £3 million and the owner, Joe Simpson, wanted it to remain an independent free house rather than become a Fuller's, Young's or other big brewers' tied house. Within just two minutes, Clive and I had agreed to buy it for the asking price in an off-market deal, much to the chagrin of just about every other brewer and pub company in the UK.

John Young, the chair of Young's Brewery, rang to congratulate me on our latest acquisition and said he was delighted it would remain a free house and at least Fuller's, his great London rival, had failed to buy the Anglesea. John added he would like us to sell Young's Bitter in our latest free house and asked if I cared to dress up with him for a fun PR initiative close to Christmas. He said he would be Father Christmas and asked what fancy dress I'd wear. I consulted Danese, my PA, and she suggested I could be the front or the back end of a reindeer, or one of Santa's little helpers – an elf. None of her suggestions appealed to me until she came up with the idea of me being a Christmas fairy, which I certainly would never have thought of myself!

On 12 December, John Young arrived at the Anglesea Arms on a Young's Brewery horse-drawn dray with a wooden firkin of his finest ale. The 81-year-old, dressed as Father Christmas, then presented his firkin to the Christmas fairy dressed in white tights, a pink tutu, white stilettos, diaphanous wings, a wand and flowing blonde wig.

David with John Young and his horse-drawn dray delivering beer to the Anglesea Arms

The photoshoot outside the pub resulted in brilliant publicity in the *Daily Telegraph* and the *Evening Standard*. I then adopted Louise's suggestion that I really should be the Christmas fairy on top of the Christmas tree. She'd bought a 3 ft-high plastic tree with nasty flashing lights that I plugged into a wall socket in the bar. This enabled me to stick the top of the small tree up and under my tutu so I really was the fairy on top of the tree. It did mean, however, that I couldn't move far from the socket to join in the celebrations as the lights would stop flashing.

The first two rounds of EIS fundraising had brought in £14.3 million. As a result, in the new year of 2003, Clive and I discussed creating a brand-new EIS company we would call The Capital Pub Company 2 plc. Seventy-three per cent of our 565 shareholders had invested in both rounds since our first company was set up and they were keen to invest further, so a new company had to be launched rather than turning away the prospect of yet more money piling in. One of our wealthy shareholders, who had sold his insurance company and needed to roll over some of his capital gains tax, agreed to invest £1 million in our second Capital Pub Company on top of the £1 million he'd already put into the first one.

My fundraising roadshows continued in order to reach the £16 million target, and during February I visited Leeds, Bristol, Exeter, Birmingham, Glasgow, Hull, Edinburgh, Manchester, Belfast, Cardiff and Norwich. It was exhausting but proved to be well worth the effort. By the end of March we'd raised £15.5 million and decided to stop fundraising, pending setting up the new company to see if we could do it all over again. The achievement was recognised in the *Publican* newspaper in March 2003 as 'the most successful company yet in the EIS universe', adding it was 'now the biggest-ever EIS company, attracting over 700 investors'.

On top of all the new equity raised, sales from our 12 pubs, in just one year from start-up, had grown from zero to £8 million a year. Clearly, our initiative was set for a rosy future. On 17 January 2004, the *Times* announced that Clive and I were launching a brand-new EIS venture, The Capital Pub Company 2 plc. We aimed to raise £10 million to emulate the success of our first EIS-funded pub company.

A new board would be formed and Clive and I would be joined by David Maxwell Scott as non-executive chair and Sheila McKenzie as non-executive director. David had been chair of Highland Distillers while Sheila was the former chief executive of Slug & Lettuce and the founder of the Pitcher & Piano chain of bars.

To attract maximum publicity, Clive and I dressed up again, this time with me as Sherlock Holmes and Clive, fittingly, as Dr Watson. The photos were taken outside our flagship pub, the Anglesea Arms, with a caption saying we were 'on the trail of new investment for our new company'.

In line with our first Capital Pub Company, new funds were soon flowing in and by December 2005 we had not only £10 million from our offer for subscription but also a further private placing of shares that created a total of £13.7 million from 425 shareholders. These funds were used to purchase some brilliant London freeholds, such as The Mitre in Greenwich (with its 16 bedrooms), The Tea Clipper in Knightsbridge and The Crown & Anchor in Chiswick.

From January 2006, the new Noble & Co fundraising team of Shane Elliott and Gordon Leatherdale were working flat out with me to try to raise £16 million by the end of the tax year. By 21 March, following a final frenzy of roadshows around the country, we'd achieved our objective and fundraising had to stop. Unbelievably, between Capital Pubs and Capital Pubs 2, we'd raised more than £31 million and yet another record had been broken.

On 30 November, I was one of several hundred people who attended the thanksgiving service at Southwark Cathedral for my old friend John Young, the chair of Young's Brewery. True to form, there were several Young's horse-drawn drays lined up outside. One of the most poignant facts from John's eulogy was that he'd died on the very morning the last brew was mashed at Young's Brewery, before the Wandsworth site was sold to property developers. What a spooky coincidence.

Two of the rules when raising equity under the Enterprise Investment Scheme are that investors must hold their equity for a minimum of three years and the company must at some stage after that offer liquidity to its EIS investors by either selling the company or floating on the London Stock Exchange. Either rule provides an exit route for investors to cash in their shares, preferably with a tax-free profit. This explains my crude expression 'flog it or float it'.

The board of The Capital Pub Company decided in January 2007 that, as the company was six years old, it was high time we offered investors the opportunity to sell their shares if they so wished. The company was still on a roll, so selling to a rival in the pub trade wasn't an option any of us would consider. We agreed to float the company on the London Stock Exchange's Alternative Investment Market (AIM) by way of an initial public offering (IPO).

This was uncharted territory for both Clive and me as neither of us had launched an IPO before, so we were on a steep learning curve.

We spent the spring of 2007 researching and appointing a whole new raft of specialist corporate advisors. For secret commercial reasons, our IPO project needed a code name for all our new advisors to use. The stockbrokers initially started using Project Hangover, which I objected to as being inappropriate for a pub company. They changed it, without consultation, to Project Headache – something that often accompanies a hangover. I vetoed that as well and suggested Project Bacchus. Bacchus was the god of wine in ancient Rome, and as his name was pronounced 'back us' it was ideal for our IPO application. Everyone endorsed my suggestion and the hard work could begin in earnest. Fees for all our professional advisors were estimated at around £1 million, which was a frightening prospect, but we couldn't float without their expertise.

At first we intended to raise £5 million to invest in buying more pubs but when we were offered £9.5 million for the Hog in the Pound on the corner of Oxford Street and Bond Street, we decided not to raise the £5 million of new equity and instead only go for an admission to the Alternative Investment Market of the London Stock Exchange. This would provide liquidity for any EIS investor who wanted to cash in his or her chips and run for the hills.

Our focus was on the IPO of The Capital Pub Company plc but it was important that we didn't abandon the future of The Capital Pub Company 2 plc and its eight pubs, especially as so many people had invested under the EIS in both companies. In order to avoid any future conflicts of interest over site selection and management time, it was agreed to hive off The Capital Pub Company 2, with its existing separate board, and change its name to Convivial London Pubs plc, with Kris Gumbrell as its CEO, who could develop his own management team.

On 17 May 2007, the *Financial Times* announced that Clive and I were floating our company and featured a large 10" x 6" photo of us each holding a foaming pint at the Anglesea Arms. On 4 June that year, all our hard work paid off and we achieved our objective of floating the company. Little did we know then that four years later we would sell up when 'flog it and float it' became reality.

In the six and a half years since Clive and I teamed up to create our first venture together, we'd raised about £31 million under the Enterprise Investment Scheme; developed an estate of 23 free-of-tie pubs in Greater London, 20 of which were freehold; the estate was valued at £70 million; and annual turnover had grown to some £12 million and pre-tax profit to nearly £2 million.

Within a month of the company's IPO, the government brought in a smoking ban in all enclosed public areas. Luckily, 90 per cent of our pubs had outside trading areas and 55 per cent already had non-smoking areas, especially in our food-led pubs, and this draconian measure didn't affect our business too badly.

I was delighted when The Capital Pub Company plc was awarded 'Best Managed Pub Company' at the 2010 Publican Awards. At the time, Clive and I escorted two directors of Fuller, Smith & Turner, round some of our Capital pubs, starting at the Square Pig in Holborn. At the end of the tour, they said they liked everything they'd seen and what we'd achieved and added, 'If you ever decide to sell up, we're only a phone call away and would love to have first refusal.'

Clive and I assured them we had absolutely no intention of selling up for the foreseeable future and if we ever did decide to do so, we'd put the business up for sale on the open market to secure the best possible price for our loyal EIS investors. We were shocked to find that they grew impatient waiting for us to phone and say, 'Please buy us cheap.' As a result, Fuller's launched a hostile takeover bid to buy the company without any warning other than phoning Clive at home at 7 am one day to let us know they were about to launch a bid as soon as the London Stock Exchange opened at 8 am.

On 23 June 2011, the London *Evening Standard* ran the headline, 'Gloves are off as Fuller's and Capital Pubs fight turns nasty'. It was accompanied by a large colour photo of Michael Turner superimposed in front of our beloved Anglesea Arms, smiling smugly and holding a pint. We refused to engage with Fuller's in spite of them offering 200p per share but, unfortunately, their unsolicited hostile approach had 'put us in play' and other predators could start to circle. On 20 July 2011, my board accepted an offer for our 34-strong pub company from Greene King, a big regional brewer based in Bury St Edmunds, Suffolk, valuing each share at 235p or an enterprise value for the company of £93 million.

The Independent reported, 'David Bruce, who co-founded Capital in 2000, will receive more than £2 million.' Better than a poke in the eye with a sharp stick, as someone once said. Clive and I had proved that not only could we create a new company from scratch but we could also float it and flog it along the way.

Lessons and learnings

🍺 **Lesson 1: Follow your instincts and demonstrate your motivation to succeed**

After the costly failure of my first and only joint venture company, I was determined to have another go to restore my reputation and recover some of my financial losses. If you've enjoyed building up and then selling your own business, then you've probably got the aptitude and attitude to see if you can do it all over again.

🍺 **Lesson 2: Build a trusted support network**

Teaming up with Clive Watson to start and develop a new company worked well, as we enjoyed working together and, as a chartered accountant, he provided crucial financial advice. Only work with people you like and respect and who provide commercial synergies as well as different skills and experience.

🍺 **Lesson 6: Control the cash**

Use your hard-won reputation to attract new equity and reduce any dependence on bank debt. Both Clive and my track records were sufficient to raise more than £31 million for our first two start-up companies.

🍺 **Lesson 8: Encourage and nurture free PR, even if it entails fancy dress**

Never miss an opportunity to attract national free PR. When fundraising for our first two ventures together, Clive and I attracted front page, full colour photos in the national press of us dressed up as a beefeater, a guard, Dick Whittington and Lord Nelson, and especially me as a Christmas fairy. Perhaps wearing fancy dress isn't so acceptable nowadays but think up ways to attract the media to publicise your unique selling proposition. Online social media and podcasts are far more the way forward today.

21

From pubs to farm shops and a vineyard

2007–2011

Clive and I thought we could relax and enjoy the summer after successfully floating our company. However, on 29 July 2007, I had my first formal meeting with Gordon Leatherdale. He'd been part of the fundraising team at Noble & Company and wanted to talk about a new business idea he'd been nurturing.

Gordon was impressed with the approximately £31 million that had been raised for the two Capital Pub Companies and wondered if I might be interested in helping him raise equity for his new venture under the Enterprise Investment Scheme. He proposed creating a new company, The Country Food & Dining Company Ltd, which would initially buy and develop an existing farm shop. The business would focus on selling local farm produce and also include a café serving locally sourced food.

Gordon had identified an existing farm shop, Highclose, which quite by chance was only a few miles from my home near Hungerford. I went there with Gordon to view it and considered it as a good example of how it could be developed to meet Gordon's vision. The board of the new company was made up initially of me as the founder investor with 175,000 shares; Gordon as CEO, reporting to the founding investor (me as quasi-chair!); and Kris Gumbrell as non-executive director. We launched the fundraising with Smith &

Williamson Investment Management Ltd in the City of London and 97 investors had soon raised £1.9 million under the EIS. This enabled us, in October 2007, to buy the freehold of Highclose Farm Shop and its 53 acres of 'Pick Your Own' farmland for £1.6 million. There was one initial problem: the business was known locally as Highcost Farm Shop, a reputation we'd have to change without delay.

As a result, Smith & Williamson decided to launch a second new company, The Country Food & Dining Company (2), and it quickly raised £1.2 million from 30 investors.

By the autumn of 2008, we'd increased the size of what had been renamed Cobbs Farm Shop by 50 per cent to include a 66-seater café, a butcher, baker, fishmonger, florist and a children's play area. The company was growing so rapidly that several key appointments had to be made. They included Tom Newey as operations director in August 2008, and Gordon Montgomery FCA as finance director the following May. In June 2009, Gordon Leatherdale took us by surprise by deciding to resign and pursue other business interests and as a result I had to become executive chair.

Fundraising continued and Country Food & Dining soon passed £3.9 million from 106 shareholders, Country Food & Dining (2) raised £1.6 million and Country Food & Dining (3) £1.08 million by August 2009. In August 2008, Country Food & Dining (2) bought a freehold farm shop with ten acres of land at Norton St Philip, seven miles south of Bath. I changed its name from Springleaze Farm Shop to Woody's Farm Shop.

In April 2009, our first farm shop company, Country Food & Dining, purchased the freehold of a farm shop near Donnington in Shropshire called, appropriately, Green Fields Farm Shop. Within two years of starting the new farm shop venture, more than £6.5 million had been raised and three existing freehold businesses had been bought – all paid for out of the new EIS equity and, gloriously, with no bank debt at all, meaning we were in a strong position for future expansion.

To add to that achievement, in March 2010 Country Food & Dining (3) bought the freehold of The Good Life Home and Garden

Centre at Headbourne Worthy, near Winchester, for £700,000. On 12 March 2010, the *Times* featured me acquiring our fifth farm shop with a quote from me about its location: 'If you're within ten miles of a Waitrose, you're doing the right thing!' Of the switch from pubs to catering, I added: 'It's the same kind of thing, except I don't have to get the train into London every day.'

A new venture for me came in August 2010, when we decided to plant a vineyard at Cobbs Farm Shop. It was to be called Alder Ridge, as there was one alder tree on a ridge close to where we located the vines. The chalky, flinty, south-sloping *terroir* was almost exactly the same as in the Champagne region of France and as a result, in 2011, we planted 6,000 vines comprising 4,500 Pinot noir and 1,500 Chardonnay.

Once the vineyard was planted, we bought our next outlet, Fielder's Farm Shop at Englefield, on the western outskirts of Reading. The shop was small but behind it were some beautiful old barns that were ripe for conversion into a mega farm shop. The tortuous process of obtaining planning permission to develop one of my new ventures began, yet again.

Equally good *terroir* as Champagne

The Firkin Saga

Lessons and learnings

🍺 **Lesson 3: Be brave, ambitious and determined to overcome all obstacles**
Always expect the unexpected, especially just when you think you're safe. Soon after floating our company on the London Stock Exchange, Clive and I were completely thrown one day by an unexpected, unsolicited hostile takeover bid from a rival company. Even if the challenge is something you haven't encountered before, remind yourself of obstacles you've overcome in the past, then work out how to deal with this one.

🍺 **Lesson 4: Seize opportunities as they arise**
Explore new avenues as your company grows. Neither Clive nor I had ever put any of our companies onto the London Stock Exchange, so as soon as we were big and profitable enough, that's exactly what we did, thereby giving some of our investors the chance to cash in their chips.

🍺 **Lesson 10: Savour the special moments**
Never grow tired of celebrating your success. Soon after repelling the hostile takeover bid, we received a cash offer for our company of £93 million, which we were more than happy to accept on behalf of all our happy shareholders and, of course, ourselves.

22

Success breeds success

2011–2015

When we sold The Capital Pub Company plc to Greene King, there were hundreds of very happy investors who'd turned their 70p into a 235p share, a threefold tax-free increase. There was a 30 per cent income tax rebate off a £1 share under the Enterprise Investment Scheme. Clive and I were obviously delighted with the result of our teaming up just over a decade earlier. When several significant shareholders asked if we might attempt to do it all over again, we didn't take too much persuading.

On 11 October 2011, the *Times* reported, 'Pub veterans opt for another round'. The article said we wanted 'to roll over some of the "few bob" we had made' by investing ourselves in a proposed new venture. On 2 November 2011, Clive and I had our first meeting with our lawyers to discuss how best to structure our new pub venture. With our confidence boosted by the success of starting, developing and then selling Capital Pubs, it was agreed that this time round we would create not one but two new EIS-funded pub companies, The City Pub Company (East) plc and The City Pub Company (West) plc, each of which would initially raise up to £1.87 million.

Clive and I decided to strengthen our inaugural board for our latest venture and invited John Roberts to join us as a co-founder. John was a kindred spirit and, having been the strategic planning director for Scottish Courage, he then became the managing director of the Fuller's Beer Company.

I was appointed non-executive chair of each company, with both Clive and John as non-executive directors, until Clive became the chief executive of the two companies in April 2012. As founding shareholders, the three of us each invested £75,000 in our new venture, totalling £225,000, with Clive and I each investing a further £75,000 once fundraising had started. Our two new companies were launched on 20 December 2011, with the highly appropriate headline in the London *Evening Standard*: 'Pub pair make it a double with two new businesses'. Little did I know then that our two pub companies would soon develop new breweries in Bath, Bristol, Cambridge, London, Norwich and Southampton.

I was delighted when Clive Watson and I decided there should be a third EIS fundraising for our City Pub Companies (East) and (West) in February 2013. The two previous fundraisers had already brought in £7.8 million between the two companies and this time we planned to raise a further £5 million for each company at a premium of £1.10 per share.

In June 2012, I received a phone call from Len Wright, asking me if I'd like to meet Dave and Helen Maggs. I said I'd love to be introduced to them as I'd enjoyed their beers ever since they had started the West Berkshire Brewery back in 1995. We met for lunch at the Royal Oak in Yattendon, and they explained that, after 17 years, they were looking for someone to protect and take forward their pioneering initiative, rather than just selling up and retiring. We got on really well and I left the lunch saying I'd go away and think about their proposal. However, I warned them that, as I was soon to be 65 years old, I might not need such a big challenge again at the official retirement age, especially as 25 years had passed since I'd sold my own breweries.

While I was ruminating on whether to hold further discussions with Dave and Helen, the second round of fundraising was launched in July for my latest pub venture, The City Pub Companies East and West. The initial offer for subscription in December 2011 had been oversubscribed within just three months of the launch, with each company raising £2 million. The next fundraising exercise aimed to raise a further £1.9 million for each company under the EIS at a premium of £1.10 per share.

On 8 April, the *Times* announced my new appointment at the West Berkshire Brewery (WBB) and I chaired my first board meeting, where it was agreed I'd help Dave and Helen Maggs to sell the majority of their shares to new investors in their brewery. A meeting was held with the Maggs' close friend and investor, Andy Baum, and Paul Etherington of Grant Thornton to decide the best way forward.

I'd hoped, as a result of raising millions of pounds for my pub companies and farm shops, that I could attract new investors using the Enterprise Investment Scheme. But Paul made it clear that the EIS was designed to attract new shareholders to help fund a start-up venture and it couldn't be used to buy out shareholders from an existing company. It was agreed, therefore, that I should use my reputation in the brewing industry to attempt to raise around £1.4 million for the founding shareholders of WBB while leaving them with at least 10 per cent of the company.

Back at WBB, I'd arranged to meet the senior management team of Will Twomey (head brewer), Tom Lucas (finance) and James Tomlinson (sales). It was a strange meeting. I outlined my initial thoughts on how best to take the company forward without Dave and Helen and the three sat round in a circle and glowered in silence, much to the chagrin of the Maggs, who were furious with them for their attempts to frighten me off. It later transpired that the three had been working on a plan for a management buyout and my appearance on the scene had scuppered their chances as Dave and Helen wanted me to take over as brewery chair when they retired.

I offered to raise enough money for them to retire by selling the majority of their shares to their loyal supporters and the beer drinkers of West Berkshire. This would protect their brewery from asset strippers and hedge fund managers in the City who'd love to pounce on the opportunity to own a brewery. In December 2013, I launched a fundraising document to sell to new shareholders 11,516 of the founders' shares at £125 per share to raise the £1.4 million I'd told them I'd achieve to buy out their majority shareholdings. Any excess funds raised above the £1.4 million, up to a maximum of £2 million, would be allocated to provide additional working capital for the company.

The founders' shares were made available to their family and friends along with the beer drinkers, licensed retailers and residents of Berkshire and its neighbouring counties. In other words, there would be no involvement with hedge fund managers, venture capitalists, private equity firms or other financial predators. I took the opportunity to top up my initial purchase in July 2013 of £100,000 worth of the Maggs' shares and bought an additional £50,000 worth of their shares. It's what I call leadership from the front… or my balls on the block.

The Sunday Times reported on 29 December that I was launching an initial £2 million fundraising for the West Berkshire Brewery to build a war chest to buy out all but 10 per cent of the founding shareholders' equity. The article, featuring a large photo of me in the brewery holding a pint (as usual!), also mentioned my further £50,000 investment.

Once I'd settled into my responsibilities as the new chair of the brewery, I thought it would be fun to resurrect my legendary Dogbolter ale for WBB to produce and wholesale. Will Twomey, the head brewer, and I discussed how we could adapt the original recipe from its Firkin days to a grown-up commercial plant. As dawn broke on 21 May, Will and I brewed 30 barrels of Dogbolter with an ABV (alcohol by volume) of 6 per cent, which was as strong as my original brew with an original gravity of 1060 degrees. After two weeks of conditioning, it tasted as good as the original. Sadly, my ambition to add Dogbolter to our portfolio was promptly dashed when, 48 hours after starting to sell it, an injunction was slapped on me out of the blue. One of my Firkin brewers from years ago, Eddie Gadd, had started Gadds' Brewery in Ramsgate, Kent, and when Punch Taverns stopped operating the Firkin pubs, Eddie bought the intellectual property and recipe for Dogbolter and started to brew it again. He threatened to sue me if I ever produced another drop of my much-loved brew. I had to 'cease and desist', as a lawyer would say, and agree never to brew another drop of my own creation ever again.

While I was still peeved at the threat of being sued by one of my former Firkin brewers, I was delighted to be featured in a major article in the *Times* on 11 September 2014 by Dominic Walsh with the headline 'Serving up success in a crafty pint' and referring to me as 'the godfather of craft brewing'.

The publicity could not have been better timed, as on 26 November I launched the West Berkshire Brewery fundraising document to raise £4 million at £3 per share under the EIS with two strap lines: 'There's something exciting brewing!' and 'A refreshing opportunity to get involved with some proper liquid assets'. The new equity raised would be used to build a new, high-specification brewery with bottling, kegging and canning lines together with a visitor centre, shop and taproom.

City Pubs East and West launched its fourth round of fundraising just before Christmas 2014. This time, Clive and I intended to raise a further £5 million for each company at a premium of £1.25 per share, having already raised a total of £17.8 million for our latest venture. The second fundraising document for the West Berkshire Brewery announced that I was strengthening the board with Clive Watson and Simon Robertson-Macleod as non-executive directors. Clive had recently succeeded me as chair of the City Pub Companies East and West while I became the senior independent director. Simon brought a wealth of brewing experience as a former director of Scottish & Newcastle Breweries and Fuller, Smith & Turner.

As a thank you and a gesture of goodwill to Dave and Helen Maggs, who still owned around 10 per cent of the company they'd founded almost 20 years earlier, I appointed both of them to be life presidents of the WBB and to serve with Andy and Karen Baum on the newly formed Founders' Advisory Committee.

In July I was delighted, as chair of the West Berkshire Brewery, to be admitted to the livery of the Worshipful Company of Brewers, thanks to Billy Whitbread, who had put my name forward. It was a great honour to become a liveryman of the company, which had been established by a Royal Charter granted by Henry VI in 1438, although the origins of the Brewers' Guild go back to

1292 in support of 'The Mystery or Art of Brewing Ale or Beer'.

I was never one to rest on my laurels, and therefore Clive Watson and I decided that as our City Pub Companies were fully funded – we'd raised a total of £27.8 million for them – we should start yet another new venture together. On 25 November 2014, the *Daily Telegraph* reported that Clive and I were starting the City Pub EIS Fund to raise £75 million of equity together with £25 million of debt to create a new £100 million venture with the aim of buying 50 primarily freehold pubs. The initial proposal was to raise up to £25 million under the Enterprise Investment Scheme to be spread across up to five new pub companies, subject to the amount raised. I would be chair of each company while Clive would be the investment consultant to the Mayfair Fund Manager, Thompson Taraz.

The first three companies were each named after a variety of brewers' hop, Galaxy, Pioneer and Sovereign with, for example, The Galaxy (City) Pub Company Ltd. The following three new companies would be named after the hops Liberty, Phoenix and Summit. The spring of 2015 was spent fundraising for our latest venture, which was boosted by an article in the London *Evening Standard* with the headline 'Raise your glass to this £100 million venture' with the obligatory photo of me with a pint in my hand.

Lessons and learnings

🍺 **Lesson 4: Seize opportunities as they arise**

Apart from building up several new pub companies, I also ventured into developing a chain of farm shops, a vineyard and even investing in an existing brewery just to keep my hand in from all those years ago. Keep on enjoying seizing new opportunities and applying all your hard-won experience to making a success of your new ventures.

Epilogue

By 2015, I was spinning plates on all fronts, including West Berkshire Brewery, the City Pub EIS Fund and the Bruce Trust and I was about to enter my 50th year in the international brewing and pub industries. It was difficult to believe I'd spent close to half a century doing just what I loved, through both good and bad times.

I really hope that I'm living proof that true entrepreneurs never retire – only employees who don't enjoy their work want to retire. Entrepreneurs thrive on creating and developing new businesses and above all enjoy a fun and stimulating life working alongside kindred spirits.

The highlights of that 50th anniversary year included the City Pub EIS Fund launching its second fundraising in March to raise £15 million for three new pub companies, after raising £14.3 million for its first three companies. When all six new companies had been fully funded, it was agreed that a generic trading name for them was required and we chose Mosaic Pub & Dining Ltd: Mosaic is yet another hop variety. I was the chair of each company with James Watson, Clive's brother, and Peter McDonald as joint CEOs.

West Berkshire Brewery produced a special 50th-anniversary beer, Firkin Ale, to celebrate my 50 years as a brewer. Needless to say, the recipe was almost identical to the one Will Twomey and I had brewed for our one-off version of Dogbolter and the colourful label naturally pictured me holding my ubiquitous pint.

I also launched a crowdfunding campaign for the brewery to attract a further £1.5 million on top of the £4 million already raised to fund its state-of-the-art brewing and packaging facilities to be located in its new 38,000 square feet of converted cowsheds.

On a more philanthropic front, in 2016 the Bruce Trust entered into a strategic alliance with the Kennet & Avon Canal Trust by lending its four boats to be operated by the Canal Trust with a view to their eventually being gifted by the Bruce Trust to secure their future as Louise and I grow older.

David in the empty cowshed before developing it into the taproom and (below) shiny new tanks of the WBB

Whether it's been developing commercial or charitable interests, the past 50 years have been an exciting, adventurous, entrepreneurial journey that continues to evolve nine years into my second half century of being an entrepreneur and philanthropist. *Carpe diem*!

Watch this space for Volume 2 of The Firkin Saga.

The Firkin end!

Brewing Bruce's brilliant beers!

Having been a brewer since 1966, I'm delighted to share my basic step-by-step guide to the traditional brewing process, which was first referred to during the formation of the City of London's ancient Guild of Brewers in 1292 as 'The Mystery or Art of Brewing Ale or Beer'.

1. There are only three basic ingredients in brewing beer: malted barley, hops and water. Assemble these.
2. The water (liquor) is heated in the hot liquor back while the husks of the malted barley are cracked by the rollers of the mill, after which the grain is referred to as the grist, hence the idiom 'grist to the mill'.
3. The grist is then corkscrewed along a cylinder to the mash tun where the hot liquor is mixed with the grist. During the next 90 minutes the starch in the grist is converted into brewing sugars known as the wort.
4. The mash is then sparged (sprayed) with hot liquor so the wort can percolate down through the mash and is then pumped into the copper. The 'spent grains' can then be used as pig and cattle feed.
5. The wort in the copper is brought to a rousing boil before the hops are added to give the wort its bitter flavour.
6. After boiling for 90 minutes, the hopped wort is pumped into the hop back, which acts as a filter for the 'spent hops', which can then be used as garden fertiliser.
7. The wort is then cooled down before being pumped into the fermenting vessel.
8. Yeast is added to the wort and converts its brewing sugars into alcohol and CO_2.
9. After four to five days of fermentation, this liquid can at last be called BEER!

10. The beer is then racked (poured) into barrels and a gelatine is added to clarify the beer by coagulating the yeast and protein particles, which otherwise would cloud the finished product.
11. The beer is then left for at least a couple of days in a cool cellar to mature and condition, hence 'cask-conditioned beer' or 'real ale'.
12. Finally, from the barrel, the beer is sucked up to the customer's glass by a beer engine, which is the pump/tap on the bar top. Simple, eh?!

Here endeth the lesson delivered from the pulpit at the Fox & Firkin

Pros and cons for the Firkin sale

REASONS FOR SELLING THE FIRKIN PUBS

Commercial

Pros

Property values are now twice USM/City values.

Liquidate assets now rather than risk future recession, bear market or property crash.

Include Brentford and less profitable assets in the package.

Only one out of last year's three sites is a roaring success.

Clear £2m of debts and have £4m to roll over into something new within three years.

Increasing plagiarism.

Increasing competition.

Bruce's beer volumes in continuing decline.

The most successful Firkin pubs are trading at their best and can now only decline.

MMC Report - ? relaxation of the brewers' tie could affect marketing and therefore the value of free houses.

Flexible licensing hours will change the industry - increased costs and little benefit to Firkin locations.

Get out while on top!

Get rid of 3i.

All DB's interesting jobs now delegated so loss of job satisfaction.

Company has grown into an administrative bureaucracy - just like DB's old jobs.

Cannot think of any diversification ideas if Firkin formula wanes.

Dried up on any new Firkin ideas.

Firkin concept almost played out - now we are lager retailers rather than tradtional ale brewers.

End of an era.

Cons

Abandon 22 years contacts and experience and therefore the ability to capitalise on them.

Abandon DB's reputation as a brewer/pub operator.

Losing future good sites: Tooting, Kew, Chiswick.

Lose corporate identity and respect.

Could things get even better if we hang on?

Abandon USM experience and achievement/prestige.

Lose receptive banking contacts.

Betray loyal customers and staff.

Abandon profits growth trend.

Commercial pros and cons for a sale (see page 172)

REASONS FOR SELLING THE FIRKIN PUBS

Personal

Pros

£2m in personal bank or £4m in company bank for 9 years work.

Need a new challenge.

Chance to achieve charitable ambitions.

Want to spend more time with family, especially with new baby arriving.

Burnt out, poor health and no energy.

Want to enjoy life before health and energy declines (any further!).

More leisure time.

Wish to return to being husband/wife team again.

Would rather get more involved locally.

Been there, done that!

Nice to do the unexpected, i.e. sell out! (The sting!).

Want to start a new life - male menopause!

Wish to be free to travel the world.

Wish to become a slob for a change!

Wish to write a book - The Firkin Saga.

Possible huge pension contribution for D. and L.B. from this year's accounts.

Bored with job.

No more fun/laughs at work.

DB not a 'City' type - would be upset easily by outside shareholders.

No more commuting and sleeping bags in office.

Fed up with working in London.

Never wanted to build an Empire - only wanted one pub to get off the dole - victims of being swept along by our own success.

Cons

Lose personal identity -
(Bruce the Brewer,
 Bruce the Entrepreneur),
therefore risk of possible identity crisis.

Abandon: carving out a niche
 cocking a snook
 taking on the
  establishment.

Personal pros and cons for a sale (see page 172)

Acknowledgements

Everything I have strived to achieve as an entrepreneur has been focused on not only initially attracting customers to my various new ventures but also then trying to satisfy their consumer needs, so they kept wanting to come back for more.

Without their enthusiastic and loyal support, none of my initiatives or investments would ever have succeeded. Therefore, top of my list of people to thank are my innumerable customers for the vital part they have each played in my story.

After my customers, there are so many wonderful people who have provided invaluable support and advice that it is impossible to name them all here. However, most of them already feature personally throughout this book and I cannot thank each of them enough for the positive impact they have had influencing me through all the good and the bad times.

However, absolutely key players who I want to thank especially are:

Louise, my long-suffering wife for over 52 years and to whom this book is dedicated.

Danese, my indispensable, indefatigable executive PA, who has supported me for over 36 years, during 22 of which she was also the administrator of my charity. Her loyal support, hard work and advice while I have been creating, developing and operating new ventures, both commercial and charitable, have been invaluable.

All the Firkin team, who helped me achieve my first commercial success, especially Sally, Paul, Rory and Colin.

Ken Pyne, who has been producing brilliant, bespoke cartoons for over 46 years, several of which feature in these pages.

Charlie Papazian, who first introduced Louise and me to the pioneering days of craft-brewing in North America over 42 years ago.

Rev Mike Shaw, who has not only shared since 1988 all his experience and contacts in helping my Trust design, develop and operate its canal boats but also blessed each boat at its launch.

Clive Watson, with whom I have enjoyed co-founding several new pub companies during the past 25 years.

Roger Protz and all the other authors and journalists who have kindly featured me so favourably over the years.

All the dedicated volunteers of both the Bruce Trust and the Kennet & Avon Canal Trust, who have enabled over 30,000 people with special needs to enjoy canal holidays for the past 35 years.

All the team at the Right Book Company whose professional guidance and expert advice on how best to publish this book has been invaluable.

To everyone else who I have encountered over the years, please forgive me for not mentioning you personally but thank you for your support and you will know who you are and what part you have played in my journey.

Index

A

Adams, Paul, 144, 146, 172, 180, 206
Akers, Barry, 81
Alder Ridge vineyard, 253
Alexandra pub, 242
Alistair's pet parrot, 61–62
Allied Arab Bank, 145
Allied Breweries, 41–42, 66, 81, 82–83, 85, 94, 113, 150, 162
Allied Irish Bank, 146, 163–164
Alternative Investment Market (AIM), 245
Ambishus Pub Company, 211, 224
American Brewers' Association, 188, 213, 216
American Craft Brewers' Conference, 154, 216, 222
American Homebrewers Association, 96, 101, 188
Amos, Vic, 50
Anchor Hotels and Taverns, 37
Andrews, Tim, 219, 221, 222
Anglesea Arms, 242, 243, 246
Anheuser Busch (AB InBev), 227
Arkell, Claude, 21
Artesian (pub, Notting Hill), 51–54, 55, 128
Austin, Peter, 21, 59, 74, 80, 84, 116
awards, 161, 211, 247

B

Balloon Tavern, 114–115
Bannister, Tricia, 85
Barbican Bitter, 101, 106
Bar Central restaurant, 210
Barings Bank, 119–120
Barker-Harland, Richard, 22, 25, 27, 30, 65, 69, 76, 83, 99, 100, 118–119, 124, 192
Baum, Andy, 257, 259
Baum, Karen, 259
Bee & Bee!, 231
Belcher's Brewery, 206–207
Bennett, Jeremy, 96–97, 115, 131
Bertie Belcher, 206–208, 209
Bisacca, Joe, 218, 227
Blanc, Raymond, 176
Bodhipakti, Virabhongse, 223
Bo Junglies (children's play area), 156
Booth, Roger, 21, 30
Booth-Clibborn, Patrick, 237, 239
Bootlace Bitter, 100

Bourne, Richard, 73
Bourne, Robert, 73
Bovis, 118–119, 131, 141
Bowes, Simon, 209
Brakspear's Brewery, 229–234, 237
Branson, Richard, 94, 134–135
Brauring, 107
Brewers' Society, 116–117
brewing equipment, 12, 21, 22, 30, 59, 60, 84, 113, 129, 150, 230
brew kit providers, Bruce's Brewery as, 109, 179
Brew Moon, 220–222, 224–226
Brewpubs, 21, 59, 84
Brew Securities Ltd, 218, 219, 224, 227, 230–233
Brierley, Richard, 189
Brighton Breezy Bitter, 206
British Rail, 96, 97, 115, 118, 123, 131, 135, 141–143, 144, 180
Brock Court Developments, 205, 206, 209
Brooklyn Brewery, 215–217, 225, 226
Brown, Matt, 238
Bruce, Hannah (daughter), 174, 189
Bruce, Louise (wife), 11, 12, 15, 16, 20–24, 26, 30–31, 43, 46–51, 55–56, 92–94, 101–102, 105–107, 138, 151–152, 162–166, 172–176, 269
Bruce, Rachel (mother), 33, 35, 43, 180, 195, 196
Bruce, Rebecca (daughter), 37, 138, 151, 162, 166, 199
Bruce Charitable Foundation, 199–202
Bruce Charitable Trust, 190–197
Bruce's Barbarian Bitter, 106
Bruce's Borough Bitter, 9, 13
Bruce's Brewery, 9, 12, 101, 108–109, 124, 139, 155, 174, 179, 181, 189, 205, 206
 (Bristol) Ltd, 91–92
 (Denmark Hill) Ltd, 115
 (Hackney) Ltd, 153
 (Highbury) Ltd, 145
 (Lewisham) Ltd, 69–70
 (Portobello) Ltd, 82, 85, 86
 (Southwark) Ltd, 25, 30
 (World's End) Ltd, 118, 178
Bruce's Bristol Bitter, 100
Bruwel Ltd, 84–85, 87, 91, 92, 96, 97, 107, 113, 120, 129, 150
Budd, David, 83, 218
Buhler, Dave, 218, 219
Bullfrog Bitter, 90
bureaucracy, 69–86, 89, 92–93, 123–131, 132, 188, 198
Burns, Paul, 164
Burrell, Barbara, 224
Burrows, Jim, 233
Business Expansion Scheme (BES), 126–127, 146

C

Campaign for Real Ale (CAMRA), 8, 12, 41, 61, 77, 174
Canal & River Trust, 198
Canary Wharf, 161
Cantwell, Dick, 218
Capital Pub Company plc, 238–240, 244, 245, 246, 247, 251, 255
Capital Pub Company 2 plc, 243–244, 245, 246, 251, 255
Carpenter's Arms, 29
Caruso, Jim, 224
CCRPPO, 127
Chantler, Paul, 209–210
Chaplin, Henry, 237
Charles Kinloch, 37
Charram Ltd, 47–49, 53, 64, 65
Charrington Brewery's Moss Hall Tavern, 16
Charrington's, 28, 69, 123–124
Christon, Andy, 227
City Pub Company East plc, 255, 256, 259–260
City Pub Company West plc, 255, 256, 259–260
City Pub EIS Fund, 260, 263
Cobbs Farm Shop, 252, 253
Cocksedge, Charles, 192
Coe, Lord Sebastian, 201
Country Food & Dining Company Ltd, 251, 252
County Bank, 127, 214
Courage Brewery, 36, 38, 67, 95, 229
Cousins, Dave, 77
Cremorne Gardens, 119
Crown & Anchor, The, 245
Crown Commissioners, 152, 154

D

Dark de Triomphe, 210
Davies, Nick, 179
Dean, Rob, 197
Denmark Hill railway station, 96–97, 107, 115, 123, 131, 142–145, 161, 196
Diana (canal boat), 196, 200–201
Dick (Bruce's uncle), 72, 163
Dogbolter, 12, 100, 109, 117, 118, 179, 206, 258, 263
du Boulay, David, 22, 65, 69, 135–136, 142–143, 150, 210, 218
du Boulay Construction, 22, 83, 119, 141, 149, 156, 163, 167, 218
Duke and Duchess of Cambridge, 201
Duke of Gloucester, 161, 200
Duke of York (pub), 12, 15–31, 64, 67
Dunbrewin plc, 181

E

Earthstopper, 12
Elliott, Shane, 237, 245
Elysian Brewery, 218, 219, 225, 227
Enterprise Investment Scheme (EIS), 126–127, 238–260, 245
Etherington, Paul, 257

F

Falcon & Firkin, 153–157, 159, 172, 174, 191
father of David Bruce, 34–35, 39, 44, 45
Fawcett, Chris, 114, 126
Feiner, Elliott, 220, 222, 224, 225
fermenting vessels, 11, 60, 78, 86, 91, 141
Ferret Ale, 117, 119, 126
Ferret & Firkin in the Balloon up the Creek, 107, 118–119, 178–179
Fielder's Farm Shop, 253
Firkin Club, 73–74, 87
Fitzpatrick, Patrick, 116
Flanagan's Black Bull, 64–65, 67, 69
Fleece & Firkin, 91, 100, 107–108, 113, 115, 127, 128, 132
Fletcher, Antony, 72, 82, 107, 118, 126, 133, 139, 145, 146, 147, 217
Fleurets, 106, 130, 133, 149, 171, 173, 179
Flounder & Firkin, 7, 149, 151, 152, 154
Flower, The, 180–181
Foster, Mike, 229, 230, 231, 232
Fox & Firkin, 75, 76, 79, 92, 93, 144, 175, 187, 189, 204, 266
Freedom of the City of London, 230
free trade loans, 24–25, 80–81, 83, 85, 146, 156
Frog & Firkin, 82, 84–86, 89, 90, 101, 118, 129, 139, 150, 187
Froghopper, 90
Frog & Rosbif, 210
Fuller's, 16, 247
Fuzzock & Firkin, 163

G

Gadd, Eddie, 258
Galaxy (City) Pub Company Ltd, 260
Garden, Rory, 97, 144, 151, 172, 180
Gill, Tom, 224
Gillham, Barry, 171–173, 179
Giuliani, Rudy, 217
Good Beer Guide, 8, 61
Good Life Home and Garden Center, 252–253
Goose & Firkin, 7, 9–13, 14–32, 33, 62–67, 69, 73, 147, 148, 187

Great American Beer Festival, 188, 218
Greater London Council, 93
Greene King, 248, 255
Green Fields Farm Shop, 252
Griffiths, Harrington, 116
Griffiths, Michael, 66
Grosvenor Estates, 29
Grosvenor Inns plc, 209–211, 217, 219
Gudmundsson, Thor, 209–210
Gumbrell, Kris, 246, 251

H

Half Moon Brewing, 219
Hall, Alan, 66
Hallett, Keith, 86, 91, 99, 100, 107–108
Hannah (canal boat), 194, 196
Hannam, Peter, 192, 205
Harding, Stephanie, 91, 109
Hare-Scott, Peter, 22
Harvey, Colin, 91
Hayes, Mike, 77
Hedgehog & Hogshead, 206, 208, 210–211
Heriot-Watt University, 97, 150–151, 163
Herridge, Colin, 216
Hickenlooper, John, 216–219, 221–222, 224–225
Highbury Brewery Tap, 130, 133–134, 138, 139, 145, 149
Highclose/Highcost Farm Shop, 251–252
Hill, Roger, 85
Hindy, Steve, 215, 217, 226
Hogbolter, 206
Home Farm Trust, 194
Honeypot Inns, 229–234, 237
Hopf, Hans, 96, 107, 120, 129, 219, 223
Hopf, Wilma, 219
Hopf Lodge Brew House, 223
Hopf Weissbierbrauerei, 96
Hotel du Vin, 234
Howard, Roger, 85
Hungerford massacre, 166–167

I

Ind Coope, 130, 133, 149
Inglewood Farmhouse, 177–180
Inland Revenue (HMRC), 19, 92
Inntrepreneur Ltd, 206
INSEAD Business School, 209–210
Inseine, 210
Ippolito Christon, 227
Irish Republican Army (IRA), 130

J

Jackson, Michael, 85
J A Welch & Sons, 84–85
J D Wetherspoon, 163
Jessop, Johnny, 37

Jimmy, Crazy, 30
Joe Allen, 210
Jones, Terry, 97

K

Kaye, Michael, 25, 206
Kemp, Terry, 191–192
Kennet & Avon Canal, 190, 191–193, 194, 196, 197, 200, 263
Kennet & Avon Canal Trust, 192, 196, 263, 270
Kew Gardens, 167, 180
Kintbury Lock, 191
Kirby, Tim, 80, 84, 91
Kneetrembler, 12
Krug, Henri, 179

L

Ladbroke Arms, 242
Laker, Freddie, 94
Leatherdale, Gordon, 245, 251–252
Leisure Sales Development (LSD), 50–56
Lewisham Narrow Boat Project, 189–190
Ley, Andy, 238
Littler, John, 95, 115, 123, 125–126
Lloyds Bank, 10–11, 24–25, 69, 85, 99, 108, 113–114, 118–119, 126, 128, 133–134, 138, 145
logos, 25, 73, 80, 117, 118, 119, 152, 154, 208, 229
London Narrow Boat Project, 189–190, 204
London Weekend Television, 147, 148
Looker, Roger, 209–219, 221, 224–225, 232
Loosley, Bob, 37, 206
LSD Entertainment, 54
Lucas, Bob and Gloria, 192
Lucas, Tom, 257
Luitpold, Crown Prince of Bavaria, 129

M

Maggs, Dave and Helen, 256–259
Manhattan Brewing Company, 214–215
marathons, 80, 92–95, 102
Martin, Tim, 163
Maxwell Scott, David, 244
McDonald, Andy, 54, 62, 65, 80, 90, 106, 119, 126, 128, 133
McDonald, Peter, 263
McKenzie, Sheila, 244
Middlemas, Mike, 105, 106
Midsummer Leisure, 173–176, 178–180
Mike Gration (Steelcraft), 192, 193, 194
Mindboggler, 12
Mitchell, Colin, 85
Mitre, The, 245
Monopolies and Mergers

Index

Commission, 165
motorhome for disabled people, 176, 199, 201–202

N

Nail City Brewing, 219
National Association of Licensed House Managers, 162–163, 167, 172
National Front march, 93–94
National Giro Bank, 146
Neame, Bobby, 83–84
nepotism in business, 42, 44
Newey, Tom, 252
New Zealand Breweries, 160–161
Nichol, John, 106–107, 108
Nicholson, Kirsty, 198
Nimmo, Jamie, 25, 74–75, 118, 119, 152, 154, 167, 208
Noble & Company, 237–240, 245–246, 251
Norstrand, Lenny, 238
North American Brewery Investment Trust (NABIT), 219, 221
Notting Hill Carnival, 52–53

O

O'Dwyer, Mike, 167
Old Market Brewing, 219
Old Peculier (beer), 40–41
Oliver, Garrett, 215, 217
Owen, John, 45

P

Page, Adam, 174
Pallett, Neil, 199, 201–202
Papazian, Charlie, 96, 101, 116, 120, 154, 187–188, 213, 216, 219, 221–222, 227
Paralympic Games, 200–201
Parislytic, 210
Paris Real Ale Brewery, 210, 216
Pearson, Ron, 226
Pewter Platter Tavern, 231
Phantom & Firkin, 162–163, 169
Pheasant & Firkin, 95–98, 101–102, 106, 116
philanthropic work, 189–202
philanthropy, 93, 129, 189–205, 264, 269
Phoenix & Firkin, 107, 113, 123–127, 129–130, 135–138, 143–147, 183, 200, 160180
Pilkington Glass, 89–90, 150
Pope, Mike, 28
Portobello Porter, 90
Potter, Tom, 215–218, 226
Power, John, 105, 172, 179
Prickletickler, 206
Prodigal's Return, 241
Project Bacchus, 246
Project Hangover, 246
Project Headache, 246
Protz, Roger, 7–8
Pub Company Asia Pacific Pte Ltd, 223

Pullman, Nigel, 230
Punch Taverns, 258
puns, 7, 12, 70, 100, 162, 163, 183, 187
Putland, Dick, 10–11, 24–25, 27, 62, 69, 85, 96, 108–109, 133
Pyle, Martin, 70
Pyne, Ken, 81, 109, 129, 195

Q

Queen Elizabeth Training College, 35
Queen's Hotel (Hackney), 152–153

R

Rachel (canal boat), 195, 196
Rail Ale, 143
railway memorabilia, 135–137, 144
Rea Bros, 219–220
Reach Out for Kids (ROK), 191–193
Rebecca (canal boat), 190–194, 202
Reed, Michael, 218
Roberts, Dave, 91
Roberts, John, 255–256
Robertson-Macleod, Simon, 259
Royal Bank of Scotland, 179, 232–233
Rudd, Danese, 193, 199, 222, 242, 269
Ryan, Michael, 166–167

S

Saccone & Speed, 37–38
Shaw, Mike, 191–193, 194
Shearman, John, 79, 144
Shell-Mex and Courage, 36
SIBA (Small Independent Brewers' Association), 116–117, 165
Simpson, Joe, 242
SLOBA (Small London Brewers' Association), 116–117
slogans, 12, 25, 41, 80, 90, 100, 109, 118, 152, 159–160, 162, 163, 167, 175, 180, 206, 213, 214
Slug & Lettuce, 211
Smith, Sally, 100–101, 135, 137–138, 150, 152, 154, 160, 172
Smith & Williamson Investment Management Ltd, 252
Snook, Philip, 224
Southwark Development Corporation, 114
Southwark Environment Trust, 96–97, 115, 123
Sperling, Michael, 26, 27, 65, 69
Springleaze Farm Shop, 252
Springleaze/Woody's Farm Shop, 252
Square Pig, 241, 247

Index

squatters, 7, 130–131, 134, 138–139, 145, 149
Stericker, Charlie (Louise's brother), and his wife Debbie, 22
Staveley, Simon, 42
Steinlager, 160–161
Stoat, 117
Summers, Colin, 97, 150–151
Sunday Times Fun Run, 62–63, 129
Swales, Jonathan, 175
Sykes, Malcolm, 50–51

T

Tavistock Hotel, 82, 83–86
tax, capital gains, 127, 205–206, 238, 244
tax problems, 105
Tea Clipper, The, 245
Teddington Arms, 242
Tetley pub, 150
Thatcher, Margaret, 164, 169, 189
Theakston, Frank, 39
Theakston, Michael, 42–43
Theakston, Paul, 21, 39–42
Theakston's Brewery, 21, 39–43, 45, 47, 72, 175
Thompson Taraz, 260
Thwaites, Tim, 209, 217
Tomlinson, James, 257
Touche Ross, 105–106, 113, 128, 133, 137–138, 167, 172, 179

Tutti-men, 160
Twin City Investments, 47
Twomey, Will, 257–258, 263
Twort, Alan, 146, 163–164, 167, 172, 179

U

Unlisted Securities Market (USM), 147, 155, 164, 209

V

Vernon, Richard, 21
Vickers, Pippa (sister), 25, 92, 217
Vickers, Tony, 217
Virgin, 134
Vulture's Perch, 135

W

Wadsworth, David, 167, 172, 179
Walsh, Dominic, 259
Water Rat, The (pub), 208–210
Watney Combe Reid, 178
Watney's Red Barrel, 41–42
Watson, Clive, 232, 237–248, 255–256, 259–260, 269
Watson, James, 263
Watson, Neil, 67–68, 70, 80, 84
Watson, Tint and Alistair, 26–27, 30–31, 120
Weasel Water, 117
Welch, John and Jim, 84–85, 92

Welman, Jo, 219, 222
Weschler, James, 223
West Berkshire Brewery (WBB), 256–259
Wetherland Ltd, 23, 25
wheelchair-accessible motorhomes, 199
Whitbread, Billy, 259
Whitbread, Humphrey, 35
White, Graeme, 173
Whiteley, Candy, 50
Whiteley, Richard, 47
Wicks, Raymond, 17–22, 25, 64–67
Williams, Jerry, 23, 56
Williams, Richard, 172
Williams & Glyn's, 145–146
Wing Tai Investments, 223
Witty, Mark, 215
Woody's Farm Shop, 252
Wool Hall Company, 91–92
Worshipful Company of Brewers, 259–260
Worshipful Company of World Traders, 230
Wright, Nick, 191–192
Wrigley, Richard, 214
Wynkoop Brewing Company, 216–225

Y

Yosemite, 213, 214
Young, John, 29, 242–243, 245
Young's Bitter, 242
Young's Brewery, 242, 245

EU Safety Representative: euComply OÜ Pärnu mnt 139b-14 11317 Tallinn
Estonia hello@eucompliancepartner.com +33 756 90241

www.ingramcontent.com/pod-product-compliance
Lightning Source LLC
Chambersburg PA
CBHW061245170426
43191CB00039B/2359